T0074144

Lecture Notes of the Institute for Computer Sciences, Social Informatics and Telecommunications Engineering 216

More information about this series at http://www.springer.com/series/8197

Petr Matoušek · Martin Schmiedecker (Eds.)

Digital Forensics and Cyber Crime

9th International Conference, ICDF2C 2017
Prague, Czech Republic, October 9–11, 2017
Proceedings

 Springer

Editors
Petr Matoušek
Brno University of Technology
Brno
Czech Republic

Martin Schmiedecker
SBA Research Vienna
Vienna
Austria

ISSN 1867-8211   ISSN 1867-822X (electronic)
Lecture Notes of the Institute for Computer Sciences, Social Informatics
and Telecommunications Engineering
ISBN 978-3-319-73696-9   ISBN 978-3-319-73697-6 (eBook)
https://doi.org/10.1007/978-3-319-73697-6

Library of Congress Control Number: 2017963758

Printed on acid-free paper

This Springer imprint is published by Springer Nature
The registered company is Springer International Publishing AG
The registered company address is: Gewerbestrasse 11, 6330 Cham, Switzerland

Preface

It is our pleasure to introduce the proceedings of the 9th EAI International Conference on Digital Forensics and Cyber Crime (ICDF2C) 2017. Since its start in 2009, the ICDF2C conference each year brings together leading researchers, practitioners, and educators from around the world to advance the state of the art in digital forensics and cybercrime investigation. After nine years of existence, the conference has received worldwide recognition. Scores of researches and experts of digital forensics and cybercrime come together each year to meet at this event.

The Technical Program Committee (PC) of ICDF2C received about 50 submissions that were carefully evaluated by the team of international reviewers. After the review, 18 papers were invited for oral presentation at ICDF2C 2017. The authors of the papers come from 11 countries over the world: UK, China, Czech Republic, Germany, Austria, Switzerland, USA, Portugal, Sweden, Ireland, Australia, and South Korea.

Traditionally, the program of ICDF2C features keynote speeches. This year we had the privilege to welcome Joshua I. James, a professor and researcher from Hallym University, South Korea, whose research focuses on event reconstruction in post-mortem digital investigations. The second keynote speaker was Felix Freiling from Friedrich-Alexander-Universität in Erlangen-Nürnberg, Germany, who is an expert on safety and security. For the third keynote, Domingo Montanaro and Cyllas Elia presented their results of a two-year long investigation of cyber criminals in Brazil. The program also accommodated three tutorials given to the ICDF2C audience: Bitcoin analysis by experts from the cybersecurity lab Neutrino, Switzerland; an application of NetFlow data for network forensics given by Flowmon Networks Ltd., Czech Republic; and an introduction to the GRR Rapid Response framework for remote live forensics, given by Google.

We would like to thank everyone who offered their help and support during the conference organization. We appreciate the thorough work and flexible approach of all PC members during the reviewing process. Also, we would like to express our sincere thanks to all members of the Organizing Committee for their hard work in the realization of the conference. The conference could not have been organized without the support of the European Alliance for Innovation (EAI) and Flowmon Networks Ltd., Czech Republic.

December 2017

Petr Matousek
Martin Schmiedecker

Organization

Steering Committee

Sanjay Goel	University at Albany, State University of New York, USA
Imrich Chlamtac	EAI, CREATE-NET
Pavel Gladyshev	University College, Dublin, Ireland
Marcus Rogers	Purdue University, USA
Ibrahim Baggili	University of New Haven, USA
Joshua I. James	DFIRE Labs, Hallym University, South Korea
Frank Breitinger	University of New Haven, USA

Organizing Committee

General Co-chairs

Petr Matoušek	Brno University of Technology, Czech Republic
Martin Schmiedecker	SBA Research, Vienna, Austria

Technical Program Committee Chair

Sebastian Schinzel	University of Applied Sciences, Münster, Germany

Workshop Chair

Marc Scanlon	University College Dublin, Ireland

Publicity and Web Chair

Sebastian Neuner	SBA Research, Vienna, Austria

Publications Chair

Ondřej Ryšavý	Faculty of Information Technology, Brno, Czech Republic

Local Chair

Matěj Grégr	Brno University of Technology, Brno, Czech Republic

Conference Coordinator

Alzbeta Mackova	EAI

Technical Program Committee

Harald Baier	University of Applied Sciences Darmstadt, Germany
Spiridon Bakiras	Hamad Bin Khalifa University, Qatar
Nicole Beebe	University of Texas at San Antonio, USA
Frank Breitinger	University of New Haven, USA
Mohamed Chawki	University of Lyon III, France
Kim-Kwang Raymond Choo	University of South Australia, Australia
David Dampier	Mississippi State University, USA
Virginia Franqueira	University of Derby, UK
Pavel Gladyshev	University College Dublin, Ireland
Joshua I. James	DigitalFIRE Labs, Hallym University, South Korea
Ping Ji	City University of New York, USA
Umit Karabiyik	Sam Houston State University, USA
Nhien An Le Khac	UCD School of Computer Science, Ireland
Michael Losavio	University of Louisville, USA
Stig Mjolsnes	Norwegian University of Science and Technology NTNU, Norway
Alex Nelson	NIST, USA
Sebastian Neuner	SBA Research, Austria
Bruce Nikkel	UBS AG, Switzerland
Richard E. Overill	King's College London, UK
Gilbert Peterson	Air Force Institute of Technology, USA
Golden G Richard III	Louisiana State University, USA
Vassil Roussev	University of New Orleans, USA
Neil Rowe	U.S. Naval Postgraduate School, USA
Ondřej Ryšavý	Brno University of Technology, Czech Republic
Mark Scanlon	University College Dublin, Ireland
Bradley Schatz	Queensland University of Technology, Australia
Michael Spreitzenbarth	Siemens CERT, Germany
Krzysztof Szczypiorski	Warsaw University of Technology, Poland
Vladimír Veselý	Brno University of Technology, Czech Republic
Timothy Vidas	Carnegie Mellon University, USA
Christian Winter	Fraunhofer Gesellschaft, Germany

Contents

Malware and Botnet

FindEvasion: An Effective Environment-Sensitive Malware Detection System for the Cloud

Xiaoqi Jia[1,2,3,4], Guangzhe Zhou[1,2,3,4], Qingjia Huang[1,2,3,4(✉)],
Weijuan Zhang[1,2,3,4], and Donghai Tian[5]

[1] Institute of Information Engineering, CAS, Beijing, China
{jiaxiaoqi,zhouguangzhe,huangqingjia,zhangweijuan}@iie.ac.cn
[2] School of Cyber Security, University of Chinese Academy of Sciences,
Beijing, China
[3] Key Laboratory of Network Assessment Technology, CAS, Beijing, China
[4] Beijing Key Laboratory of Network Security and Protection Technology,
Beijing, China
[5] Beijing Key Laboratory of Software Security, Engineering Technique,
Beijing Institute of Technology, Beijing, China

Abstract. In recent years, environment-sensitive malwares are growing rapidly and they pose significant threat to cloud platforms. They may maliciously occupy the computing resources and steal the tenants' private data. The environment-sensitive malware can identify the operating environment and perform corresponding malicious behaviors in different environments. This greatly increased the difficulty of detection. At present, the research on automatic detection of environment-sensitive malwares is still rare, but it has attracted more and more attention.

In this paper, we present FindEvasion, a cloud-oriented system for detecting environment-sensitive malware. Our FindEvasion system makes full use of the virtualization technology to transparently extract the suspicious programs from the tenants' Virtual Machine (VM), and analyzes them on our multiple operating environments. We introduce a novel algorithm, named Mulitiple Behavioral Sequences Similarity (MBSS), to compare a suspicious program's behavioral profiles observed in multiple analysis environments, and determine whether the suspicious program is an environment-sensitive malware or not. The experiment results show that our approach produces better detection results when compared with previous methods.

Keywords: Cloud security · Environment-sensitive malware · MBSS
Transparent extraction · Multiple operating environments

1 Introduction

In recent years, increasing malwares have gradually become an important threat to the construction of cloud computing. These malwares can not only occupy

© ICST Institute for Computer Sciences, Social Informatics and Telecommunications Engineering 2018
P. Matoušek and M. Schmiedecker (Eds.): ICDF2C 2017, LNICST 216, pp. 3–17, 2018.
https://doi.org/10.1007/978-3-319-73697-6_1

the computing resources maliciously, but also attack other tenants and even the underlying platform to steal the other tenants' private data. As more and more data with sensitve and high commercial value information is migrated to the Cloud, researchers paid more attention to the malware detection for the Cloud.

Among the various kinds of malwares, environment-sensitive malwares are growing rapidly. This kind of malware can identify the current operating environment and perform corresponding malicious behaviors in different environments. According to Symantec's security threat report [1], 20% of new malwares are environment-sensitive currently and the number of environment-sensitive malware is increasing at a rate of 10–15 per week.

In order to detect environment-sensitive malwares, some methods have been proposed gradually, such as BareCloud [2] and Disarm [3]. BareCloud is based on the bare-metal and only considers the operations that cause a persistent change to the system. This will lead to many meaningful non-persistent malicious operations being ignored, for example, the remote injection. Besides, Bare-Cloud uses a Hierarchical similarity algorithm to compare the behavioral profiles, however, the detection ability of this algorithm will be greatly affected if the environment-sensitive malware performs a lot of independent interference behaviors. Disarm deploys two kinds of sandbox with different monitoring technologies. However, two kinds of environments are not enough to detect a variety of evasive behaviors within the environment-sensitive malware. Therefore, how to make the environment-sensitive malware exhibit the evasive behavior and cope with the interference behaviors is the key issue for the detection.

In this paper, we present FindEvasion, a cloud-oriented system for automatically detecting environment-sensitive malwares. The FindEvasion performs malware analysis on multiple operating environments, which include Sandbox environment, Debugging environment, Hypervisor environment and so on. In order to analyze the suspicious program running in the guest VM, we make use of the virtualization technology to transparently extract it from the guest VM and the suspicious program will not be awared of this whole process. We propose an algorithm to compare the suspicious program's behavioral profiles and determine whether it is an environment-sensitive malware or not.

Our work makes the following contributions:

- We present a system called FindEvasion for detecting environment-sensitive malwares. Our system makes full use of the virtualization technology to transparently extract the suspicious program from the guest VM, and then performs suspicious program analysis on multiple operating environments to make the environment-sensitive malware exhibit the evasive behavior.
- We introduce a novel evasion detection algorithm, named MBSS, for behavioral profiles comparsion. Our algorithm can cope with the interference behaviors to make the detection more effective.
- We present experimental evidence that demonstrates that the operations of eliminating interference behaviors are effective for detecting enviornment-sensitive malwares, and the recall rate is increased to 60% with 100% precision.

The rest of this paper is organized as follows. The next section presents the system architecture of FindEvasion. Section 3 shows the implementation in detail. In Sect. 4, we design four experiments for evaluating our system and MBSS algorithm. Finally, we discuss related work in Sect. 5 and conclude the paper in Sect. 6.

2 System Architecture

As Fig. 1 shows, the FindEvasion architecture consists of two parts. One is the Cloud service node, which provides service to the tenants. It contains an Extraction module in the VMM. The Extraction module can extract a suspicious program running in the guest VM and transfer it to the multiple environments analysis platform for analyzing. More details are provided in Sect. 3.1. The other is the multiple environments analysis platform, which includes Sandbox environment, VM environment, Hypervisor environment and debugging environment, etc. It contains an Environment-sensitive detection module, which can compare the behavioral profiles extracted from multiple analysis environments and make a judgment that whether the suspicious program is environment-sensitive malware or not. This is achieved by our MBSS algorithm.

The purpose of deploying multiple environments analysis platform is to identify the deviations in the behaviors of a suspicious program. That is, if a suspicious program is environment-sensitive, then it would have different behaviors obviously in a specific environment compared to the other environment. Besides, it is necessary to point out that the Hypervisor used in multiple environments analysis platform is modified particularly. It can not only transparently monitor a suspicious program based on the virtualization technology, but also avoid being detected by the malware. This can be achieved by some skills, for example cheating the guest. We insert a kernel module in the VM environment and debugging environment for monitoring. As for Sandbox environment, it contains own in-guest monitoring components. Various monitoring technologies can also help us to find the environment-sensitive malware that targets a specific monitoring technique.

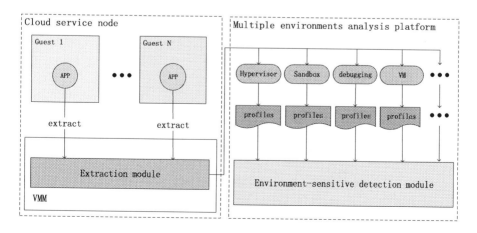

Fig. 1. FindEvasion system architecture.

3   Implementation

3.1   Transparent Extraction

In order to analyze a suspicious program which is in the guest Operating System (OS), we should extract it to the multiple environments analysis platform transparently. Note that the suspicious program is running in the guest VM. So the simple socket operation, like FTP, is easy to be awared by environment-sensitive malware because of the abnormal network behaviors. For this reason, we need to make use of the virtualization technology to extract the suspicious program and the whole process will not be awared by the malwares in the guest VM.

The detail is illustrated in Fig. 2. It is necessary to point out that the kernel module in the Guest OS has no HOOK operations and it can be completely hidden and protected by the VMM. Hence, the suspicious program is hard to detect inside the VM. For instance, if the Guest OS is win7, we can hide the module through monitoring the *NtQuerySystemInformation* function in the VMM. While a malware calls the function to query the modules in system, the VMM will intercept it and return the fake information to the malware. In this way, the kernel module can be hidden.

To better understand the procedure, we introduce the step details in Fig. 2. (1) While a suspicious program is going to run in the Guest OS, the Extraction module can capture this behavior. Then the Extraction module injects an event to notify the kernel module in the Guest OS. (2) The kernel module in the Guest OS receives notification from the Extraction module, then locates the suspicious program's executable file and copies it to a buffer. (3) The kernel module in the Guest OS calls instruction *VMCALL* to cause a VM-Exit. Now,

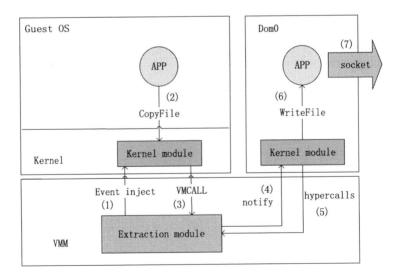

Fig. 2. Extract suspicious programs from Guest OS using virtualization technology.

the Extraction module obtains the binary executable file. (4) The Extraction module notifies the kernel module in Dom0. (5) The kernel module in dom0 reads the Extraction module through hypercalls. (6) The executable file is saved in Dom0. (7) We use socket operation to send the file from Dom0 to the multiple environments analysis platform. Here, we can use the socket operation, because the extracted suspicious program in Dom0 is only a static executable file and it can not be aware of the network behaviors. By this way, we can extract the suspicious program from Guest OS transparently.

3.2 Behavioral Profile

While the analysis of a suspicious program finishes in multiple operating environments, we need to extract it's behavioral profiles. Bayer et al. [6] have proposed an approach about how to extract behavioral profile from system-call trace. We will use a similar method in our system.

Similar to the model proposed by Bayer et al., we define our behavioral profile BP as a 4-tuple.

BP := (obj_type, obj_name, op_name, op_attr)

Where, *obj_type* is the type of objects, *obj_name* is the name of objects, *op_name* is the name of operation and *op_attr* is a corresponding attribute to provide additional information of a specific operation.

The *obj_type* is formally defined as follows.

obj_type := File(0) | Registry(1) | Syspath(2) | Process/Thread(3) | Network(4)

The *File* type represents this Behavioral Profile (BP) is a file operation, such as creating a file. The *Registry* type represents this BP is a registry key/value operation. The *Syspath* type represents this BP is a system key path operation, for example the *%systemroot%*. The *Process/Thread* type represents this BP is an operation about a process or a thread, such as terminating a process. And the *Network* type represents network behaviors, which include the remote IP and port. Each type is represented by integers 0, 1, 2, 3, 4 to reduce the complexity of behavior comparison later.

An operation must have a name, which is the API in reality. Besides, a corresponding attribute is needed to provide additional information about the operation. For example, the kernel function *NtDeviceIoControlFile* is used uniformly to represent all the socket functions related. Hence, we need additional information to tell us what exactly it is. That is, if we set the *op_attr* to the string "send", then we can clearly know this operation is the *send* function.

3.3 Behavior Normalization

In order to eliminate the influence of irrelevant factor and get a more reliable result, it is necessary for us to perform a series of normalization steps. As we all know, the same object may be represented differently in different systems, however, this will bring great differences in the behavioral profiles and then lead to a wrong judgment. Hence, we perform the following actions:

(1) We transformed uniformly all of the behavioral profiles into lowercase. The same behavioral profiles in different environment usually have different format. Some use uppercase and some use lowercase. In order to eliminate the differences, we use lowercase uniformly.

(2) We set a fix value to the *SID*. The registry key *HKEY_USERS\<SID>* is a secure identifier and the value is generally different in each system.

(3) We performed repetition detection. Some malwares perform many times with the same behaviors, which will cover up the real malicious acts. Therefore, if the number of repetitions is more than five times, the processing of duplicate removal is executed.

3.4 Behavior Comparison

The environment-sensitive malware often performs a lot of independent interference operations for anti-detection. The interference behaviors will appear in each environment, and if we do not deal with them, they will make up a large proportion of the behaviors and impact on the calculation of similarity. The previous methods, such as Hierarchy similarity [2], did not consider this issue, and it would lead to an absolutely opposite analysis result. Therefore, we propose a novel algorithm, named MBSS, which can eliminate interference behaviors and make the comparison more robust.

The algorithm model. Let $X = \{x_1, x_2, x_3, \ldots x_n\}$, $Y = \{y_1, y_2, y_3, \ldots y_m\}$, where x_1–x_n, y_1–y_m, each element represents a BP defined as Sect. 3.2, such that the set X represent all the Behavioral Profiles captured from a specific environment. Let L(X) be the number of elements of the set X and L(Y) be the number of elements of the set Y. Let set S be the intersection of set X and set Y, that is $S = X \cap Y$. We recursively define Sim as:

$$Sim(X,Y) = \begin{cases} 1 & \text{if } 0 < L(X) \leq \beta \text{ and } 0 < L(Y) \leq \beta \\ 0 & \text{if } L(x) == 0 \text{ and } L(Y) == 0 \\ cpt(X,Y) & \text{if } S == \varnothing \text{ and } L(X) > \beta \text{ and } L(Y) > \beta \\ Sim(X - x_i, Y - y_j) & \text{if } S \neq \varnothing \text{ and } x_i == y_j \end{cases} \quad (1)$$

where,

$$cpt(X,Y) = \frac{AB}{|A||B|} = \frac{\sum_{i=1}^{n} A_i B_i}{\sqrt{\sum_{i=1}^{n} A_i^2} \sqrt{\sum_{i=1}^{n} B_i^2}} \quad (2)$$

Here, β is a configurable parameter and we designed an experiment in the Sect. 4.1 to try to search an optimal value for it. x_i is an element in set X and y_j is an element in set Y. A is a vector transformed from set X and $A_i \in A$. Also, B is a vector transformed from set Y and $B_i \in B$. We realized a method to transform the set into vector in Algorithm 2. The expression (2) is derived from the cosine similarity algorithm and it represents the similarity between set X and set Y after the interference operators are eliminated from set X and set Y. Therefore, $Sim(X,Y)$ represents the similarity score. More details about how to eliminate interference behaviors are provided hereinafter.

We can clearly see that $Sim(X,Y)$ always lies between 0 and 1. Hence, the deviation score between set X and set Y can simply be defined as:

$$Dis(X,Y) = 1 - Sim(X,Y) \tag{3}$$

Also, $Dis(X,Y)$ is in interval [0,1], that is if the value tends to 0, the deviation between set X and set Y is small. On the other hand, if the value tends to 1, the deviation is large. We define a deviation threshold t. If the $Dis(X,Y)$ is greater than t, we consider the suspicious program as an environment-sensitive malware.

Eliminate interference behaviors. Here, we use a simple but effective method to eliminate interference behaviors. First we scan the behavioral profiles captured from different environments, if there is a common behavioral profile, that is all the elements in the 4-tuple defined as Sect. 3.2 are the same, we record the position until all the common behavioral profiles are found. Then we remove common behavioral profiles according to the positions we record. In this way, we can eliminate most of the interference behaviors and leave the real malicious behaviors behind. This simple method works well in our experiment.

We implement the above algorithm with pseudo code.

Algorithm 1. MBSS algorithm

Input: a suspicious samples behavioral profiles extracted in different environments
Output: the sample is environment-sensitive or not

```
1  def Judge(bp1,bp2):
2       Dis = 1 - Sim(bp1,bp2)
3       if Dis > t:
4            return TRUE
5       else:
6            return FALSE
7  def Sim(bp1,bp2):
8       if 0 < len(bp1) ≤ β and 0 < len(bp2) ≤ β:
9            return 1
10      elif len(bp1) == 0 and len(bp2) == 0:
11           return 0
12      lines=[line for line in bp1 if line in bp2]
13      if len(lines) == 0:
14           return cpt(bp1,bp2)
15      for line in lines:
16           bp1.remove(line)
17           bp2.remove(line)
18      return Sim(bp1,bp2)
```

In Algorithm 1, the parameter t in the line 3 is a threshold. Lines 3–6 give the result that the sample is environment-sensitive or not. Lines 7–18 is the mainly part of our algorithm to compute the similarity score. Line 12 is to get the common behavioral profiles between *bp1* and *bp2*. Lines 13–14 represent that if there is no common behavioral profile, then we compute the similarity score. More details are going to be described in Algorithm 2. Lines 15–17 represent that if there are a few of common behavioral profiles, then we do the processing of eliminating interference, which just removing the common behavior profiles from the set.

We implement the Algorithm 2 with pseudo code. Lines 2–3 is to split all the 4-tuple behavioral profiles into words. Line 4 is to union all the words into a set. Lines 6–14 transform the set into vector, that is if an element not only in the set *allwords* but also in the set *word1*, then the *vector1* appends a value 1, otherwise, appends a value 0. Line 15 makes use of the cosine similarity algorithm to compute the similarity score.

Algorithm 2. Function cpt()

Input: a suspicious samples behavioral profiles after the interference behaviors are eliminated
Output: the similarity score

```
1  def cpt(bp1,bp2):
2      word1 <- split the bp1 into words
3      word2 <- split the bp2 into words
4      allwords <- union all the words in word1 and word2
5      vector1 = [], vector2 = []
6      for w in allwords:
7          if w in word1:
8              vector1.append(1)
9          else:
10             vector1.append(0)
11         if w in word2:
12             vector2.append(1)
13         else:
14             vector2.append(0)
15     return cosine(vector1,vector2)
```

---

4   Evaluation

We use Xen-4.4.0 [4] to build the Cloud service node. The Hypervisor environment used in multiple environments analysis platform is also based on Xen-4.4.0. We use cuckoo [5] to build Sandbox environment. Moreover, we deploy debugging environment with windbg and Ollydbg, and deploy VM environment using VMware workstation 12. And we choose Windows 7 SP1 (32bit) as the operating system for all analysis environments in the experiment.

We use the precision and recall [7] to measure the detection effectiveness.

$$Precision = \frac{TP}{TP + FP}, \ Recall = \frac{TP}{TP + FN} \tag{4}$$

where, TP represents true positive, FP represents false positive and FN represents false negative.

We designed four experiments for the following purposes. The first experiment was to look for the optimal parameter β used in MBSS algorithm. The second was to evaluate MBSS algorithm by performing the precision-recall analysis. The third was to demonstrate the effectiveness of eliminating the interference behaviors on detecting the environment-sensitive malwares. The last experiment was a large scale test for evaluating the feasibility and usability of FindEvasion.

In order to evaluate our approach, we selected the BareCloud [2] as a comparison in the following experiments. The BareCloud was developed to detect environment-sensitive malware in 2015, and used the Hierarchy similarity algorithm to compare the behavioral profiles. It has the 40.20% recall rate with 100% precision.

4.1 Optimal Parameter β Selection

In this experiment, we try to look for the optimal parameter β used in our algorithm.

Dataset. We randomly selected 140 environment-sensitive malwares and 140 common malwares as the dataset of this experiment. For simplicity, we just considered Win32 based malware in PE file format.

We extracted the behavioral profiles of these samples from all the analysis environments and computed the deviation score by varying the parameter β between 2 and 20. The result is illustrated in Fig. 3. We can clearly see that when the parameter β exceeds 8, the precision keeps on 100%. According to our algorithm defined in Sect. 3.4, when we choose a higher value for the parameter β, the similarity score will get higher so that the deviation score will become lower. That is, if a malware is judged as environment-sensitive, it will always be true with the 100% precision. However, from the Sect. 3.4, the expression (1) tells us that if we select the β too high, the similarity score will have great chance to be 1. This will cause the deviation score to be 0 and the recall rate will be lower relatively. Therefore, we can choose β between 9 and 12. Here, we selected $\beta = 10$.

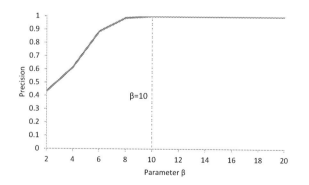

Fig. 3. The selection of parameter β

4.2   Algorithm Evaluation

In this experiment, we evaluated our MBSS algorithm by comparing with the Hierarchy similarity algorithm.

Dataset. We selected 542 environment-sensitive malwares and 319 common malwares. Also, we just considered Win32 based malware in PE file format for simplicity.

We extracted the behavioral profiles of above malwares from all the analysis environments and computed the deviation score using MBSS algorithm and Hierarchy similarity algorithm.

We performed a precision-recall analysis by varying the threshold t for these deviation score. If the deviation score exceeds the threshold t, the sample is considered as environment-sensitive. The result is presented in Fig. 4. We can clearly see that the MBSS algorithm gives better results. The reason is that the interference behaviors can impact on the detection of environment-sensitive malwares and our algorithm is able to cope with this issue. In the Sect. 4.3, we demonstrated the effectiveness of eliminating the interference behaviors.

Figure 5 illustrates the precision-recall characteristics of the MBSS algorithm by varying the threshold t between 0 and 1. We can clearly see that when the threshold $t = 0.75$, we get 100% precision with the recall rate of 60%. Compared to the recall rate of Hierarchy similarity algorithm, our algorithm's recall rate increases by 20% approximately.

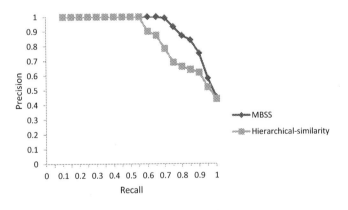

Fig. 4. Precision-Recall analysis of the MBSS and Hierarchy similarity behavior comparison

4.3   The Effectiveness of Eliminating Interference Behaviors

Since the Hierarchy similarity does not consider the influence of interference behaviors, we can therefore demonstrate the effectiveness by comparing the detection number of environment-sensitive malwares.

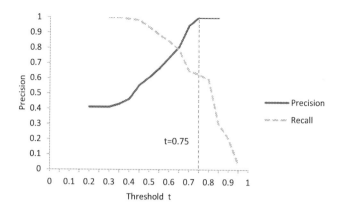

Fig. 5. Precision-Recall analysis of the behavior devision threshold value t

Dataset. We selected 380 environment-sensitive malwares as the dataset of this experiment. Each of the above malwares can perform a lot of interference operations. We only considered Win32 based malware in PE file format.

We extracted the behavioral profiles of these samples from all the analysis environments and computed the MBSS-based deviation score. We used the threshold $t = 0.75$ and parameter $\beta = 10$ that were selected in the previous experiments. We also used the Hierarchy similarity to calculate deviation score. The comparion result is shown in Fig. 6. We can clearly see that the MBSS algorithm gives better results. The MBSS algorithm was able to detect a total of 351 environment-sensitive malwares, which accounted for 92.4%. By contrast, the Hierarchy similarity only detected a total of 93 environment-sensitive malwares, which accounted for 24.5%. In other words, if an environment-sensitive malware performs a lot of interference operations, our MBSS algorithm works better than Hierarchy similarity algorithm. It also proves that the operation of eliminating interference behaviors is useful to detect the environment-sensitive malware.

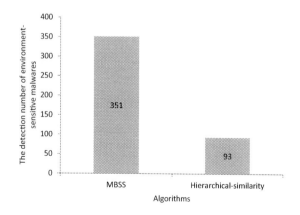

Fig. 6. The detection effect of MBSS algorithm compared to Hierarchy similarity algorithm

4.4   Large Scale Test

In this experiment, we evaluated the feasibility and usability of our FindEvasion system on a larger dataset, using BareCloud [2] system as a comparison.

Dataset. We have used VXHeaven Virus Collection [8] database which is available for free download in the public domain. We selected a total of 7257 malware samples and only considered Win32 based malware in PE file format. Note that, since we do not have a ground truth for this dataset, we cannot provide the precision rate and recall rate.

We ran FindEvasion and BareCloud using the same dataset, and made a judgment. The result is presented in Fig. 7. We can clearly see that our FindEvasion system detected 176 more samples than BareCloud did. Through manual reverse analysis, we confirmed that these samples are environment-sensitive malwares.

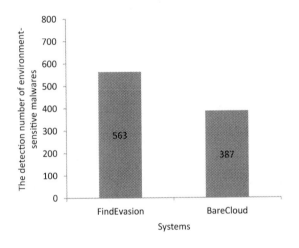

Fig. 7. The detection effect of FindEvasion and BareCloud

5   Limitations

Through the experiments result, we can clearly see that FindEvasion is able to detect environment-sensitive malwares. However, some samples using specific technologies can escape the detection. In this section, we describe the limitations of our system.

Firstly, if a sample uses stalling code to wait for some times before performing malicious behaviors, our system will lead to a wrong analysis result. The reason is that, our system's analysis time is limited. Within the limited time, the malware sample may be sleeping and escape the detection.

Secondly, our system can only identify the environment-sensitive malwares and it can not find out the provenance of the infection which may lead back to the offender. Our log files can only record the behaviors of malwares which do not include the attack's information.

6   Related Work

6.1   Dynamic Analysis

Dynamic analysis is the testing and evaluation of an application during runtime. Recently, many dynamic analysis tools have been developed for automatically analyzing malware. Most of them make use of the sandbox techniques. A sandbox is implemented by executing the software in a restricted operating system environment. Some tools like CWSandbox [9] and Norman Sandbox [10], making use of in-guest techniques for intercepting Windows API calls. This method is easy to be awared by environment-sensitive malware and be bypassed. The emulation or virtualization technologies are also universally used, for example VMScope [11], TTAnalyze [12], and Panorama [13], which are based on the Qemu [14] to record the API. Besides, Ether [15], VMwatcher [16] and HyperDBG [17] are the representative of hardware-supported virtualization technology.

6.2   Transparent Monitoring

In order to prevent the environment-sensitive malware from escaping the detection, it is necessary to develop transparent analysis platforms. Cobra [18] uses dynamic code translation, fighting with the environment-sensitive malware with anti-debugging techniques. It performs the behavioral analysis by modifying the memory properties. There are also a number of tools based on the out-of-VM monitoring which can provide transparent monitoring. Examples include Ether [15] which makes use of the hardware-supported virtualization. However, the tools above only provide very few kinds of environments which is not conducive to identify the environment-sensitive malware.

6.3   Evasion Detection

Chen et al. [19] proposed a detailed classification of anti-virtualization and anti-debugging techniques used by environment-sensitive malwares. According to their experiments, if an environment-sensitive malware is under a debugger or virtual machine environment, it showed less malicious behaviors. Lau and Svajcer [20] have proposed a method to detect VM detection by dynamic-static tracing technique. Disarm [3] deployed two kinds of analysis environments to compare the behavioral profiles. It requires each sample to be analyzed multiple times in each analysis environment. This procedure would reduce the influence of random files name. After that, it computes the deviation score through the inter-sanbox distance and intra-sanbox distance based on the Jaccard similarity. BareCloud [2] use the bare-metal environment, which has no monitoring component in the Guest OS. They only consider the persistent change to the system and they proposed a hierarchical similarity algorithm based on the Jaccard similarity to compute the deviation score. The major difference between BareCloud and our work is that we deployed multiple analysis environments and we proposed a novel algorithm, which can deal with the interference behaviors.

7   Conclusions and Future Work

In this paper, we present FindEvasion, a malware detection system for the Cloud. Different from traditional system, our system introduces a novel evasion detection algorithm that can effectively detect environment-sensitive malwares. As mentioned above, the environment-sensitive malwares can identify the operating environment and perform corresponding malicious behaviors in different environment. With the development of cloud computing, they have gradually become an important threat to cloud platforms. In order to make the environment-sensitive malware exhibit the evasive behavior and cope with the interference behaviors, we perform malware analysis on multiple operating environments and propose an algorithm to compare the suspicious programs behavioral profiles. Our approach can tranparently extract the suspicious programs from the guest VM and eliminate the influence of the interference behaviors. We have empirically demonstrated that this approach works well in practice and that is efficient.

In future, we would like to focus on adding the capability of human-computer interaction and handling stalling code. A malware can sleep for a long time to escape the analysis or the malicious behaviors need human to interact. Within a limited analysing time(e.g., five minutes), our system can not observe the malicious behaviors and this will lead to a wrong analysis result. Besides, our log files should record the provenance of the infection for leading back to the offender. We will deal with these issues in the future. Moreover, we plan to evaluate the robustness of our proposed technique on a customized dataset.

Acknowledgments. This paper is supported by National Natural Science Foundation of China (NSFC) under Grant No. 61572481, National key research and development program of China under Grant No. 2016YFB0801600 and Nation key research and development program of China under Grant No. 2016QY04W0900.

References

1. Symantec. https://www.symantec.com/security-center/threat-report
2. Kirat, D., Vigna, G., Kruegel, C.: Barecloud: bare-metal analysis-based evasive malware detection. In: Malware Detection (2014)
3. Lindorfer, M., Kolbitsch, C., Milani Comparetti, P.: Detecting environment-sensitive malware. In: Sommer, R., Balzarotti, D., Maier, G. (eds.) RAID 2011. LNCS, vol. 6961, pp. 338–357. Springer, Heidelberg (2011). https://doi.org/10.1007/978-3-642-23644-0_18
4. Linux Foundation: The Xen project. http://www.xenproject.org/. Accessed 4 Mar 2017
5. Cuckoo Sandbox. http://www.cuckoosandbox.org
6. Bayer, U., Comparetti, P.M., Hlauschek, C., Krgel, C., Kirda, E.: Scalable, behavior-based malware clustering. In: Network and Distributed System Security Symposium, NDSS 2009, San Diego, California, USA, February 2009
7. Powers, D.M.W.: Evaluation: from precision, recall and f-factor to ROC, informedness, markedness and correlation. J. Mach. Learn. Technol. **2**, 2229–3981 (2011)

8. VX Heaven Virus Collection: VX Heaven. http://vx.nextlux.org. Accessed 4 Mar 2017
9. Willems, C., Holz, T., Freiling, F.: Toward automated dynamic malware analysis using CWSandbox. IEEE Secur. Priv. **5**(2), 32–39 (2007)
10. Norman Sandbox. http://www.norman.com/
11. Jiang, X., Wang, X.: "Out-of-the-Box" monitoring of VM-based high-interaction honeypots. In: Kruegel, C., Lippmann, R., Clark, A. (eds.) RAID 2007. LNCS, vol. 4637, pp. 198–218. Springer, Heidelberg (2007). https://doi.org/10.1007/978-3-540-74320-0_11
12. Bayer, U., Kruegel, C., Kirda, E.: TTAnalyze: A Tool for Analyzing Malware (2006)
13. Yin, H., Song, D., Egele, M., Kruegel, C., Kirda, E.: Panorama: capturing system-wide information flow for malware detection and analysis. In: ACM Conference on Computer and Communications Security, CCS 2007, Alexandria, Virginia, USA, pp. 116–127, October 2007
14. Bellard, F.: QEMU, a fast and portable dynamic translator. In: Conference on USENIX Technical Conference, p. 41 (2005)
15. Dinaburg, A., Royal, P., Sharif, M., Lee, W.: Ether: malware analysis via hardware virtualization extensions. In: ACM Conference on Computer and Communications Security, CCS 2008, Alexandria, Virginia, USA, pp. 51–62, October 2008
16. Jiang, X., Wang, X., Xu, D.: Stealthy malware detection through VMM-based "Out-of-the-Box" semantic view reconstruction. In: ACM Conference on Computer and Communications Security, CCS 2007, Alexandria, Virginia, USA, pp. 128–138, October 2007
17. Fattori, A., Paleari, R., Martignoni, L., Monga, M.: Dynamic and transparent analysis of commodity production systems. In: IEEE/ACM International Conference on Automated Software Engineering, pp. 417–426 (2010)
18. Vasudevan, A., Yerraballi, R.: Cobra: fine-grained malware analysis using stealth localized-executions. In: IEEE Symposium on Security & Privacy, p. 15 pp. -279 (2006)
19. Chen, X., Andersen, J., Mao, Z.M., Bailey, M.: Towards an understanding of anti-virtualization and anti-debugging behavior in modern malware. In: IEEE International Conference on Dependable Systems and Networks with FTCS and DCC, pp. 177–186 (2008)
20. Lau, B., Svajcer, V.: Measuring virtual machine detection in malware using DSD tracer. J. Comput. Virol. Hacking Tech. **6**(3), 181–195 (2010)

Real-Time Forensics Through Endpoint Visibility

Peter Kieseberg[1]([✉]), Sebastian Neuner[1], Sebastian Schrittwieser[2],
Martin Schmiedecker[1], and Edgar Weippl[1]

[1] SBA Research, Vienna, Austria
pkieseberg@sba-research.org
[2] Josef Ressel Center for Unified Threat Intelligence on Targeted Attacks,
St. Pölten University of Applied Sciences, St. Pölten, Austria

Abstract. In the course of the last years, there has been an established forensic process in place known by every investigator and researcher. This traditional process is regarded to produce valid evidence when it comes to court trials and, more importantly, it specifies on a very precise level how to acquire a suspects machine and handle the data within. However, when new technologies come into play, certain constraints appear: Having an incident in a network containing thousands of machines, like a global corporate network, there is no such thing as shutting down and sending an investigation team. Moreover, the question appears: Is this an isolated incident, or are there any other clients affected?

In order to cover such questions, this paper compares three tools aiming at solving them by providing real-time forensics capabilities. These tools are meant to be deployed on a large scale to deliver information at any time, of any client all over the network. In addition to a feature comparison, we deployed these tools within a lab environment to evaluate their effectiveness after a malware attack, using malware with pre-selected features in order to allow for a more precise and fair comparison.

Keywords: Digital forensics · Real-time forensics · Forensic process
Endpoint visibility

1 Introduction

Through several years of accumulated practical experience and academic research, forensic investigators were able to establish a standardized and well-known routine for digital investigations [3,10]. This is especially important, since relying on a common ground is critical for forensic investigations that have to back a legal trial, in order to provide soundness to claims of both sides, the defendant as well as the prosecutor (for different reasons obviously). However, there are forensic investigations that do not have the convenient features of physical access, sufficient investigation time or close to unlimited storage capacity. In

© ICST Institute for Computer Sciences, Social Informatics and Telecommunications Engineering 2018
P. Matoušek and M. Schmiedecker (Eds.): ICDF2C 2017, LNICST 216, pp. 18–32, 2018.
https://doi.org/10.1007/978-3-319-73697-6_2

times of fast growing storage capacities and even commodity hardware bringing more than two terabytes to the end-user as a USB stick, the well-established forensic process has to be re-invented. A first step to this new process has been shown by Neuner et al., who opted for a whitelisting approach that allows to exclude already known files from the acquisition process [18]. However, this still relies on the assumption that the computers which have to be investigated are physically accessible and are already (or at least can be) shut down.

Large companies such as Google, Facebook and Mozilla are challenged with the downsides of those standardized approaches. Like many other companies, they experienced several incidents [2], however they suffer from the problem of scales, having to investigate on thousands and thousands of computers. Relying on the established forensic approach and turning every computer off, making a 1:1 hard drive copy and so forth, is not only unfeasible in reality, but would cost millions of Dollars every hour [15]. Thus the three mentioned companies are developing solutions called *real-time forensic tools*, namely *Google's GRR Rapid Response* (GRR) [8,16], Facebooks *osquery* [12] and *Mozillas InvestiGator* (MIG) [17]. In this paper we compare these three tools with respect to their feature set and capabilities. Furthermore, we evaluate their effectiveness in a scenario where a presumable administrator detected multiple infections on different machines. Main questions answered include whether it is possible to detect the infections if the malware features are known and whether it is possible to detect every infected machine. More precisely, the contributions of our work are as follows:

- We survey the current state-of-the-art forensic approach with respect to real-time forensics.
- We compare the three real-time forensic tools regarding their features and applicability.
- We evaluate their effectiveness for a successful attack with a known malware.

The rest of the paper is structured as follows: Sect. 2 provides the needed background information to this work and also offers insights into the related work. Section 3 provides an overview on the three selected real-time forensic tools, but also discusses alternatives in the open-source sector as well as other commercial tools. Section 4 describes the methodology and the evaluation details of our work. This section furthermore describes the lab setup used for the evaluation as well as the selected malware and its features. Section 5 outlines the results of the evaluation. Section 6 discusses the limitations of our approach and future work in the direction of live forensics. Finally, Sect. 7 summarizes and concludes our paper on real-time forensics.

2   Background and Related Work

Forensics in a traditional sense is a standardized process - standardized in academic work [4] and by the National Institute of Standards and Technology

(NIST) for law enforcement organizations such as the U.S. Department of Justice [19]. This process ensures that the investigator is carrying out reproducible steps in order to acquire a suspects data. Figure 1 [20,21] shows a typical illustration of the process.

Fig. 1. Flow of a traditional forensic process.

However, the process requires the suspect to have its data stored on a manageable number of devices, preferable only possessing low storage capacities. As shown in related work [10], storage is a very limiting factor during the acquiring process, since several copies have to be made for each device. These copies include the actual working copy for the investigator, a backup copy in case the working copy is tampered and, in some cases, a copy directly sent to the client (e.g. the court). Having all these copies means a high recoverability against data loss, however, this also means that the investigator needs huge amounts of storage capacities and enough computing power to process the data for investigative tasks. This problem was already predicted before in 2010 by Garfinkel [10] and since then discussed in academic work. One suggestion in 2016 by Neuner et al. [18] is the utilization of file whitelisting of known files to reduce both, the required capacity and the required process power. Additionally there is not only academic work describing the traditional forensic process, but also suggestions by the NIST [13]. These suggestions for acquiring data include a graceful shutdown, once the volatile memory (e.g., RAM) is acquired.

Considering a typical suspect having one computer, several hard disks and a mobile phone, this traditional forensic process works well in practice. But considering modern storage techniques, like distributed storage (cloud storage), the standardized process mentioned above will not work in every detail [11]. Considering large companies such as Google, Facebook and Mozilla having an incident within their infrastructure of tens of thousands of clients, shutting down every (probably) affected computer will not work without causing huge costs to the infrastructure provider. Therefore companies like those three developed frameworks, called real-time forensic tools which do not require shutting down the client, but are able to copy important data over the network to a centralized station for further investigation. Considering an infected client, these real-time forensic tools are able to scan all clients in range for infection details to find other infected clients, with some of those frameworks being able to directly access the client and prevent further spreading of the malware, e.g. by disabling certain network interfaces. On the one hand, this approach is definitely considered tampering with the data on the client, however, on the other hand this approach is fast and does not affect the clients (or the networks) up-time. Certain frameworks (e.g. Googles GRR) are able to produce AFF4 images of the clients,

which could be considered as a starting point for a forensic standard targeting
live environments using real-time forensic tools. Nevertheless, it should not be
unmentioned that carrying out real-time forensics is at no point compliant with
any standardized forensic process as it is currently demanded by court.

3   Real-Time Forensic Tools

In contrast to traditional tools as outlined in Sect. 2 real-time forensic tools do
not work upon the standardized forensic process. To tackle huge amounts of data
in real-time, without turning off the suspected computer, several tools have been
developed by various companies [23]. In this section we provide insights into the
three tools selected for evaluation, including an illustration of their capabilities
with Table 1 providing a compact overview.

Table 1. Capabilities of real-time forensic tools

		osquery	MIG	GRR
File interaction	Read access on files	✗	✓	✓
	Client write access	✗	✗	✗
	File timelining	✓	✗	✓
Endpoint statistics	Host statistics (e.g. uptime)	✓	✓	✓
	Process listing	✓	✓	✓
	Connected users	✓	✓	✓
Network statistics	Users	✓	✓	✓
	Connected machines (IP)	✓	✓	✓
	Connected machines (MAC)	✓	✓	✓
Endpoint monitoring	Windows registry	✓	✗	✓
	Linux packages	✓	✓	✗
	Memory inspection (userland memory)	(✓)	✓	✓
Agent compatibility	Windows	✓	✓	✓
	Linux	✓	✓	✓
	MAC OSX	✓	✓	✓
	Embedded devices (e.g. switches)	✗	✓	✗
Digital evidence acquisition	AFF4	✗	✗	✓

3.1   osquery

osquery was first released by Facebook in October 2014 as a simple way for
extracting properties from a life system that can be helpful in a forensic investigation. It currently targets Linux, Ubuntu, CentOS, FreeBSD and OSX and was

very recently extended to the Windows world [22]. The main idea behind osquery lies in providing an abstraction layer between the analyst and the operating system internals, allowing querying of information like changes in the file system, loaded kernel modules, information on processes and users, from a database-like structure. For this, all information is abstracted as so-called "tables" that follow the same syntax as SQLite tables and can be queried using SQL-commands.

Basically, there exist two ways of invoking osquery: Using an interactive shell called *osqueryi*, or configuring the *osqueryd* daemon. The osqueryi shell is completely stand-alone and typically used for prototyping, as well as ad-hoc analysis of the system. The osqueryd daemon on the other hand is used for structured and regular analysis of key features of the system, e.g. the list of running processes or changes in the file system. It is primarily configured by a scheduler, where defined queries are executed regularly. The daemon provides means for aggregation of these results over time and generates logs, thus can be used to easily show changes on the operating system level.

The main configuration work is done using so-called *query schedules*, SQL-style definitions of the data to be retrieved, including an interval definition for the recurring execution of the retrieval. Several queries can be packed together in so-called *packs* that allow for more fine-grained options on the logging, as well as the use of predefined packs for specific cases, including specific malware. Figure 2 shows a simple query schedule for retrieving all files opened by processes. The interval was set to 10 s, i.e. the daemon checks for these variable every ten seconds, events that take place in between will not be recorded and are lost for the analysis. Contrary to e.g. GRR, osquery is meant to be executed permanently to monitor changes on the fleeting aspects of the operating system, it is not capable of actually analyzing the actual content of files.

```
{
  "files_by_process": {
    "query": "select pid, fd, path from process_open_files",
    "interval": 10
  }
}
```

Fig. 2. A query schedule for osquery.

3.2 GRR

The Google GRR Rapid Response (GRR) was first announced by Cohen et al. in 2011 and intended to handle Google's internal infrastructure regarding remote live forensics [5]. Basically, GRR is a Python agent that is installed on the clients to be managed. The GRR front-end servers, that are under the control of a system administrator (sysadmin), receive the messages sent by the GRR agents. This sysadmin initiates a so-called "flow" via the front-end server on the agents. This message contains code that is executed on the agents, which are requested to return the required information to the front-end server for aggregation and evaluation. The concept of "hunts" on the other hand describes massive amounts of flows, targeting a huge number of agents.

Most of the "basic" capabilities are built into GRR, such as file interactions, live memory analysis and endpoint monitoring. Strong points of GRR are on the one hand the possibility to manage the agent live by using an IPython shell that is capable to run on all major operating systems (Windows, Linux, OSX). On the other hand, GRR offers the possibility to extract forensic evidences using the open-source file format *Advanced Forensics File Format 4* (AFF4) [6].

3.3   MIG

To tackle problems like accidental private key pushes to github in a large environment (such as every computer and every server owned by Mozilla) Julien Vehent proposed Mozillas own real-time forensic tool, the Mozilla InvestiGator (MIG) [17], in 2015. MIG is written in GO and compiled into a statically linked binary for easy sharing and easy deployment. Although the binary has to be installed as a root service, activated MIG modules are locked down in terms of requested privileges. For secure communication between the clients on which a MIG agent is installed and the MIG master, Rabbit MQ is used to exchange PGP signed JSON messages. The underlying architecture is shown in Fig. 3.

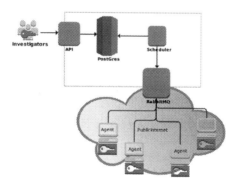

Fig. 3. Architecture of the Mozilla InvestiGator   (Image source: http://mig.mozilla. org/doc/.files/mig_workflow.gif. Accessed: 13.09.2016).

As soon as the agents are finished working on the tasks requested by the master, the results are sent back to the investigators and stored in a postgreSQL database. Table 1 outlines capabilities of MIG not mentioned here. The developers of MIG, besides various other features, managed to deploy MIG agents on rather restricted embedded systems like switches. This, on the one hand, adds a large amount of additional systems to be managed and analyzed, but on the other hand creates the possibility to monitor and protect these kinds of systems.

3.4   Commercial Solutions

Besides open-source real-time forensic tools there are also commercial tools available. This includes Mandiant's MIR, Encase Enterprise, as well as the real-time forensic tool of F-Response. These frameworks could not be evaluated due to the limited availability of the software, e.g. demo versions, however, even if a demo would be available for all of these commercial frameworks, they are typically limited and therefore cannot be compared to fully fledged open-source solutions.

4   Methodology

4.1   Lab Setup

Figure 4 depicts the setup of the lab environment used for the evaluation of the real-time forensic tools. As a first step (1), the control panel prepares the malware that is subsequently sent to the virtual machines. The malware can be chosen based on a range of pre-classified features (see Sect. 4.3 for details on the selection for our work). Step (2) initializes the VMs for a first use.

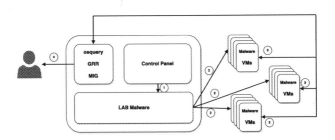

Fig. 4. The lab setup used for evaluating the real-time forensic tools.

In our case this includes the installation of the operating system Windows 7 Service Pack 1 (64 bit) for GRR and Windows 10 Pro (64 bit) for MIG and osquery, as well as an agent corresponding to all three real-time forensic tools we are evaluating. In step (2) the malware is loaded onto the machines, enabling certain types of malware to infect the virtual machine at boot time or at time of the start of the operating system, respectively. Step (3) is bi-directional: The real-time forensic tools are polling for data, which results in data sent to the infected virtual machines. The way the data is sent (methods, protocols used) depends on the communication techniques of each real-time forensic tool. As soon as the data is available for each tool it is evaluated and made available for the investigator in step (4).

4.2 Malware Sample Selection

Based on the methodology described in Sect. 4, the malware used for evaluation was selected on the following feature set:

Feature (F1), Process spawning: Malware is often running as processes in the background in order to carry out their malicious activities. However, the names of those processes are often either publicly known or easy to spot [14]. Feature (F2), Persistence: Certain kinds of malware persists themselves on the system, either somewhere on the filesystem but also e.g. in the registry. Persistence ensures the malware staying on the system after a reboot, as well as the possibility to restart the malware process after manual termination [1]. Feature (F3), Network connection: Processes that start outgoing, as well as accept incoming connections without any user interaction, are often malware [24]. Outgoing connections can indicate data that is being exfiltrated or the establishing of a connection to a botnet server (Command and Control server) [9]. Incoming connections can indicate patching of the malware or dropping additional payload on the attacked system [7].

Therefore, the following samples of malware have been selected based on the feature list above: Sample (S1) containing the banking trojan *retefe*, a malware that installs a root CA on the infected machine and starts to intercept e-banking connections, sample (S2) containing the *Locky* ransomware that encrypts files on the user's hard disk for asking for ransom for the decryption key, as well as sample (S3) containing the *Win32.Viking* worm.

Feature *F1* is fulfilled by all of the three samples *S1*, *S2* and *S3*. Each of them spawns several processes, some running in the background in order to carry out the malicious behavior. These processes include notoriously dangerous executables like "powershell.exe", "certutil.exe" and "tor.exe". All malware samples persist themselves on the system, more precisely the file system, fulfilling feature *F2*. Finally, feature *F3* is also fulfilled by all three samples to a varying degree: While the banking trojan does open several connections, the Win32.Viking worm works much more stealthy.

Sample S2, the Locky ransomware, was also chose, because it possesses a specialty: Contrary to other malware like ebanking trojans, ransomware stays hidden only for a specific time, until enough user files (or even the whole disk, depending on the actual malware) have been encrypted. Then the malware actually informs the user in order to make him/her pay the ransom. Thus, the detection capabilities evaluated in our scenarios are evaluated with respect to the "dormant" ransomware, i.e. the ransomware before or during the encryption phase, since its presence afterwards, in the ransom phase, is detected trivially.

4.3 Evaluation

The goal of the evaluation was to study the behavior and detection possibilities of the three live forensic tool-kits under real-life conditions. To this end we selected three malware examples and tested them on a system. Furthermore, we had a look on the capabilities of the different tool-kits and extrapolated their typical applicability in real-life scenarios.

For the evaluation, we infected a running system, with each malware separately, in order to get a good comparison of the results. While this evaluation yields good results for the detection of malware with known or at least expected feature, it does yield the problem that many artifacts are quite typical for the malware in question. Thus, we concentrated on utilizing the artifacts for detection that are more uncommon, like changes to system routines, changes to specific keys in the registry, or spawning of suspicious processes.

5 Results

In this section we provide a comparison of the analyzed tools with respect to our research scenario and outline major differences, as well as shortcomings based on the three malware samples selected before.

5.1 osquery

osquery mainly targets the monitoring of operating system internals, i.e. it is a constant monitor of the system state and does not target the reconstruction of deleted files. Regarding the banking trojan retefe, this helps detection in case of continuous monitoring through the osqueryd daemon. Here, the following artifacts could be found that identified this malware. It has to be noted though that the malware does generate many more artifacts, we reduced our analysis to those issues that possess high significance. This also implies that we did not concentrate on artifacts that can be the result of arbitrary other programs running on the respective machine like memory usage or checking for needed third party software:

- For file interaction, osquery is capable to detect the changes done to the file system on a pure metadata level. The malware generates and changes several files in the AppData directories for Microsoft Office and Tor, using file names like "Microsoft.Win32.Task Scheduler.dll", as well as the TOR-AppData.
- On the endpoint statistics level, it created various process, the most notorious including instances of "powershell.exe", "certutil.exe" (for adding the root CA) and "tor.exe".
- Regarding the network level, it generates various connections to the outside world, which can be detected by constant querying of the respective interfaces using osquery.
- On the endpoint monitoring level, there is a change happening to the Windows registry, deleting and recreating a specific key "HStartupItem" for MS Office and creating several other keys. Furthermore, a new root CA is installed, also resulting in the respective changes in the registry. Altogether, the process changes the registry which can be detected by osquery.

For the Locky ransomware, we detected the following artifacts that indicate an infection with malicious software:

- On the file level, it generates an executable in the system32 directory of Windows, as well as a file containing decryption instructions. Furthermore, as soon as the ransomware process is started, in starts accessing and updating files and changing their names to the ".locky" suffix.
- On the endpoint statistics level, it generates some processes, with "cmd.exe" being the most notable.
- Regarding the network level it does some DNS-lookups and downloads executable code during the infection. This of course is only visible in osquery in case the malicious code is not already downloaded before. Furthermore, it opens a connection to the well-known Locky distribution site "greenellebox.com". In addition, it uses a known web browser user agent for HTTP communication, which can be filtered using osquery.
- On the endpoint monitoring level, while of course activity was shown that can be attributed to the infection, there was nothing outstanding recorded that enabled us to identify the infection with Locky with a high certainty, while, of course, the randomly generated key in the registry was visible and could be a starting point for further investigations.

Regarding the Win32.Viking worm, we detected the following artifacts that indicate an infection with malicious software:

- On the file level, it generates the dll-file "FastUserSwitchingCompatibility.dll" in the system32-directory, as well as deletes a file in this directory. Furthermore, it generates a randomly named file in the root directory (typically "c:").
- While only spawning a few processes, these include several instances of "reg.exe" for modifying the registry, as well as a (changed) instance of Internet Explorer.
- On the network level, this malware is invisible to osquery, as no direct network connections are opened, but the (modified) Internet Explorer is used for hiding the communication.
- On the endpoint monitoring level, the malware makes changes to the registry by adding a new key and creating a Windows Service pointing to the executable "FastUserSwitchingCompatibility.dll".

5.2   GRR

The main benefit of GRR is its capability to check actual file content and search for strings that can be attributed to known malware samples. Furthermore, it still allows for file timelining and looking for changed files in the overall OS structure. This also holds true for the analysis of running processes. Still, the typical idea of GRR, in contrast to osquery, does not lie in the permanent observation and monitoring of the system looking for changes that might hint at an infection, but more on analyzing a system suspected for an infection already having taken place. Regarding our first sample, the banking trojan retefe, the following artifacts can be detected:

- Regarding changes to the file system, GRR is capable to detect the changed files in the AppData directories for Microsoft Office and Tor. Furthermore, the docx-document used for infection contains several deviations to typical docx-files like irregular field values in the summary information. It also contains a stream with embedded javascript code. This is especially valuable, as it helps to reveal the actual source of the infection.
- GRR is capable of detecting the processes spawned by the malware, still, since GRR is typically used as ad-hoc tool in the course of an investigation and not as constant system monitoring, it might miss most of these processes.
- The same holds true for the networking level. Since a banking trojan is meant to be active regularly in order to intercept the e-banking connections, GRR can be used for detection.
- The same holds true for the connections on the network level, especially since relevant information on the connection parameters can be extracted from the infected file, thus giving a valuable hint on what to look for.
- Finally, GRR is perfectly capable on extracting the changes that happened to the registry, the recreated "HStartupItem" key, as well as the root CAs.

For the Locky ransomware, the capabilities to check the actual file content are especially valuable. Furthermore, the following artifacts were be used for detecting this infection:

- GRR is capable of detecting the files generated by the malware, especially the executable in the system32 directory of Windows. Furthermore, since the timeline of the files is accessible by GRR, arbitrarily changed files become visible. In addition, the file system can be checked for files that should be readable (e.g. Office files), but only contain gibberish, hinting at encrypted data. Furthermore, the statistics also reveal the suffix changes. In addition, specific URLs can be found in the documents, as well as a dropped file, where the content does not match the file extension.
- While the encryption is taking place, GRR is capable of detecting the respective processes, especially running an executable with a randomly generated name from the local temporary directory (e.g. "b7uG0vk9g4qsBc5Z.exe").
- Locky contacts the distribution site "greenellebox.com" which can be detected using GRR during the connection. Furthermore, GRR could detect the known web browser user agent used for HTTP, in case Locky communicates during the investigation, still, the ransomware is typically limiting itself to small amounts of communication.
- GRR is also capable to see the randomly generated key in the registry, still, we found it rather hard to detect Locky solely by this artifact, especially in the presence of the much more distinctive artifacts on the file level.

Also with respect to the Win32.Viking worm, the capability to search for the content inside files helped a lot:

- The generated dll-file in the systems32-directory can be detected easily. Furthermore, it generates an executable with a random name in the root directory "C:" that contains search strings for anti-malware evasion.

- GRR was capable of detecting the spawning of the "reg.exe" command for editing the registry, if this is done during the investigation.
- While in theory GRR should be capable to see the network channel opened by using Internet Explorer, we were not able to detect this in our example environment using GRR.
- GRR is perfectly capable to detect the changes to the registry by adding a new key and creating a Windows Service pointing to the executable "FastUserSwitchingCompatibility.dll".

5.3   MIG

The MIG framework proposed by Mozilla, like GRR, is used in ad-hoc investigations and not for permanent monitoring. Furthermore, like GRR, it is also capable to provide read access to the actual content of files. Still, since the main goal was to tackle the problem of accidental pushes of information, it does not allow for file timelining, somewhat limiting the detection capabilities compared to GRR. Thus, in this section, we will mainly outline the differences to GRR.

With respect to the *retefe* banking trojan, the following artifacts could be observed in the lab environment:

- While it is possible to analyze the actual contents of the files, the detection of actually changed files is harder due to missing file timelining. Still, the detection is possible, especially when routinely looking for the ill-formatted docx-files.
- One major drawback for the detection, is the incapability to access the Windows registry, as the tool misses the recreated "HStartupItem" key, as well as the root CAs. This information is especially valuable, as it is (i) far more specific for this malware, (ii) typically not the effect of an user error (like badly formatted docx-files could be) and (iii) very simple to spot.

Still, even though the Windows registry could not be accesses, MIG is capable to detect the malware based on the other characteristics. For the Locky ransomware, the picture looks almost the same:

- Having no file timelining seems a bit problematic for getting the best picture on the changes taking place in the overall file system, still, we were able to detect the malware,
- Again, having access to the randomly named keys in the registry would add to the analysis.

For the Win32.Viking worm, the following artifacts were especially useful:

- Since the filename that is generated is known, and the malware generates an executable holding search strings for anti-malware evasion, we were able to detect it using MIG.
- Again, accessing the Windows registry would have helped a lot finding the Windows Service created by the malware.

It must be noted though that MIG is the only product of the three evaluated approaches that can be used for embedded devices, thus possesses a feature that must be taken into account as especially interesting in other real-life scenarios.

6   Limitations and Future Work

In terms of limitations of our evaluation, there is clearly the limited number of deployed clients. This accompanies one of our targets for future work: For follow-up work we plan to contact companies such as Google, Facebook and Mozilla to share their insights after several months (or even years) of deployment and execution of those real-time forensics tools. This would provide data from real-world deployments rather than from a lab environment, allowing to answer research questions like statistics on the typical time between detection and cleanup of a certain incident, or on the most commonly experienced incidents, and so on. However, the lab environment is indispensable without having access to the company data.

In case we do not get access to the requested data, a fallback plan is to imitate a large network by deploying thousands of cloud instances, running the real-time forensic tools. This would also provide insights into the long-term applicability of the evaluated tools. Additionally, this would bring shed light onto the effectiveness of the tools, e.g. in terms of time: How long does it take from detection until cleanup of a given incident?

Among further future work planned, we also intend to deploy more open source real-time forensics tools (or at least freeware tools) on the cloud instances mentioned. This would extend the insights on different frameworks, but would raise the problem of increasingly unmaintained frameworks.

7   Conclusions

In conclusion, all the tools reviewed in this work were able to detect the samples, still the artifacts most probably used seem to differ. In the selected examples, especially MIG's incapability to check the Windows registry was noted, as this would offer a lot of additional capabilities. Still, it must be noted that MIG is capable of dealing with embedded systems, which is an additional benefit worth noting. From the point of view of usage, the use of osquery differs quite a lot from GRR and MIG: While GRR and MIG are made to be used during an investigation, i.e. at a specific point of time after e.g. an infection was suspected, osquery, while offering this capability too, is typically configured to automatically monitor the system based on different attributes and artifacts that are prepared to be queried like tables. Still, on the other hand, it does not offer the user the possibility to check actual data on the file system, especially reconstructing deleted files and checking for search strings inside suspicious files.

In conclusion, we would recommend to use a mixed approach by having the osquery daemon permanently monitoring a selection of artifacts, especially the process list, changes to the file system and changes to the Windows registry, as well as using either MIG or GRR for getting into the issue of file checking in case new and suspicious file generation or changes are detected by the monitoring. For choosing between GRR and MIG, this mainly depends on the system at hand. In case of a Windows system, GRR outperforms MIG due to its capabilities of file timelining and accessing the Windows registry. On the other hand, in case of a more complex system structure including embedded systems or low-end hardware, MIG is simply capable to generate a much more complete picture, as information from these sources can be incorporated into the analysis.

Acknowledgements. The financial support by the Austrian Federal Ministry of Science, Research and Economy and the National Foundation for Research, Technology and Development is gratefully acknowledged.

References

1. Alsagoff, S.N.: Malware self protection mechanism. In: 2008 International Symposium on Information Technology, vol. 3, pp. 1–8 (2008)
2. Auchard, E.: Major security breaches found in Google and Yahoo email services. Accessed 13 Sept 2016
3. Carrier, B.: File System Forensic Analysis. Addison-Wesley Professional, Boston (2005)
4. Casey, E.: Digital Evidence and Computer Crime: Forensic Science, Computers, and the Internet. Academic Press, Orlando (2011)
5. Cohen, M.I., Bilby, D., Caronni, G.: Distributed forensics and incident response in the enterprise. Digit. Invest. **8**, S101–S110 (2011)
6. Cohen, M., Garfinkel, S., Schatz, B.: Extending the advanced forensic format to accommodate multiple data sources, logical evidence, arbitrary information and forensic workflow. Digit. Invest. **6**, S57–S68 (2009)
7. Comparetti, P.M., Salvaneschi, G., Kirda, E., Kolbitsch, C., Kruegel, C., Zanero, S.: Identifying dormant functionality in malware programs. In: IEEE Symposium on Security and Privacy. IEEE (2010)
8. Cruz, F., Moser, A., Cohen, M.: A scalable file based data store for forensic analysis. Digit. Invest. **12**, S90–S101 (2015)
9. Dittrich, D., Dietrich, S.: Command and control structures in malware. Usenix Mag. **32**(6), 8–17 (2007)
10. Garfinkel, S.L.: Digital forensics research: the next 10 years. Digit. Invest. **7**, S64–S73 (2010)
11. Guo, H., Jin, B., Shang, T.: Forensic investigations in cloud environments. In: 2012 International Conference on Computer Science and Information Processing (CSIP), pp. 248–251. IEEE (2012)
12. Facebook Inc. osquery performant endpoint visibility. Accessed 13 Sept 2016
13. Kent, K., Chevalier, S., Grance, T., Dang, H.: Guide to integrating forensic techniques into incident response. NIST Spec. Publ. **10**, 800–886 (2006)
14. Kolbitsch, C., Comparetti, P.M., Kruegel, C., Kirda, E., Zhou, X.-Y., Wang, X.: Effective and efficient malware detection at the end host. In: USENIX Security Symposium, pp. 351–366 (2009)
15. Mosendz, P.: Lets calculate how much money Facebook just lost during todays outage. Accessed 13 Sept 2016
16. Moser, A., Cohen, M.I.: Hunting in the enterprise: forensic triage and incident response. Digit. Invest. **10**(2), 89–98 (2013)
17. Mozilla. Mig: Mozilla investigator. Accessed 13 Sept 2016
18. Neuner, S., Schmiedecker, M., Weippl, E.: Effectiveness of file-based deduplication in digital forensics. Secur. Commun. Netw. **9**(15), 2876–2885 (2016). Wiley Online Library

19. National Institute of Standards, Technology (NIST), and United States of America. Forensic examination of digital evidence: a guide for law enforcement (2004)
20. Pollitt, M.: Computer forensics: an approach to evidence in cyberspace. In: Proceedings of the National Information Systems Security Conference, vol. 2, pp. 487–491 (1995)
21. Pollitt, M.M.: An ad hoc review of digital forensic models. In: Second International Workshop on Systematic Approaches to Digital Forensic Engineering, SADFE 2007, pp. 43–54. IEEE (2007)
22. Ty, S.: osquery: cross-platform, lightweight, and performant host visibility. In: 7th Annual Open Source Digital Forensics Conference (OSDFCon) (2016)
23. Wahnon, M.: Awesome-incident-response: all-one-tools. Accessed 13 Sept 2016
24. Yin, H., Song, D., Egele, M., Kruegel, C., Kirda, E.: Panorama: capturing system-wide information flow for malware detection and analysis. In: Proceedings of the 14th ACM Conference on Computer and Communications Security, pp. 116–127. ACM (2007)

On Locky Ransomware, Al Capone and Brexit

John MacRae[1,2] and Virginia N. L. Franqueira[2(✉)]

[1] Department of Research and Impact, Ulster University,
Belfast BT37 0QB, UK
j.macrae@ulster.ac.uk
[2] Department of Electronics, Computing and Mathematics,
University of Derby, Derby DE22 1GB, UK
v.franqueira@derby.ac.uk
j.macrael@unimail.derby.ac.uk

Abstract. The highly crafted lines of code which constitute the Locky cryptolocker ransomware are there to see in plain text in an infected machine. Yet, this forensic evidence does not lead investigators to the identity of the extortionists nor to the destination of the ransom payments. Perpetrators of this ransomware remain unknown and unchallenged and so the ransomware cyber crimewave gathers pace. This paper examines what Locky is, how it works, and the mechanics of this malware to understand how ransom payments are made. The financial impact of Locky is found to be substantial. The paper describes methods for "following the money" to assess how effectively such a digital forensic trail can assist ransomware investigators. The legal instruments that are being established by the authorities as they attempt to shut down ransomware attacks and secure prosecutions are evaluated. The technical difficulty of following the money coupled with a lack of registration and disclosure legislation mean that investigators of this cybercrime are struggling to secure prosecutions and halt Locky.

Keywords: Locky · Ransomware · Cryptolocker · Bitcoin · Brexit
Digital forensics · Money laundering

1 Introduction

Ransomware is not new. In fact the first reported example of a ransomware attack dates back to around 1989 and masqueraded as AIDS education software [1]. Ransomware is the name given to a class of software programs that prevents users from accessing their computer resources until a ransom is paid. In the earliest instances of ransomware this meant a screen lock or installing password protection on user's files. More recently a particular class of ransomware has been discovered called cryptolockers which encrypts a user's files using the AES and RSA algorithms [2]. Locky is an instance of cryptolocker ransomware. The AES and RSA algorithms require keys for encryption and decryption. The private key for decryption is provided only on payment of the ransom. Most recent versions of cryptolocker ransomware are also able to self-propagate and delete or encrypt backup files [3]. This means that the standard defence against ransomware, that of restoring files from backup, may not be effective.

© ICST Institute for Computer Sciences, Social Informatics and Telecommunications Engineering 2018
P. Matoušek and M. Schmiedecker (Eds.): ICDF2C 2017, LNICST 216, pp. 33–45, 2018.
https://doi.org/10.1007/978-3-319-73697-6_3

Additional tools to perpetuate the extortion have been observed such as countdown timers after which no ransom payments are accepted and ransom payments which increase with time. Ransom amounts have increased with the sophistication of ransomware so that amounts equivalent to thousands of dollars are now commonly demanded by the extortionists [4].

Section 2 of this paper is an overview of how Locky works. This is known as the Locky infection chain. Section 3 looks in detail at two steps within the infection chain; the spam email which initiates the Locky download, and the Tor page where Locky payments are made. These steps inform how any digital forensic investigation of Locky can be undertaken. Section 4 observes that the impact of Locky and ransomware in general is significant. The potential cost to society goes beyond financial so there is an urgent need to find the perpetrators and shut down attacks. Section 5 expands on the detail of the Tor payment page, noting that the ransom payments are in Bitcoin. Bitcoin is particularly attractive to ransomware perpetrators due to its anonymity. Section 6 evaluates what tools are presently available and their likely effectiveness against Bitcoin anonymity. Tools are one way of supporting investigators, legal instruments and cooperation between jurisdictions are another. Efforts to introduce legislation and information sharing within the EU is described in Sect. 7. Consideration is given to the consequences of Brexit for the UK's legislation and participation in these EU arrangements. In the concluding section the combined value of tools, legislation and cooperation arrangements are assessed against the backdrop of cryptocurrency money laundering techniques being increasingly used by ransomware cybercriminals. It is shown that virtual currency processors located beyond the reach of legislation and information sharing agreements remain an unsolved problem.

2 How Locky Works

A diagrammatic summary of the Locky infection chain is shown in Fig. 1 [5]. Locky is delivered as an email attachment, ostensibly an invoice for payment. The email itself could be spam email, or the victim's email address could have been collected as part of a preliminary phishing attack. The attachment is a Word document with an embedded macro function. The function can only execute if Word macros are enabled. In order to encourage the user to enable macros, distorted text is shown along with the message "*enable macro if data encoding is incorrect*". When the Word document is opened the macro downloads the Locky code which then encrypts files on the machine and simultaneously renames the filenames and changes the file extension to .locky. The first instances of Locky appeared early in 2016 and a number of variants have appeared since, namely bart, odin and thor. Bart simply moves the victim's files into a password protected zip archive and demands 3 Bitcoin for the password, unless the default language of the computer is Russian or Ukrainian in which case bart uninstalls itself. Emails with an odin malware payload have a slightly different subject line and append the extension .odin to the encrypted files. The thor variant of Locky was released in October 2016 [6] and is distributed using a javascript-based downloader and a DLL file. The DLL is executed using the rundll32.exe file. rundll32.exe is a normal windows executable which enables the thor variant of Locky to install itself stealthily [7].

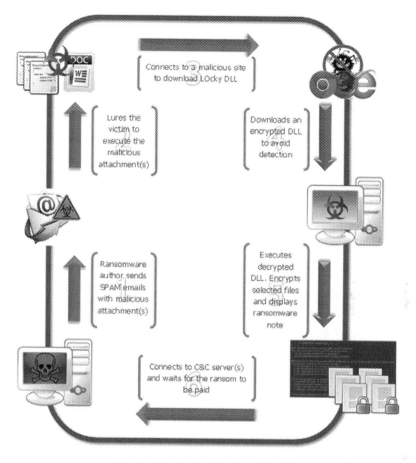

Fig. 1. The Locky infection chain [5]

3 Mechanics of the Locky Malware

The distribution and activation mechanism for Locky mirrors that of the dridex botnet and in fact may use a subnet of this botnet [8]. It is reported that this botnet has a database of 385 million email addresses so can generate significant amounts of spam targeted mainly at accounts departments of companies and enterprises rather than individuals. A typical Locky spam email is shown in Fig. 2 [9]. Note how the email masquerades as a payment invoice with a spurious purchase order reference in the subject line. The phraseology of the email is deliberately worded so that the invoice cannot readily be disregarded as fake unless the details are checked by opening the attachment.

The actual download code for Locky is obfuscated meaning that it is not directly visible within the Word macro. Instead a function CallByName is passed a string, the output of which is a visual basic script similar to that in Fig. 3 [9]. Note the section highlighted in red which shows the construction of the URL from which Locky is to be downloaded. For forensics investigators trying to find the download source of Locky, this is the start of the trail.

> Subject **ATTN: Invoice J-62818225**
>
> To   ☆   Other Actions ▾
>
> Dear John,
>
> Please see the attached invoice (Microsoft Word Document) and remit payment according to the terms listed at the bottom of the invoice.
>
> Let us know if you have any questions.
>
>
> We greatly appreciate your business!
> Abram Brewer
>
>
> ▷ 📎1 attachment: invoice_J-62818225.doc   ⬇ Save ▾

Fig. 2. Sample email with which Locky has been associated [9] (Color figure online)

Once Locky is downloaded it renames itself svchost.exe so that it looks like a regular windows executable. The renamed process initiates a secondary process to delete backup files and prevent a system restore. Before file encryption can commence the ransomware must communicate with the command and control servers to report that a system has been infected and to obtain the RSA public key. A unique ID of the infected machine is generated and stored on the command and control server. However even this communication is encrypted so as to prevent ethical hackers observing the traffic. As of 2016, nine of the command and control servers were reported to be in Russia and therefore beyond EU law enforcement [9].

Locky can encrypt a wide range of file types – 164 according to Threat Intelligence Team [9] – which means that a very wide range of businesses can be impacted. The strength of the encryption algorithm is such that it is not possible to decrypt the affected files without the matching private key downloaded from the command and control servers. The servers provide the correct private key by cross referencing against the unique system ID provided when the infection process commenced. Figure 4 shows the ransomware payment page within the tor network [9]. Note the payment instructions in Bitcoin. This payment mechanism has substantial implications for forensic investigators whose task is to "follow the money". These implications are discussed throughout the remainder of this paper.

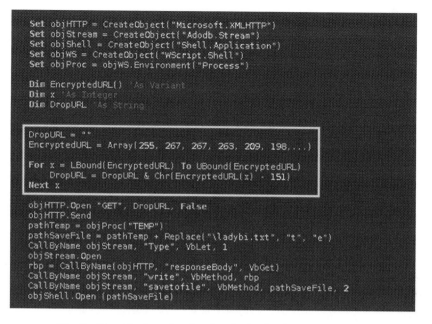

```
Set objHTTP = CreateObject("Microsoft.XMLHTTP")
Set objStream = CreateObject("Adodb.Stream")
Set objShell = CreateObject("Shell.Application")
Set objWS = CreateObject("WScript.Shell")
Set objProc = objWS.Environment("Process")

Dim EncryptedURL() As Variant
Dim x 'As Integer
Dim DropURL 'As String

DropURL = ""
EncryptedURL = Array(255, 267, 267, 263, 209, 198,...)

For x = LBound(EncryptedURL) To UBound(EncryptedURL)
    DropURL = DropURL & Chr(EncryptedURL(x) - 151)
Next x

objHTTP.Open "GET", DropURL, False
objHTTP.Send
pathTemp = objProc("TEMP")
pathSaveFile = pathTemp + Replace("\ladybi.txt", "t", "e")
CallByName objStream, "Type", VbLet, 1
objStream.Open
rbp = CallByName(objHTTP, "responseBody", VbGet)
CallByName objStream, "write", VbMethod, rbp
CallByName objStream, "savetofile", VbMethod, pathSaveFile, 2
objShell.Open (pathSaveFile)
```

Fig. 3. Visual basic script showing the Locky download code [9]

Fig. 4. Locky payment page within the Tor dark web [5]

4 Impact of Locky is Substantial

A Symantec report on ransomware published in 2016 [4] makes the point that it is impossible to measure how much money has been paid to ransomware extortionists. Anubis Networks detected 4500 infected machines between 16th and 18th February 2016 [10]. If every machine pays a decryption cost of 1 bitcoin, which is worth £800 in February 2017, then that adds up to £1.2 million per day. However that infection rate is a 2016 figure: since then more sophisticated versions of Locky have been released which encrypts backups and shared drives. Accordingly the cost of decryption has increased. FBI researchers have estimated that the revenue from ransomware collectively could be as high as a billion dollars annually [11].

However the revenue being collected by the extortionists is only part of the economic cost of Locky. The other part is the cost incurred by organisations that have their work disrupted. Hospitals have been a particular target for Locky. In February 2016 Hollywood Presbyterian Medical Centre in Los Angeles paid $17,000 to regain access to their patients data [12]. There were attacks on other US and Japanese hospitals [13]. Attacks on hospitals mean that patients medical records may be inaccessible leading to delays in administering treatments and medications. This has the consequence of putting lives at risk and exposing the hospital to fines and legal claims.

5 Ransomware and Cryptocurrency Have Become Either Side of the Same (Bit)Coin

For cyber criminals the most problematic aspect of the ransomware model has always been that of receiving payment in a way that did not lead to their detection. Early methods involved sending an SMS message to a premium account or use of an anonymous PO Box mailing address. Law enforcement soon learnt to stake out the PO Box until someone came along to pick up the payments. PayPal, Western Union, iTunes and gift cards have also been used as payment methods but they all suffer from limited anonymity; the money cannot be spent unless it ultimately goes through a conventional bank account or online retailer.

The scale and sophistication of ransomware attacks has accelerated in recent years. This is partly due to the spread of botnets that are distributing the Locky infection email. It is partly due to reorganisation within the crime gangs which have turned to offering cybercrime-as-a-service business models. Philadelphia [14] is an example of ransomware-as-a-service in which the ransomware attack and payment infrastructure is leased out, allowing criminals with no IT knowledge to take advantage of the ransomware extortion. However the success of ransomware is mostly to do with the technical sophistication of ransomware itself. This means efficient implementation of the public private key encryption so that infected computers cannot be decrypted without the private key. It means traffic between infected computers and the command and control computers (C&C) is encrypted so that the URL of the C&C computers cannot be traced, and it means virtually untraceable payments made in Bitcoin or another cryptocurrency.

Bitcoin is a peer-to-peer cryptocurrency in which transactions are recorded in a distributed ledger called blockchain. There is no central repository or single administrator. The information which is used to perform Bitcoin transactions is stored in a software application called a wallet. Bitcoin uses public key cryptography: the information contained in the wallet is essentially the public and private keys relating to a user's Bitcoin ownership. Blockchain contains the public key hashes of all Bitcoin transactions. Since there is no single administrator the entire blockchain must be distributed across the internet and these public key hashes are visible.

The connection between visible public key hashes and the private keys only takes place in whatever way the wallet is implemented. Increasingly the function of the wallet is provided by Bitcoin processors. Such processors can move money between the Bitcoin virtual currency and real bank accounts. They can take the form of ATMs or of online payment intermediaries similar to the services provided by MasterCard and VISA as used by merchants. Wallets are also implemented as smartphone applications that can be used to pay for goods and services directly. An example of the rich functionality that such smartphone wallets now provide can be seen in the CoinsBank wallet app [15].

6 Review of Tools for Bitcoin and Blockchain Deanonymisation

Strictly speaking, Bitcoin transactions are pseudonymous rather than anonymous. The public key hashes of the transactions are visible, but the link between the public keys and their owners is not visible or accessible. Deanonymisation is the process of using other sources of information to try to connect public key hashes to Bitcoin owners or to their bank accounts. This process uses a combination of traditional policing methods otherwise known as the classical forensic approach [16] and more recently dedicated tools such as BitIodine [17], BitCluster [18], Elliptic [19] and Chainalysis [20] all of which involve collection to some extent of open source forensics. The term open source forensics refers to information and potential evidence publically available from internet blogs, forums and social media.

The so-called classical approach is analogous to a blunt instrument in which a legal demand is served on Bitcoin processing businesses to reveal the owner or bank account of public key hashes of interest to investigators. As it is the purpose of Bitcoin processors to enable the transfer of money from Bitcoin to and from traditional currencies, these processors hold the link between the anonymous public key hashes and their owners. However the classical forensic method is fraught with difficulty. A particular problem is connecting a public key hash suspected to be associated with cyber criminality with a specific Bitcoin processor on which to serve the information demand. The Bitcoin processors may themselves be illegal and may be operating outside of the legal jurisdiction of the investigators such that they cannot be compelled to provide information. This problem is discussed in Sect. 7.

In contrast BitIodine could be described as a covert approach to Bitcoin forensics. This method, which relies on open source forensics, is described as trying to correlate Bitcoin transaction activity with Facebook account activity [15]. A more comprehensive description of BitIodine is that it consists, inter alia, of a set of "crawlers" which search the web for Bitcoin addresses which can be associated with real users. The types of domains that are searched include usernames on Bitcoin forums, details of known scammers and tagged data from blockchain.info, news sites and from social media.

Meiklejohn et al. [21] describe the application of BitIodine to a ransomware investigation. It is not stated in the paper if the destination of the ransom money was ultimately determined, but BitIodine was able to detect Bitcoin clusters belonging to the ransomware perpetrators and cross reference that to a reddit thread where victims had been posting addresses.

BitCluster is an open-source data mining tool which allows its users to group Bitcoin transactions by their participants. The goal of BitCluster according to [18] was to gather data on users of the Bitcoin network, and attempt to aggregate Bitcoin wallets which otherwise would seem to be anonymous and isolated from one another. BitCluster therefore enables investigators to detect significant payment patterns which could be linked to ransomware schemes. BitCluster is a way to link public key hashes to campaigns using the scale of transactions linked to the timing of spam attack. If the relevant public key hashes can be determined then investigators can follow-up with the classic forensics approach of demanding information from the Bitcoin processors. However BitCluster only works as long as the same public key hashes are used for ransom payments. The effectiveness of the tool is defeated if each new ransom payment uses a new public key hash.

Elliptic is a startup company founded in 2013. The Elliptic product is a data mining tool with similarities to BitCluster but with ongoing development and support commensurate with a commercial product [19]. Elliptic started life as a Bitcoin vault platform but found that Bitcoin forensics was of particular interest to financial institutions worried about the consequences of anti-money laundering regulations that would leave them exposed were they inadvertently be involved in processing of Bitcoins obtained as proceeds of crime. The technology underlying Elliptic is not described in the public domain. However according to a 2017 paper [15] it traces transactions through the blockchain, uncovers relationships between different entities and uses artificial intelligence techniques to enable mapping between public hash keys and their real owners. It is a logical step from Elliptic's history as a Bitcoin vault, that is as a store of Bitcoin transaction, to analysing and visualising the transaction history.

A typical Elliptic screenshot is shown in Fig. 5 [19]. This visualisation indicates the relationships between the illegal marketplace "Silk Road" and other entities processing Bitcoins. Elliptic claims to provide forensics intelligence to ransomware investigators and thus facilitate the arrest of ransomware cybercriminals and assist financial institutions in refusing to process Bitcoins collected through ransomware attacks.

Chainalysis was formed in 2014 and has already signed an MoU with Europol [22] on the provision of technical services to spot connections between Bitcoin transactions and cyber criminals. The Chainalysis Reactor tool is specifically aimed at forensics investigation of virtual currency transactions.

There is little material in the public domain linking these data mining tools to successful prosecutions of cyber criminals. The most convincing is the application of the BitIodine tool to the Dread Pirate Roberts case described by Meiklejohn et al. [21].

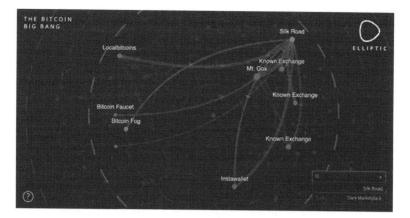

Fig. 5. Elliptic screenshot showing Bitcoin trading relationships [19]

This might be due to the need to maintain confidentiality for prosecutions which have not yet come to court. Or it might be the case that cyber criminals have already learnt to outwit the data mining tools by changing transaction patterns: essentially money laundering within virtual currencies. For forensic investigators, these tools are unlikely to possess the specificity to withstand court scrutiny - if they provide any evidence at all - and at best may provide some complementary investigative direction.

7 Legal Instruments Facilitating Ransomware Digital Forensics

On the 30th November 2016 a federal court in the northern District of California authorised the tax authorities in the US, known as the Internal Revenue Service (IRS), to serve a "John Doe" summons [23] on the Bitcoin processor Coinbase Inc [24]. The purpose of the summons is to demand that Coinbase releases the names and financial trading history of owners of Bitcoin and other cryptocurrencies so that the IRS can collect any unpaid taxes. The John Doe summons is considered a brute force approach by the IRS yet is also an acknowledgement that the pseudonymous nature of cryptocurrencies means that it is otherwise difficult for the tax authorities to detect hidden wealth and potentially taxable capital gains. Note that the IRS have chosen the approach of forcing the cryptocurrency processor to disclose information rather than using other means - such as the data mining tools described above - to try to link the public key hashes that are visible on the bitcoin exchanges with their owners and bank accounts.

There is an interesting parallel with the notorious American prohibition-era gangster Al Capone. Despite Capone's involvement in a criminal syndicate that supplied illegal alcohol, he was eventually tried and convicted by the FBI on a charge of tax evasion. This was considered a novel strategy by the FBI in 1931. The suspicion of tax evasion is therefore being used to challenge the pseudo-anonymity of cryptocurrencies in a strategy which may provide information and lead prosecutors to the recipients of the proceeds of ransomware. The strategy relies on being able to link public key hashes with ransomware payments, and it relies on the relevant cryptocurrency processors operating within the jurisdiction covered by the US court summons.

The UK's first money laundering national risk assessment was published by UK Government in 2015 [25]. Although the report is concerned with money laundering in all its respects, it acknowledges the speed of trade, anonymity and cross border nature of virtual currency transactions. It assesses this threat as principally related to the activities of cyber criminals. The report concluded that there was a strong case for anti-money laundering legislation in order to create a hostile environment for illicit users of virtual currencies. Contemporaneously, legislation was being developed by the European Commission known as the 4th Money Laundering Directive (4MLD). The 4MLD was published on 20th May 2015 and was essentially implementing the recommendations of the international Financial Action Task Force dating back to 2012 [26]. The Commission proposed that 4MLD was implemented into the national legislation of EU member countries by 26 June 2017. 4MLD did not, at this stage, make any reference to disclosure requirements for virtual currencies.

In response to terrorist attacks across Europe during 2015, a number of European bodies, specifically the Justice and Home Affairs Council [27], the Economic and Financial Affairs Council [28] and the European Council [29] stressed the need to intensify the work within the EU on addressing terrorism and enhancing the provisions within 4MLD. This led, on 5th July 2016, to the Commission adopting an Action Plan [30] as amendments to 4MLD to tackle the abuse of the financial system for terrorist financing purposes. This document also brought forward to 1st January 2017 the date by which the 4MLD including these amendments was to be implemented in member states.

The effect of the amendments is to add virtual currencies and wallet providers as entities to whom the obligations of the 4MLD apply. These obligations are, inter alia, know-your-customer requirements, suspicious activity reporting, licensing and registration. The consequence of these additional obligations on virtual currency processors is that anonymous virtual currency ownership and trading will no longer be possible within EU-based entities. The 4MLD legislation will therefore increase the forensic material available to ransomware investigators. This information will have to be used alongside other sources of forensics, such as the data mining tools described above in Sect. 6, in order for investigators and cryptocurrency processors to identify and link ransomware payments with cryptocurrency transactions.

The European Commission's action plan of amendments to 4MLD states that the proposed objectives cannot be achieved by member states alone and can be better achieved at the European Union level: the lack of an effective anti-money laundering framework in one member state can have consequences across the other member states and undermine the disclosure and transparency aims of 4MLD. As well as the legislative momentum for 4MLD and its later amendments coming from the EU, the proposed information sharing mechanisms will be EU-wide under the proposal to establish and then interconnect national central registers which would hold information on virtual currency transactions.

Despite Brexit, the UK Government has given a commitment to implement the 4MLD in the UK as the Money Laundering and Transfer of Funds (Information on the Payer) Regulations 2017. As yet unanswered is the question of the UK's participation post Brexit in the information sharing aspects of 4MLD between EU Financial Intelligence Units. Information sharing is an important aspect in achieving the desired transparency on ownership of virtual currency. Also unanswered is the UK's ongoing participation, post Brexit, in the various European bodies from which legislative momentum is derived. Post Brexit, without participation in such European bodies, without the legislative momentum derived from European Commission proposals and without access to shared information, there is a risk that ransomware forensic investigators in the UK are substantially blindfolded compared with their European counterparts. There is a corresponding risk that outside of European frameworks of cooperation the UK could become a preferred destination for the cryptocurrency transactions of cybercriminals.

8   Conclusions

According to Cisco, the ability to demand payment in Bitcoin, a pseudonymous virtual currency not controlled by any country, was 'the birth of ransomware' and has led to a substantial increase in number of ransomware attacks since the currency's introduction in 2009. Since the source and control of ransomware involves botnets and servers invariably hidden in uncooperative jurisdictions, the best strategy for digital forensics investigators is to "follow the money" to see if recipients of the Bitcoin ransomware payments can be identified. Some research projects and corresponding tools were identified and examined.

The commercial tools especially make bold claims concerning the deanonymisation of Bitcoin public key hashes, but there is little in the public domain about how they work. There are no case studies with demonstrated convictions. The exception is Meiklejohn et al. [21] who describe in detail the algorithms and approaches designed into the BitIodine open source tool and demonstrate its effectiveness in several real world use cases. It can be inferred from the terminology used that the commercial tools use similar approaches with similar outcomes.

The best that might be said of the state of the art in Bitcoin forensics tools is that they can provide leads for investigators to follow alongside investigative processes. However since the tools are based on the data mining techniques of pattern matching and clustering, these algorithms can be defeated if the cyber criminals start to use multiple independent Bitcoin keys, each transaction being of a small Bitcoin amount. A further obfuscation technique the criminals use is to vary transaction patterns: the cryptocurrency version of money laundering. Clearly data mining tools are not a panacea for ransomware investigators, although it is worth keeping an eye on the capabilities of the commercial tools as a complement to traditional investigative processes.

In the US and Europe the experience of chasing Al Capone has not been forgotten and so the approach to increasing the forensics available to ransomware investigators is not on the crime itself, but via the financial crimes of tax evasion and money laundering. However enabling legislation in cooperating jurisdictions is not yet in place. In Europe the provisions within the 4th Anti-Money Laundering Directive were substantially amended following the terrorist attacks in Europe in 2015 to include disclosure and information sharing requirements on virtual currency processors. It is not clear how Brexit will affect the UK's long term participation in this information sharing, but it will be important for ransomware investigators that the UK continues to participate in the cooperation arrangements proposed by the EU. This desire was formally expressed in the UK Prime Minister's letter to the EU President on 29th March 2017 which triggered Article 50, that is, the UK intention to leave the European Union [31].

Regardless of Brexit or 4MLD, the legislation does not address the problem of illegal processors or those operating outside the frameworks of cooperation. For example, a close examination of the CoinsBank bitcoin processor described in Sect. 5 reveals that the website is operated by CB Exchange LP with an address in Edinburgh. The underlying financial services of CoinsBank are provided by XBIT Ltd which is registered and regulated in Belize. It is not yet clear if this structure will fall within the jurisdiction of the UK's 4MLD. Virtual currency processors resident and regulated outside the jurisdiction of 4MLD will continue to represent a formidable obstacle for ransomware forensic investigators.

References

1. Alina, S.: Ransomware's stranger-than-fiction origin story (2015). https://medium.com/un-hackable/the-bizarre-pre-internet-history-of-ransomware-bb480a652b4b-.z5qxcdeyy
2. Calderbank, M.: The RSA Cryptosystem: History, Algorithm, Primes. http://www.math.uchicago.edu/~may/VIGRE/VIGRE2007/REUPapers/FINALAPP/Calderbank.pdf
3. Trendmicro.co.uk: Ransomware - Definition - Trend Micro UK. http://www.trendmicro.co.uk/vinfo/uk/security/definition/ransomware
4. Symantec: ISTR2016 Ransomware Report. http://www.symantec.com/content/en/us/enterprise/media/security_response/whitepapers/ISTR2016_Ransomware_and_Businesses.pdf
5. Valdez, J.: Meet the latest member of the Locky family: odin. https://blog.gdatasoftware.com/2016/10/29245-meet-the-latest-member-of-the-locky-family-odin
6. State of Security: The Thor Variant of Locky Virus. https://www.tripwire.com/state-of-security/latest-security-news/thor-variant-locky-virus
7. It-b.co.uk: What is Thor. http://www.it-b.co.uk/blog/what-is-thor
8. Zorz, Z.: Dridex botnet alive and well, now also spreading ransomware - Help Net Security. Help Net Security. https://www.helpnetsecurity.com/2016/02/17/dridex-botnet-alive-and-well-now-also-spreading-ransomware/
9. Intelligence Threat Team: A closer look at the Locky ransomware. Blog.avast.com, https://blog.avast.com/a-closer-look-at-the-locky-ransomware
10. Blog.anubisnetworks.com: Locky ransomware, metrics and protection. http://blog.anubisnetworks.com/blog/locky-ransomware-metrics-and-protection
11. Griffin, D.: Cyber-extortion losses skyrocket, says FBI. CNNMoney. http://money.cnn.com/2016/04/15/technology/ransomware-cyber-security/
12. Yadron, D.: Los Angeles hospital paid $17,000 in bitcoin to ransomware hackers. The Guardian. https://www.theguardian.com/technology/2016/feb/17/los-angeles-hospital-hacked-ransom-bitcoin-hollywood-presbyterian-medical-center

13. Theregister.co.uk: FireEye warns 'massive' ransomware campaign hits US, Japan hospitals. http://www.theregister.co.uk/2016/08/18/fireeye_warns_massive_ransomware_campaign_hits_us_japan_hospitals/
14. Krebsonsecurity.com: Ransomware for Dummies: Anyone Can Do It — Krebs on Security. https://krebsonsecurity.com/2017/03/ransomware-for-dummies-anyone-can-do-it/
15. Coinsbank.com: CoinsBank - the bank of Blockchain future. https://coinsbank.com/wallet
16. InfoSec Resources: The End of Bitcoin Ransomware? http://resources.infosecinstitute.com/the-end-of-bitcoin-ransomware/#gref
17. Spagnuolo, M., Maggi, F., Zanero, S.: BitIodine: extracting intelligence from the Bitcoin network. In: Christin, N., Safavi-Naini, R. (eds.) FC 2014. LNCS, vol. 8437, pp. 457–468. Springer, Heidelberg (2014). https://doi.org/10.1007/978-3-662-45472-5_29
18. Bit-cluster.com: BitCluster. http://www.bit-cluster.com
19. Elliptic: Elliptic. https://www.elliptic.co/
20. chainalysis.com: Chainalysis - Blockchain analysis. Chainalysis. https://www.chainalysis.com/
21. Meiklejohn, S., Pomarole, M., Jordan, G., Levchenko, K., McCoy, D., Voelker, G., Savage, S.: A fistful of Bitcoins. Commun. ACM **59**(4), 86–93 (2016)
22. Europol: Europol and Chainalysis Reinforce Their Cooperation in The Fight Against Cybercrime. https://www.europol.europa.eu/newsroom/news/europol-and-chainalysis-reinforce-their-cooperation-in-fight-against-cybercrime
23. Justice.gov: Court Authorizes Service of John Doe Summons Seeking the Identities of U.S. Taxpayers Who Have Used Virtual Currency. https://www.justice.gov/opa/pr/court-authorizes-service-john-doe-summons-seeking-identities-us-taxpayers-who-have-used-virtual-currency
24. Coinbase.com: Bitcoin & Ethereum Wallet - Coinbase. https://www.coinbase.com/?locale=en
25. UK Treasury: UK national risk assessment of money laundering and terrorist financing. https://www.gov.uk/government/uploads/system/uploads/attachment_data/file/468210/UK_NRA_October_2015_final_web.pdf
26. Fatf-gafi.org: Documents - Financial Action Task Force (FATF) (2017). http://www.fatf-gafi.org/publications/fatfrecommendations/documents/fatf-recommendations.html
27. Consilium.europa.eu: Economic and Financial Affairs Council configuration (Ecofin) - Consilium. http://www.consilium.europa.eu/en/council-eu/configurations/ecofin/. Accessed 15 Mar 2017
28. Consilium.europa.eu: Justice and Home Affairs Council configuration (JHA) - Consilium. http://www.consilium.europa.eu/en/council-eu/configurations/jha/
29. Consilium.europa.eu: The European Council - Consilium. http://www.consilium.europa.eu/en/european-council/
30. European Union: AML Directive. http://ec.europa.eu/justice/criminal/document/files/aml-directive_en.pdf
31. BBC News: Teresa May Article 50 letter. http://news.bbc.co.uk/1/shared/bsp/hi/pdfs/29_03_17_article50.pdf

Deanonymization

Finding and Rating Personal Names on Drives for Forensic Needs

Neil C. Rowe[(✉)]

Computer Science, U.S. Naval Postgraduate School, Monterey, CA 93940, USA
ncrowe@nps.edu

Abstract. Personal names found on drives provide forensically valuable information about users of systems. This work reports on the design and engineering of tools to mine them from disk images, bootstrapping on output of the Bulk Extractor tool. However, most potential names found are either uninteresting sales and help contacts or are not being used as names, so we developed methods to rate name-candidate value by an analysis of the clues that they and their context provide. We used an empirically based approach with statistics from a large corpus from which we extracted 303 million email addresses and 74 million phone numbers, and then found 302 million personal names. We tested three machine-learning approaches and Naïve Bayes performed the best. Cross-modal clues from nearby email addresses improved performance still further. This approach eliminated from consideration 71.3% of the addresses found in our corpus with an estimated 67.4% F-score, a potential 3.5 times reduction in the name workload of most forensic investigations.

Keywords: Digital forensics · Personal names · Extraction · Email addresses
Phone numbers · Rating · Filtering · Bulk Extractor · Naïve Bayes
Cross-modality

1 Introduction

When we scan raw drive images we can often find information about people who have used the drives and their contacts, and this information is often important in criminal and intelligence investigations using digital forensics. We call these "personal artifacts" and others have called them "identities" [8].

Our previous work [14] developed a methodology for finding interesting email addresses on drives using Bayesian methods and graphing their social networks. Personal names could provide more direct information than email addresses about users of a drive and their contacts. Candidates can be found using lists of known names. They can be combined with the email data and other information to build a more complete picture of users. However, we only are interested in "useful" names, names relevant to most criminal or intelligence investigations. We define "useful" to exclude those not being used as names, those that are business and organizational contacts, those associated with software and projects, those in fiction, and those that occur on many drives. (These criteria would need modification for an investigation involving an associated organization or an important common document.) We estimate that useful names are

© ICST Institute for Computer Sciences, Social Informatics and Telecommunications Engineering 2018
P. Matoušek and M. Schmiedecker (Eds.): ICDF2C 2017, LNICST 216, pp. 49–63, 2018.
https://doi.org/10.1007/978-3-319-73697-6_4

only 30% of the names found on drives. We shall test the hypothesis that a set of easily calculable local clues can reliably rate usefulness of name candidates with precision well beyond that of name-dictionary lookup alone, so that most candidates irrelevant to most investigations can be excluded.

2 Previous Work

Finding personal data is often important in forensics. Web sites provide much useful information about people, but only their public faces, and email servers provide much semi-public data [9]. Registries, cookie stores, and key chains on drives can provide rich sources of personal data including names [11], but they often lack the deleted and concealed information that may be critical in criminal and intelligence investigations. Thus this work focuses on more thorough search of a drive image for personal names.

Tools for "named entity recognition" in text [1] can find locations and organizations as well as personal names. Most learn sequences of N consecutive words in text that include named entities [12]. This has been applied to forensic data [15]. Capitalization, preceding articles, and absence from a standard dictionary are clues. But these methods do not work well for forensic data since our previous work estimated that only 21.9% of the email addresses in our corpus occurred within files. Secondly, only a small fraction of the artifacts within files occur within documents or document fragments for which linguistic sequence models would be helpful; for instance, articles like "the" are rare in most forensic data. Instead, other clues from the local context are needed to find artifacts. Thirdly, most forensic references to people are business and vendor contacts, not people generally worth investigating, a weakness in the otherwise interesting work of [8]. For these reasons, linguistic methods for named-entity recognition do not work well for forensic tasks.

An alternative is to make a list of names and scan drives for them using a keyword search tool. We explored this with the well-known Bulk Extractor tool [2] and its –F argument giving a file of the names. But full scans are time-consuming. An experiment extracting all delimited names from a single 8.92 gigabyte drive image in EWF (E01) format took around ten days, given the additional requirement of breaking the names into 927 runs to satisfy Bulk Extractor's limit of 300 per run. Furthermore, the percentage yield of useful names was low. Because names had to be delimited, the output did not include run-on personal-name pairs in email addresses, so it found only 21% of the name occurrences found by the methods to be described. It did find a few new name candidates beyond those of our methods since it searched the entire drive, but 98.7% of these candidates in a random sample were being used as non-names (e.g. "mark" and "good"). Another criticism of broad scanning is that finding an isolated personal name is less useful than finding it near other personal information, since context is important in an investigation; [14] showed that email addresses more than 22 bytes distant on a drive were statistically uncorrelated, and names are probably similar. It is also difficult to confirm the validity of names without other nearby personal artifacts, making it hard to train and test on them.

This work will thus pursue an approach of examining context in which useful personal names are more likely to occur in routine Bulk Extractor output, rating the candidates using machine-learning methods, and selecting the best ones. The ultimate goal of extraction of personal artifacts in forensics will be to construct graphs modelling human connections. This can provide a context for the artifacts as well as aid in name disambiguation [3], and permits cross-drive analysis to relate drives [4].

3 Test Setup

This work used the Real Data Corpus [6], a collection of currently 3361 drives from 33 countries that is publicly available subject to constraints. These drives were purchased as used equipment and represent a range of business, government, and home users. We supplemented this with images of twelve substantial computers of seven members of our research team.

The first step was to run the Bulk Extractor tool [2] to get all email addresses (including cookies), phone numbers, bank-card numbers, and Web links (URLs), along with their offsets on the drive and their 16 preceding and 16 following characters. Such data extraction is often routine in investigations, so we bootstrapped on generally available data. Such extraction can exploit regular expressions effectively and can be significantly faster than name-set lookup. Bulk Extractor can find data in deleted and unallocated storage as well as within many kinds of compressed files [5]. It found 2442 of the drives had email addresses, 1601 had phone numbers, and 10 had bank-card numbers. In total we obtained 303,221,117 email addresses of which 17,484,640 were distinct, and 21,184,361 phone numbers of which 1,739,054 were distinct. As discussed, this research assumed that most useful personal names are near email addresses, phone numbers, and personal-identification numbers. Thus we wrote a tool to extract names from the Bulk Extractor "context" output using a hashed dictionary of possible names. We segmented words at spaces, line terminators, punctuation marks, digits, lower-to-upper case changes, and by additional criteria described in Sect. 4.1.

Our hashed name dictionary had 277,888 personal names obtained from a variety of sources. The U.S. Census Bureau (www.census.gov) has published 95,025 distinct surnames which occurred at least five times in their data 1880-2015 and 88,799 last names in 1990. For international coverage, tekeli.li/onomastikon provided more names. We supplemented this with data from email user names in our corpus split at punctuation marks, looking for those differing in a single character from known names; this found variant names not in existing lists, but had to be manually checked to remove a few errors. We also mined our corpus for the formats like "John Smith <jsmith@hotmail.edu>" and "'John Smith' 555-123-4567" that strongly suggest names in the first two words. Most dictionary names were Ascii, as non-Ascii user names were not permitted by email protocols for a long time and rarely appear in our corpus. We did not distinguish surnames and family names since many are used for both purposes. Note this is a "whitelisting" approach to defining names; a blacklisting approach storing non-names is unworkable because the number of such strings is unbounded and they have too much variety to define with regular expressions.

We also created a list of 809,216 words from all our natural-language dictionaries [13], currently covering 23 languages and 19 transliterations of those, together with counts of words in the file names of our corpus to get a rough estimate of usage rates.

We created another list of 54,918 generic names like "contact" and "sales" from manual inspection of our corpus and translation of those words into all our dictionary languages, to serve as definite non-names for our analysis.

Bulk Extractor provides offsets (byte addresses) on the drive for the artifacts it finds. Offsets for nearby personal names can be computed from these; nearby artifacts are often related. Bulk Extractor gives at least two offsets for compressed files, one of the start of the compressed file and one within the file if it were decompressed; a few files were multiply compressed and had up to six offsets. It is important not to add these numbers since the sums could overlap into the area of the next file on the drive when compression reduced the size of a file. We separate the container address space by taking -10 times the offset of the container and adding to it the sum of the offsets of the artifact within the decompressed container. Since few compressions exceed a factor of 10, this maps offsets of compressed files to disjoint ranges of negative numbers.

4 Analysis of Personal-Name Candidates

Overall, 95.6% of the personal-name candidates our methods extracted were found in Bulk Extractor email records, 1.0% in phone-number records, 0.0% in ccn (bank-card) records, and 3.4% in URL records when we included them. URL paths can refer to personal Web pages, but a random sample of 1088 candidate personal-name candidates found only 71 or 6.5% useful personal names since it found many names of celebrities, fictional characters, and words that are predominantly non-names. It appeared that the "url" plugin provides too many false alarms to be useful. Output of other Bulk Extractor plugins was also unhelpful.

We obtained in total 302,242,805 personal names from 2222 drives with at least one name in our corpus, of which 5,921,992 were distinct (though names like "John" could refer to many people). The number of files on these drives was 61,365,153, so only a few files had personal names. Interestingly, several hundred drives had no recoverable files but many names, apparently due to imperfect disk wiping.

4.1 Splitting Strings to Find Names

Personal names are often run together in email addresses, e.g. "johnsmith". We can segment these by systematically examining splits of unrecognized words. Usually one should prefer splits that maximize the size of the largest piece since this increases the reliability of the names found. For instance, there are 10,785 personal names of length 4 in our name wordlist (fraction 0.024 of all possible 4-character Ascii words), 39,548 of length 5 (fraction 0.0033), 62,114 of length 6 (fraction 0.00020), 58,119 of length 7 (fraction 0.0000072), and 37,461 of length 8 (fraction 0.00000018). That suggested the following algorithm for splitting to find names:

1. Check if the string is a known word (personal name, generic name, or dictionary word); if so, return it and stop. For instance, "thompson", "help", and "porcupine". However, there must be an exception for hexadecimal strings using digits and the characters "abcdef" for which there can be false alarms for names like "ed" and

"bee". So we exclude words preceded by a digit, but not names followed by a digit since these can be numberings of identical names like "joe37".

2. Check whether the string minus its first, last, first two, last two, first three, or last three characters (in that order) is a known personal name; if so, return the split and stop. For instance, "jrthompson" and "thompsonk".

3. Split the string into two pieces as evenly as possible, and then consider successively uneven splits. Check whether both pieces can be recognized as personal names or dictionary words, and stop splitting if you do. For instance, "johnthompson" and "bigtable" can be split into "john thompson" and "big table", but only the first is a personal name.

Unicode encodings raise special problems. Bulk Extractor often represents these with a "\x" and number, and these can be easily handled. But sometimes it encodes characters in languages like Arabic, Cyrillic, and Hebrew as two characters with the first character the higher-order bits, appearing usually as a control character. We try to detect such two-character patterns and correct them, though this causes difficulties for subsequent offset-difference calculations. More complex encodings of names and addresses used with phishing obfuscation [10] need additional decoding techniques.

4.2   Combining Adjacent Personal Names

Once names are extracted, it is important to recognize multiword names that together identify an individual since these are more specific and useful than the individual names, e.g. "Bobbi Jo Riley". We do this with a second pass through the data, which for our corpus reduced the number of name candidates from 556 million to 302 million. After study of sample data, we determined that names could only be combined when separated by 0 to 4 characters for the cases shown in Table 1. These cases can be applied more than once to the same words, so we could first append "Bobbi" and "Jo", then "Bobbi Jo" and "Riley".

Table 1. Cases for appending names.

Intervening characters	Example	Extracted name
None	johnsmith	John Smith
Space, period, hyphen, or underscore	john_smith	John Smith
Period and space after single-letter name	j. smith	J Smith
Comma and space	smith, john	John Smith
Space, letter, space; or underscore, letter, underscore	john a smith	John A Smith
Space, letter, period, space; or underscore, letter, period, underscore	john a. smith	John A Smith

A constraint applied was that appended names cannot be a subset of one another ignoring case. For instance, for the input "John Smith smithjohn@yahoo.com" we can extract "John", "Smith", "smith", and "john", and we can combine the first two. But we cannot then combine "John Smith" and "smith" because the latter is a substring of the former ignoring case, though we can combine "smith" with "john". Another constraint that eliminates many spurious combinations is that the character cases must be consistent between the words appended. For instance, "smith" and "SID" cannot be combined because one is lower-case and one is upper-case; that was important for our corpus because "SID" occurs frequently indicating an identification number. We permit only lower-lower, upper-upper, capitalized-capitalized, and capitalized-lower combinations, with exceptions for a few name prefixes such as "mc", "la", and "des" that are inconsistently capitalized.

Overlapping windows found by Bulk Extractor enable finding additional names split across two contexts, as with one context ending with "Rich" and another context starting with "chard". One can also eliminate duplicate data for the same location found from overlapping Bulk Extractor context strings.

As an example, Table 2 shows example Bulk Extractor output in which we can recognize name candidates "John" at offset 1000008, "Smith" at 1000013, "j" at 1000021, "smith" at 1000022, "Bob" at 1000057, "Jones" at 1000061, and "em" at 1000070. Looking at adjacencies we should recognize three strong candidates for two-word names: "John Smith" at offset 1000008, "J Smith" at 1000021, and "Bob Jones" as 1000056. The first two-word combinations match which makes them both even more likely in context. However, possible nickname "Em" is unlikely to be a personal name here because its common-word occurrence is high, it is not capitalized, and it appears in isolation.

Table 2. Example Bulk Extractor artifacts.

Artifact offset	Artifact	Context
100000021	Address jsmith@ hotmail2.com	ylor"\x0A"John Smith" <jsmith@ hotmail2.com>, 555-623-1886\x0A"Bo
100000043	Phone number 555-623-1886	smith@hotmail2.com>, 555-623-1886 \x0A"Bob Jones", <em>Ne
6834950233	Possible bank card number 5911468437490705	222382355433193\x0A5911468437490705 \x0A101333182109778
3834394303	URL (web link) faculty. ucdi.edu/terms.pdf	Terms of use at http://faculty.ucdi.edu/terms. pdf

4.3   Rating Personal-Name Candidates

Personal names matching a names dictionary are not guaranteed to be useful in an investigation. Many names are also natural-language words, and others can label software, projects, vendors, and organizations. So it is important to estimate the probability of a name being useful. We tested the following clues for rating a name:

- Its length. Short names like "ed" are more likely to appear accidentally as in code strings and thus should be low-rated.

- Its capitalization type (lower case, upper case, initial capital letter, or mixed case). The convention to capitalize the initial letter of names provides a clue to them, but is not followed much in the digital world. Again, there must be exceptions for common name prefixes like "Mc", "De", "St", "Van", and "O" which are often not separated from a capitalized subsequent name.
- Whether the name has conventional delimiters like quotation marks on one or both sides. Table 3 lists the matched pairs of delimiters on names seen at significant rates in our corpus, based on study of random samples.

Table 3. Matched pairs of name delimiters sought.

Front delimiter	Rear delimiter	Front delimiter	Rear delimiter
"	"	<	>
(	)	[	]
<	@	(	@
[	@	>	<
>	@	:	<
:	@	;	<
;	@	'	'

- Whether the name is followed by a digit. This often occurs with email addresses, e.g. "joe682".
- Whether the name is a single word or multiple words created by the methods of Sect. 4.2.
- Whether the name frequently occurs as a non-name, like "main" and "bill". We got candidates from intersecting the list of known personal names with words that were frequent in a histogram of words used in the file names of our corpus, then manually adding some common non-names missed.
- The count of the word in all the words of the file paths in our corpus.
- The number of drives on which a name occurs. Names occurring on many drives are more likely to be within software and thus be business or vendor contacts. However, a correction must be made for the length of the name, since short names like "John" are more likely to refer to many people and will appear on more drives. Figure 1 plots the natural logarithm of the number of drives against the natural logarithm of the name length for our corpus. We approximated this by two linear segments split at 10.0 characters (the antilog of 2.3 on the graph), which fit formulas in the antilog domain of $59.7 * length^{-1.56}$ (left side) and $3.56 * length^{-0.33}$ (right side). We then divided the observed number of drives for a name by this correction factor. For instance, "john" alone occurred on 1182 drives in our corpus, and "john smith" on 557 drives, for correction factors of 6.87 and 1.64 and normalized values of 172 and 339 respectively, so "john smith" is twice as significant as "john".
- The average number of occurrences of the name per drive. High counts tend to be local names and likely more interesting.

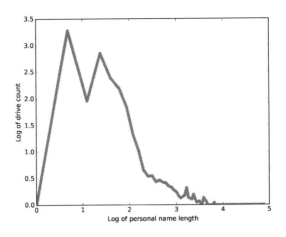

Fig. 1. Natural logarithm of number of drive appearances versus natural logarithm of name length for our corpus.

- Whether there is a domain name in the context window around the personal name that is .org, .gov, .mil, .biz, or a .com, where the subdomain before the .com is not a known mail or messaging server name. This clue could be made more restrictive in investigations involving organizations. This clue is helpful because usually people do not mix business and personal email.

4.4   Experimental Results with a Bayesian Model

We trained and tested the name clues on a training set which was a random sample of 5639 name candidates found by Bulk Extractor on our corpus. For this sample, we manually identified 1127 as useful personal names and 4522 as not, defining "useful" as in Sect. 1. Some names required Internet research to tag properly.

Our previous work developed clues for filtering email addresses as to interestingness using Bayesian methods, and we can use a similar approach for names. Probabilities are needed because few indicators are guaranteed. This work followed a Naive Bayes odds formulation:

$$o(U \mid E_1 \& E_2 \& \ldots \& E_N) = o(U|E_1)o(U|E_2)\ldots o(U|E_N)o(U)^{1-N}$$

We used previously a correction factor of $\lambda = 1$ to handle odds with zero and maximum counts:

$$o(U|E) = (n(U|E) + \lambda o(E))/(n(\sim U|E) + \lambda)$$

We calculated odds for each of the clues from the training/test set by a 100-fold cross-validation, choosing 100 times a random 80% for training and the remaining 20% for testing. Table 4 shows the computed mean odds and associated standard deviations for the clues in the 100 runs. We used maximum F-score as the criterion for setting partitioning thresholds on the four numeric parameters. So when numeric thresholds are given for the clues, they represent the values at which the maximum F-score was obtained for our training set with that parameter alone. We also tested having more than two subranges for each numeric clue, but none of these improved performance significantly. F-score weights recall and precision equally; if this is not desired, a weighted metric could be substituted.

Table 4. Odds on clues for personal names.

Clue	Odds on training set	Standard deviation on training set
Length ≤ 5 characters	0.168	0.006
Length >5 characters	0.272	0.006
All lower case	0.319	0.006
All upper case	0.150	0.015
Capitalized only	0.172	0.006
Mixed case	0.134	0.012
Delimited both sides	0.361	0.009
Delimited on one side	0.301	0.013
No delimiters	0.158	0.004
Followed by a digit	1.243	0.077
No following digit	0.214	0.004
Single word	0.236	0.005
Multiple words	0.249	0.007
Ambiguous word	0.055	0.004
Not ambiguous word	0.294	0.006
≤ 9 occurrences in corpus file names	0.451	0.011
>9 occurrences in corpus file names	0.162	0.004
Normalized number of drives ≤ 153	0.421	0.009
Normalized number of drives >153	0.112	0.004
≤ 399 occurrences per drive	0.189	0.004
>399 occurrences per drive	0.664	0.025
Organizational domain name nearby	0.009	0.001
No organizational domain name nearby	0.760	0.015
Prior to any clues	0.241	0.004

The average best F-score in cross-validation on our training set was 0.6681 at an average threshold of 0.2586 (with recall 80.7% and precision 57.0%). At this threshold, we eliminate from consideration 71.3% of the 302 million personal-name candidates found in our full corpus, and we set that threshold for our subsequent experiments. We also could obtain 90% recall at 48.9% precision and 99% recall at 30.1% precision on the training set, so even investigations needing high recall can benefit from these methods.

Such rates of data reduction do depend on the corpus, as over half the drives in our corpus appear to be business-related. Running time on the full corpus was around 120 h on a five-year-old Linux machine, or about 3.2 min per drive, not counting the time for Bulk Extractor.

All the clues except multiple words appear to be significant alone, either positively or negative. However, it is also important to test for redundancy by removing each clue and seeing if performance is hurt. We found that the capitalization clue was the most redundant since removing it helped performance the most, improving F-score by 0.94% on the full training set, and 0.6744 on 100-fold cross-validation. After capitalization was removed, no other clues were found helpful to remove. So we removed it alone from subsequent testing.

4.5 Results with Alternative Conceptual Models

We also tested a linear model for of the form $t = w_0 + w_1 x_1 + w_2 x_2 + \ldots + w_{11} x_{11}$ where the w_i values are relative likelihoods. We fit this formula to be 1 for tagged personal names and 0 otherwise. This required converting all clues to probabilities, for which we used the logistic function $1/[1 + \exp(-c * (x - k))]$ with two parameters k and c set by experiments. We obtained a best F-score of 0.6435 and a best threshold of 0.3807 with ten-fold cross-validation, similar to what we got with Naïve Bayes. The best weights were 0.1678 on length in characters (with best k = 6 and c = 6), 0.0245 for capitalization, −0.0380 for dictionary count (with best k = 5000 and c = 5000), −0.2489 for adjusted number of drives (with best k = 2000 and c = 2000), −0.0728 for rate per drive (with best k = 10 and c = 10), −0.0234 for number of words, 0.1383 for lack of explicit non-name usage, 0.1691 for having a following digit, 0.3823 for lack of having a nearby uninteresting site name, 0.0285 for number of delimiters, with $w_0 = -0.1695$.

We also tested a case-based reasoning model with the numeric clues, using the training set as the case library. We took the majority vote of all cases within a multiplier of the distance to the closest case. With ten-fold cross-validation, we got an average maximum F-score of 0.6383 with an average best multiplier of 1.97, but it took considerable time. We also tested a set-covering method and got an F-score of 0.60 from training alone, so we did not pursue it further. Thus Bayesian methods were the best, but it appears that the choice among the first three conceptual models does not affect performance much.

5 Cross-Modal Clues

Important clues not yet mentioned for personal names are the ratings on a nearby recognized artifact of a different type such as email addresses and phone numbers. For instance, "John Smith" is a common personal name, but if we find it just before "jsmith@officesolutions.com" we should decrease its rating because the address sounds like a vendor contact, and people usually separate their business mail and personal mail. Similarly, if we see the common computer term "Main" is preceded by interesting address "bjmain@gmail.com", we should increase its rating since Gmail is primarily a personal-mail site. These can be termed cross-modal clues. Our previous work [14] rated email addresses on our corpus, so those ratings can be exploited.

5.1   Rating Phone Numbers

Other useful cross-modal clues are nearby phone numbers, and their restricted syntax makes them easy to identify. Bulk Extractor finds phone numbers, but it misidentified some numeric patterns like IP numbers as phone numbers, and erred about 5% of the time in identifying the scope of numbers, most often in missing digits in international numbers. Code was written to ignore the former and correct the latter by inspecting the adjacent characters. For example, "123-4567" preceded by "joe 34-" is modified to "+34-123-4567" and "12345-" followed by "6789 tom smith" is modified to "12345-6789". Since the country of origin for each drive was known, its code was compared to the front of each phone number and the missing hyphen inserted if it matched. Some remaining 889,158 candidates proffered by Bulk Extractor were excluded because of inappropriate numbers of digits and invalid country codes. The code also regularized the format of numbers to enable recognition of different ways of writing the same number. U.S. numbers were converted to the form of ###-###-#### and international numbers to +##-######## and similar variants. Some U.S. numbers were missing area codes, and "?" was used for the missing digits.

The main challenge was in identifying the forensically interesting phone numbers, those that were personal and not of businesses or organizations, since the numbers themselves provide few clues. We evaluated the following clues for a Bayesian model:

- Whether the area code indicated a business or informational purpose as publicly announced (e.g., 800 numbers for businesses in the United States).
- Whether the number appeared to be artificial (e.g. 123-4567).
- Whether the number was in the United States.
- The number of drives on which the phone number occurred.
- Whether the number occurred on only one drive and at least four times, which suggests a localized number.
- Whether the number was preceded by "phone" or something equivalent.
- Whether the number was preceded by "fax" or something equivalent.
- Whether the number was followed by "fax" or something equivalent.
- Whether the number was preceded by "cell" or something mobile-related.
- Whether the last character preceding the number was a digit (usually an indicator of a scope error).
- Whether any of the words in the preceding 16 characters could be names.

Table 5 shows the calculated odds for each of the clues using 100 runs on random partitions of a training set of 4105 tagged random selections from our corpus, 3507 uninteresting and 446 interesting. Each of the 100 runs chose 50% of the training set for training and 50% for testing (an even split because we had little training data with positive examples). We then averaged the resulting odds over the runs. Either the clue or its absence was statistically significant, so all clues are justified to be included the model. For these tests the average best F-score with the model using all clues was 0.403 with an average best threshold of 0.0214, so most phone numbers are uninteresting and thus negative clues to nearby personal names, but there are not many. The output is also useful for rating phone numbers.

Table 5. Odds of interesting phone numbers based on particular clues.

Clue	Odds on training set	Standard deviation of odds
US	0.204	0.009
Non-US	0.121	0.045
Informational area code	0.008	0.004
Not informational area code	0.231	0.010
Artificial	0.018	0.004
Not artificial	0.204	0.009
Occurred on only one drive in corpus	0.246	0.016
Occurred on 2–4 drives in corpus	0.405	0.029
Occurred on 5 or more drives in corpus	0.012	0.004
Whether it occurred on only one drive and at least 4 times	0.378	0.061
Whether it occurred on multiple drives or less than 4 times	0.194	0.009
Personal name preceding	0.393	0.045
No personal name preceding	0.186	0.009
Preceded by "phone" or similar words	0.203	0.009
Preceded by "fax' or similar words	0.138	0.022
Followed by "fax" or similar words	0.203	0.009
Preceded by mobile-related words	0.630	0.242
No useful preceding or following words	0.209	0.010
Preceded by a digit after all possible corrections	0.136	0.011
No preceding digit after all possible corrections	0.238	0.012
Prior to any clues	0.203	0.009

5.2   Combining Cross-Modal Clues

We explored three cross-modal clues to personal names: the rating on nearby email addresses with words in common, the rating on closely nearby email addresses, and the rating on closely nearby phone numbers. Preliminary experiments showed that personal name ratings only correlated over the entire corpus with email ratings within a gap of 10 or less bytes or if they had at least half their words in common; personal name ratings only correlated with phone numbers within 20 or less bytes. So we used those results to define "closely nearby". There were 708 instances of email addresses with common words within 50 bytes, 690 instances of email addresses within 10 bytes, and 21 instances of phone numbers within 20 bytes.

Since the ratings were widely varying probabilities, for these cross-modal candidates we fit a linear rather than Bayesian model of the form $t = w_0 + w_n r_n + w_{ew} r_{ew} +$

$w_{eo}r_{eo} + w_{po}r_{po}$. Here t was 1 for valid personal names and 0 otherwise, r_n is the rating on the personal name, r_{ew} is the rating on the nearby email address sharing words, r_{eo} is the rating on the closely nearby email address, and r_{po} is the rating on closely nearby phone number. The w values were the weights on the corresponding ratings, and c_{ew}, c_{eo}, and c_{po} were default constants for r_{ew}, r_{eo}, and r_{po} when there was no nearby cross-modal clue. Evidence from more than one candidate could be used for a single personal name. We computed the least-squares fit of the linear model for the four weights and three constants applied to the training set. This gave a model of $t = -0.328 + 0.590r_n + 0.157r_{ew} + 0.005r_{eo} + 0.006r_{po}$ with $c_{ew} = 0.300$, $c_{eo} = -0.121$, and $c_{po} = 0.476$. Using these values we achieved a best F-score of 0.7990 at a threshold of 0.2889, a 19% improvement over rating without cross-modal clues. Using this model we could now achieve 90% recall with 69.5% precision and 100% recall with 66.5% precision, albeit in testing only on the subset of the training set that had evidence for at least one of the cross-modal clues. We also tested clues from the ratings on other nearby personal names, but found their inclusion hurt performance, reducing F-score to 0.7576.

6 Identifying the Principals Associated with a Drive

A secondary use of name extraction from a drive is quick identification of the main people associated with a drive, something important for instance when drives are obtained in raids apart from their owners. The most common names on a drive are not necessarily those of the owner and associates since names of vendor contacts and common words that can be used as names occur frequently. User-directory names (e.g. in the "Users" directory in Windows) can be misleading because they can be aliases, they only show people who log in, and do not give frequencies of use.

A better criterion for the owner and associates that we found is the highest-count personal names with a rating above a threshold, where the rating is computed by the methods of Sect. 5. We applied this this to 12 drives we obtained from co-workers, the only drives for which we could confirm the owner. For 8 of those 11, the owner name was the top-rated name over a 0.2 rating, for one it was second, for one it was fourth, and for one it was twentieth (for apparently a drive used by many people). So the rating threshold criterion appears to be reliable. For instance for an author's old drive, the first name rated above 0.2 was the author's first initial and last name, though it was the fifth most common name on the drive, and the second rated above 0.2 was the author's wife's name, even though it was the tenth most common name on the drive.

7 Conclusions

Personal names are among the most valuable artifacts an investigator can find on a drive as they can indicate important personal relationships not otherwise made public. This paper has shown that 71.3% of name candidates near email addresses and phone numbers can be eliminated from consideration from a representative corpus with an estimated average F-score of 67.4%. With cross-modal clues, F-score can be improved to 79.9%. Since our assumptions and methods apply to nearly any criminal or intelligence application of forensics, our methods permit a 3.5 times reduction in the workload of such investigators looking for personal names on drives who need no longer examine everything that matches a dictionary of names. At the same time, our ability to bootstrap on existing output of Bulk Extractor means our methods require only an additional few minutes per drive, far better than the days needed to do keyword search for names on a typical drive image (see Sect. 2). The work could be extended by developing a more specialized and efficient Bulk Extractor plugin; exploiting street addresses, IP addresses, names of associated organizations, and file names as additional cross-modal clues; and testing differences in strategy for different types of drives.

Acknowledgements. This work was supported in part by the U.S. Navy under the Naval Research Program and is covered by an IRB protocol. The views expressed are those of the author and do not represent the U.S. Government. Daniel Gomez started the implementation, and Janina Green provided images of project-team drives.

References

1. Bikel, D., Miller, S., Schwartz, R., Weischedel, R.: Nymble: a high-performance learning name-finder. In: 5th Conference on Applied Natural Language Processing, Washington DC, US, March, pp. 194–201 (1997)
2. Bulk Extractor 1.5: Digital Corpora: Bulk Extractor [Software] (2013). http://digitalcorpora. org/downloads/bulk_extractor. Accessed 6 Feb 2015
3. Fan, X., Wang, J., Pu, X., Zhou, L., Bing, L.: On graph-based name disambiguation. ACM J. Data Inf. Qual. **2**(2), Article No. 10 (2011)
4. Garfinkel, S.: Forensic feature extraction and cross-drive analysis. Digit. Invest. **3S** (September), S71–S81 (2006)
5. Garfinkel, S.: The prevalence of encoded digital trace evidence in the nonfile space of computer media. J. Forensic Sci. **59**(5), 1386–1393 (2014)
6. Garfinkel, S., Farrell, P., Roussev, V., Dinolt, G.: Bringing science to digital forensics with standardized forensic corpora. Digit. Invest. **6**(August), S2–S11 (2009)
7. Gross, B., Churchill, E.: Addressing constraints: multiple usernames, task spillage, and notions of identity. In: Conference on Human Factors in Computing Systems, San Jose, CA, US, April–May, pp. 2393–2398 (2007)
8. Henseler, H., Hofste, J., van Keulen, M.: Digital-forensics based pattern recognition for discovering identities in electronic evidence. In: European Conference on Intelligence and Security Informatics, August (2013)
9. Lee, S., Shishibori, M., Ando, K.: E-mail clustering based on profile and multi-attribute values. In: Sixth International Conference on Language Processing and Web Information Technology, Luoyang, China, August, pp. 3–8 (2007)
10. McCalley, H., Wardman, B., Warner, G.: Analysis of back-doored phishing kits. In: Peterson, G., Shenoi, S. (eds.) DigitalForensics 2011. IAICT, vol. 361, pp. 155–168. Springer, Heidelberg (2011). https://doi.org/10.1007/978-3-642-24212-0_12
11. Paglierani, J., Mabey, M., Ahn, G.-J.: Towards comprehensive and collaborative forensics on email evidence. In: 9th IEEE Conference on Collaborative Computing: Networking, Applications, and Worksharing, pp. 11–20 (2013)

12. Petkova, D., Croft, W.: Proximity-based document representation for named entity retrieval. In: 16th ACM Conference on Information and Knowledge Management, Lisbon, PT, November, pp. 731–740 (2007)
13. Rowe, N., Schwamm, R., Garfinkel, S.: Language translation for file paths. Digital Invest. **10S**(August), S78–S86 (2016)
14. Rowe, N., Schwamm, R., McCarrin, M., Gera, R.: Making sense of email addresses on drives. J. Digit. Forensics Secur. Law **11**(2), 153–173 (2016)
15. Yang, M., Chow, K.-P.: An information extraction framework for digital forensic investigations. In: Peterson, G., Shenoi, S. (eds.) DigitalForensics 2015. IAICT, vol. 462, pp. 61–76. Springer, Cham (2015). https://doi.org/10.1007/978-3-319-24123-4_4

A Web-Based Mouse Dynamics Visualization Tool for User Attribution in Digital Forensic Readiness

Dominik Ernsberger[1]([⌷]), R. Adeyemi Ikuesan[2], S. Hein Venter[2],
and Alf Zugenmaier[1]

[1] Department of Computer Science and Mathematics,
Munich University of Applied Sciences, Munich, Germany
ernsberger.dominik@gmail.com, alf.zugenmaier@hm.edu
[2] Department of Computer Science, Faculty of EBIT,
University of Pretoria, Pretoria, South Africa
{aikuesan, hsventer}@cs.up.ac.za

Abstract. The Integration of mouse dynamics in user authentication and authorization has gained wider research attention in the security domain, specifically for user identification. However, same cannot be said for user identification from the forensic perspective. As a step in this direction, this paper proposes a mouse behavioral dynamics visualization tool which can be used in a forensic process. The developed tool was used to evaluate human behavioral consistency on several news-related web pages. The result presents promising research tendency which can be reliably applied as a user attribution mechanism in a digital forensic readiness process.

Keywords: Mouse-dynamics · Event-visualizer · Digital forensic readiness
User identification and attribution · Behavioral dynamics

1 Introduction

A substantial aspect of Human-Computer interaction is based on pointing devices, either with the mouse, touch screens or other forms of pointing devices. The study of the behavioral components of human-mouse movement is generally referred to as mouse dynamics [1–3]. Mouse dynamics have been widely applied in user identification through authentication [3–7] or authorization [1, 8]. The integration of mouse behavioral dynamics as a biometrics for continuous and one-time authentication has gained wider attention in the recent years. This is generally attributed to the relatively cheap requirement specification, ease of data collection, and the high probability of individual uniqueness in mouse dynamics. In terms of the requirement specification, the study of mouse dynamics relies on the existing device, without a need for a specialized device. Furthermore, it does not require any specific positioning or intrusive setting for data acquisition.

Given this flexibility and robustness, the mouse-dynamics is gradually being considered as a suitable forensic mechanism [3, 9] through which human identification

P. Matoušek and M. Schmiedecker (Eds.): ICDF2C 2017, LNICST 216, pp. 64–79, 2018.
https://doi.org/10.1007/978-3-319-73697-6_5

can be evaluated in a human-computer interaction. User attribution, as a mechanism for identification of the actual user in an interaction/event in digital forensics [10, 11], relies on the reliability of the underlying identification mechanism. User attribution is generally referred to as the process of identifying a user on a digital device; the act of appending a given action/activity to a known user without ambiguity. The underlying mechanism implemented for continuous authentication based on mouse dynamics can, therefore, be adopted as a forensics attribution mechanism. However, the current reliability in the existing studies on continuous mouse dynamics falls below the 0.001 false acceptance rate, and 1.00 false rejection rate, of the European Standard for Commercial biometric technology [3]. As a step towards the actualization of this reliability, this study, a part of an ongoing behavioral biometrics for user attribution, aims to explore other probable underlying intuition of mouse dynamics for user attribution. To achieve this aim, this study developed a tool that can be used to track and visualize the behavior of human mouse actions on different websites. Various news websites were used as a means to conduct this research study. However, the integration of such mechanism into user attribution for forensics purpose can be feasible, through a digital forensic readiness framework. A digital forensic readiness framework is defined in this context in accordance with the findings from different stakeholders as presented in [12]. Digital forensic readiness is the *proactive* process of collecting, reliably storing, preprocessing and preservation of digital information which would otherwise be unavailable in a postmortem forensic process. A digital forensic readiness framework (DFRF) is therefore defined as a structural capability designed by an organization to maximize the usage of the available digital information in the event of an incident whilst minimizing the eventual cost to such an organization [13]. Given that the DFRF provide a reliable platform for user attribution, a forensic investigation process can significantly benefit from a behavioral biometrics profiling mechanism that is based on either a greater sample size of users (≤ 205-users), or a relatively smaller sample size of user (≥ 4 users) [14, 15]. This further implies that the performance of a mouse-based behavioral-biometrics is not necessarily dependent on the sample size under consideration, rather, on the capability of the mechanism adopted.

The remainder of this paper is organized as follows: a review of related works on continuous authentication and forensics, based on mouse dynamics, is shown in Sect. 2. This is then followed by the methodology employed to develop the tool and evaluation of human action. In addition, the exploratory process of other feasible intuitions which can be used to observe individual uniqueness during interaction with a mouse (or any other pointing device) is presented in Sect. 3. Analysis of result is presented in Sect. 4. Discussion and limitation of the findings of this study are presented in Sect. 5 of this paper, while the conclusion is presented in Sect. 6.

2   Related Work

Research works on behavioral biometrics (a nonintrusive method of identifying a user) in relation to human-computer interaction is gaining wider attention from the research community. Keystroke dynamics [16] and mouse dynamics are the two major focus of research in user identification. While some research focused on either mouse dynamics or keystroke dynamics, a few have attempted to integrate both mechanisms for user identification or authentication using a multimodal approach [1, 17]. A study in [18], which builds on the works in [19–21], investigated the probability of adopting mouse dynamics as a behavioral biometrics which can be used for user authentication. Raw mouse data was aggregated into high-level actions such as point-and-click, drag-and-drop. This is then characterized by action type, distance, angle, frequency, speed, duration, and direction. The aggregation process resulted in a segmentation of the raw mouse event into sessions of mouse strokes. A total of 39 mouse-action features, were further computed. Evaluation metrics include the false acceptance rate (FAR), false rejection rate (FRR), equal error rate (EER), accuracy, and pattern verification time. With an additional aim of verifying the influence of mouse device type, the study dichotomized mouse dynamics based on device. Findings from the study suggest that the type of mouse device used by a user can influence the behavior of the user. The dichotomy based on the type of device hardware yielded an accuracy of 96.7% and 97.8% respectively. Similarly, a study in [3] which builds on [22], explored the probability of user authentication based on mouse dynamics. Additional features such as single-click, double-click were included in the study. The study asserted that authentication can be performed in 11.8 s of mouse action, with a FAR and FRR of 8.74% and 7.69% respectively. This was based on 5550-data samples on 37 respondents. Recent findings in [1] observed that the multimodal approach based on C4.5 decision tree algorithm, LibSVM and Bayes Net classifiers can be used to improve the identification performance of mouse dynamics. The findings from the study showed that when authentication was based solely on mouse dynamics, the C4.5, LibSVM, and BayesNet resulted in an average accuracy of 74.26 ± 5.55, 85.53 ± 4.26, and 82.77 ± 2.96 respectively. The study was also anchored on the earlier studies of [22] and [20]. All identified existing still suffers from the limitation of poor error rate, and classification accuracy. In addition, these studies are targeted at user authentication, which does not cover some forensic processes. Whilst user authentication can be integrated into forensics, there is a need for a forensic perspective on mouse dynamics. This perspective includes the ability to visualize individual mouse paths, correlate individual mouse action from the different timeline (consistency checker), generate individual mouse dynamics for storage, subsequent analysis, as well as correlation with other users. Research targeted at improving these evaluation parameters remains a major focus, especially for usage in digital forensic readiness.

2.1 Purpose and Contribution of this Study

In addition to the development of a tool for mouse dynamics visualization and analysis, this study differs from existing studies on mouse dynamics in terms of its aim and the fundamental unit of measurement. A pixel-based single path property is considered as the fundamental unit of measurement of mouse dynamics in this study. This is intuitively distinct from the click-based [18, 21, 22], and stroke-based [1, 3] approach which is aggregated over sessions, as observed in existing studies. The current approach is based on the observation of individual path, and their corresponding behavioral characteristics. Based on the structural characteristics of an individual path in a given mouse dynamics data, this study explored the behavioral consistencies in users.

This consistency will thereafter be integrated into a forensic readiness framework. As an illustration of the forensic application, an illicit behavior can be mapped to an unknown subject within an organization based on the pre-defined template of each user gathered through a reliable forensic readiness process, within the organization. Furthermore, a deviation from the known behavioral consistency of a user can be used as a trigger for incident response and investigation. Such can also be applied to sniff out a malicious insider in an organization, by surreptitiously monitoring a triggered malicious-flag on a system. The digital forensic readiness approach defined in [23] identified event logs as a major aspect of the technology-enabled forensic process. This approach to forensics is also supported by the recommendation in [18] on the application of mouse dynamics in user attribution. User attribution in this context refers to the process of identifying a user based on their mouse dynamics. The methodology used to achieve this aim is presented in the next section.

3   Research Methodology

The approach employed to address the aim of this study is detailed in this section. The overall design process of the proposed path-pattern visualization is divided into four main parts, as depicted in Fig. 1.

1. Tracking and recording of the computer cursor and the corresponding web page elements during surfing on news web pages. This includes the mouse click, scrolling as well as the cursor movement. The extraction of the HTML objects which the user clicked or hovered over during the recording.
2. Extracting relevant information and calculating human behavior attributes based on the data captured. Furthermore, arrange and store the results in a way to provide easy access and evaluate it afterward.

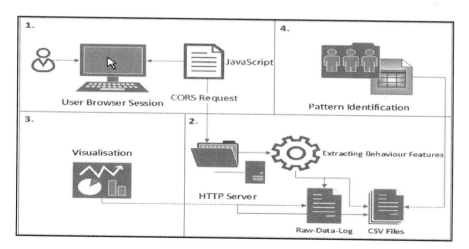

Fig. 1. Overall design approach

3. Visualize the stored data with re-drawn trajectories, tables, and timelines such that an investigator can quickly search and compare different paths.
4. Identification of user patterns based on the extracted features from the mouse actions of the user.

3.1 Mouse Navigation Tracking Process

To achieve the first goal, a client-side JavaScript is needed. It is embedded in the header of the loaded HTML page while running in the background. Two respective third-party browser extensions, i.e. Chrome: RunJS [24] and Firefox: Custom Style Script [25], which includes the stored JavaScript in the loaded pages, was used in this study. It would also be possible to use a specific proxy, which inserts the JavaScript code on the fly, into every page accessed through it, as implemented in [26]. As soon as an event (Mouse-Click-Down, Mouse-Click-UP, Scroll-Up, Scroll-Down, or Mouse-Move) occurs, the corresponding event listener is evoked. It captures the coordinates of the cursor, the precise timestamp, the HTML object of the page where the cursor is currently located, the delay (flight) between Mouse-Click-Down and Mouse-click-Up as well as the Uniform Resource Locator (URL) of the current web page. On the first Mouse-Click-Down event, it captures an additional basic user-agent information like the resolution of the page, time stamp, the type of browser and the browser version. In terms of scrolling, it captures, besides the location and timestamp, the number of scrolled pixels in the y-direction.

The coordinates, resolution and scrolled pixels are captured with *clientX, clientY, clientWidth, clientHeight* and *pageYOffset* methods. These methods return the value in Cascading Style Sheets (CSS) pixels. A CSS pixel is a software pixel which forms the unit of measurement, whereas a hardware pixel is an individual dot of light on the screen. A CSS pixel can contain a few hardware pixels and is designed to be the same size across different devices. Therefore, CSS pixels are generally used for web pages to define uniform size irrespective of the hardware pixel resolution. We considered these characteristics as an added advantage to ensure the uniformity of pixels across all devices on which data is being captured. In addition, the coordinates are relative to the upper-left edge of the content area of the browser and do not change even if the user is scrolling. This was used as a measure to distinguish between a mouse movement and scrolling.

The captured information is transmitted directly afterward to the main Java program via *XMLHttpRequests* to a local HTTP Server running on *localhost:8080/EventListener*. Given that the security model of a web browser (known as *same-origin-policy*), prevents the feasibility of sending web requests from one location to another outside the same domain, a Cross-Domain request with Cross-Origin Resource Sharing (CORS) [27], was implemented. The same-origin-policy of a web application is a security mechanism. This mechanism states that inter-access data is permitted from one web page to another if and only if both web pages have the same origin constrained by the same uniform resource identifier (URI) scheme, hostname, and port number. One of the downsides of bypassing this mechanism is server-flooding, a situation in which the server has no control over which packet to receive [28]. To prevent server flooding, the study implemented a threshold for the movement of the cursor. Whenever the

EventListener for the Mouse action is triggered, it calculates the distance between the former (position of the last data transmission request) and the new position of the mouse cursor. The data transmission request is considered acceptable if the distance of the mouse cursor is greater than the pre-defined threshold of 10-CSS Pixels, otherwise, it is rejected.

3.2   Data Pre-processing and Feature Extraction

The raw data dumped from the web browser is parsed through a preprocessing module as shown in phase 2 of Fig. 1. Feature extraction is based on the individual mouse path. A path is defined as a sequence of mouse events delineated by a time delay threshold, and/or any two consecutive mouse event clicks without the delimited threshold. A new path always starts from the last event of the preceding path, as shown in Fig. 2. A time delay threshold is defined as the idle time that satisfies the condition confined by Eq. 1.

$$Path \overset{\text{def}}{=} \begin{cases} Delay \begin{cases} \min \geq 3\,s \\ \max \leq 10\,s \end{cases} \\ 2\,consecutive\,clicks \end{cases} \tag{1}$$

Based on the mouse events, four different types of path attributes can be extracted as shown in Table 1. These attributes are consistent with features in existing studies [1, 3, 29]. A mouse click ends a current path because a click symbolize a new intention of the user (e.g. clicking on a link to open a new page). Furthermore, a movement delay (silent time) of more than 10 s between two points is interpreted as a new user intention, and consequently, starts a new path. Preliminary observation of the mouse movement showed that two consecutive mouse movement have delays $\geq$ 10-s. Existing studies considered aggregation of mouse sequence, which neither indicates a path as the fundamental unit of mouse measurement nor defined the delay between mouse actions. For instance, the exposition in [3] defined the minimum, average and maximum mouse operation task as 6.2 s, 11.8 s, and 21.3 s respectively. This does not show the actual delay between the mouse operations. However, it is logical to consider a fundamental unit of mouse movement measurement, through which pattern observation can be measured. A mouse movement path presents such an intuition.

Table 1. Labels of path

Number	Actions of a path begin	Actions of a path end	Label
1	Click	Click	cc
2	Click	Movement (>10 s)	cm
4	Movement	Click	mc
5	Movement	Movement (>10 s)	mm

A path is stored as a trajectory which contains several sequences. It includes the x-coordinate, y-coordinate, timestamp, angle of inclination, speed, mouse-click-up and mouse-click-down events, HTML object, weight, silent time, scrolled Pixel as well as the time delay between mouse-click-down and mouse-click-up events [1, 3, 18]. Furthermore, it contains the overall delay, direct distance between the start- and end-point, a distance of the path (length), average speed, overall weight, overall direction, label, and URL. Description of the relevant features and human behavioral attributes adapted in this study are explained in more detail in the proceeding subsections as.

3.2.1   Speed

The speed of mouse movement is computed for every distance between two points of movement, as well as for the scrolled pixel. For the average speed, the study excludes the scrolling points, to separate the movement speed. The speed for the ith mouse-point is described by Eq. 2. The intuition upon which speed is computed is based on existing studies [1, 3]. The average speed for the ith mouse path with n-points is defined with the expression presented in Eq. 3, where x and y represents the coordinates, and t represents the timestamp at that coordinate.

$$\Delta v_i = \frac{\sqrt{(x_i - x_{i-1})^2 + (y_i - y_{i-1})^2}}{t_i - t_{i-1}} \tag{2}$$

$$\Delta v_{i\,average} = \frac{1}{n}\sum_{k=2}^{n} \Delta v_k \tag{3}$$

3.2.2   Distance or Path Length

This study considered the shortest distance between two points, based on the general definition of slope (Euclidean distance). This can also be referred as the direct distance between two points. The shortest distance between two points (i_{th} and i_{th-1}) in a path is given by the expression presented in Eq. 4.

$$\Delta d_{i\,direct} = \sqrt{(x_i - x_{i-1})^2 + (y_i - y_{i-1})^2} \tag{4}$$

Logically, a mouse path length can be defined as the summary of the distance between all points in the path: The length of the ith path with n-points is defined by the expression in Eq. 5. This expression considers the transition from the point of path beginning to the point of path ending. This thus implies that the path length is a vector quantity. A path direction is considered with respect to the expression is Eq. 8.

$$\overrightarrow{\Delta d_{i\,path}} = \sum_{k=2}^{n} \Delta d_{k\,direct} \tag{5}$$

3.2.3   Time Delay/Silent Time/Click Delay

The delay is calculated for every point in the path. The silent time is the number of milliseconds within which the cursor was not moved. It captures the duration of all connected scrolling events. Furthermore, the click delay (flight) is computed for every click (start and end). This measures the time (t) in milliseconds between the mouse down and mouse up event. The delay at the i [th] point between time t_i and t_{i-1} is depicted by the expression shown in Eq. 6.

$$\Delta t_i = t_i - t_{i-1} \tag{6}$$

3.2.4 Angle of Inclination

The angle of inclination (the arctangent of the slope between two points) is calculated for every distance between two points. It is the angle between the horizontal axes of two the points, with the x-axis, measured in a counterclockwise direction from $0° \leq \theta < 180°$. It is defined by the expression in Eq. 7.

$$\Delta \theta_i = \tan^{-1} \frac{\Delta y_i}{\Delta x_i} \tag{7}$$

3.2.5 Direction and Weight

The direction of a mouse is calculated for the whole path as well as for the distance between two points. To compute this direction, the angle is logically assumed to have a right and a left quadrant. A left direction covers the negative left axis of a quadrant, while the converse is the right. For the direction, a path which ends with the Left $= -1$; Right $= 1$; Neutral $= 0$ is defined by Eq. 8, where $x =$ the x-coordinate, $n =$ start point, $k =$ end.

$$\Delta direction_i = \begin{cases} -1, & x_k < x_n \\ 1, & x_k > x_n \\ 0, & x_k = x_n \end{cases} \tag{8}$$

The weight of a path is calculated, from the intuition in kinematics [29], for every distance between two points as well as for the entire path length. The weight for the i [th] path is defined by the expression in Eq. 9. The overall weight for the i [th] path with n points is defined by the expression in Eq. 10.

$$\Delta w_{i\,point} = \Delta v_i * \begin{cases} \Delta d_{i\,direct} * \sin(\theta_i), & direction = 1 \\ \Delta d_{i\,direct} * \cos(360 - \theta_i), & direction = -1 \\ \Delta d_{i\,direct}, & direction = 0 \end{cases} \tag{9}$$

$$\Delta w_{i\,path} = \sum_{k=2}^{n} \Delta w_{k\,point} \tag{10}$$

3.2.6 Skewness and Kurtosis

Higher order moments as defined in [30], are statistical properties that can provide representative properties of a distribution. Skewness and kurtosis are described in this section. However, first, and second order of moment are computed using the generalized expression. Skewness is calculated for the silent time, angle of inclination and speed of a path. The skewness of the i th path is defined by Eq. 11 where n = count of values, $\bar{x}$ = mean and x_i = the i th value.

$$skew_i = \frac{\frac{1}{n}\sum_{i=1}^{n}(x_i - \bar{x})^3}{\left(\sqrt{\frac{1}{n-1}\sum_{i=1}^{n}(x_i - \bar{x})^2}\right)^3} \qquad (11)$$

Similarly, the kurtosis is computed for the silent time, angle of inclination and speed of a path. The kurtosis of the i th path is represented by the expression in Eq. 12: Where n = count of values, $\bar{x}$ = mean and x_i = the i th value.

$$kurt_i = \frac{\frac{1}{n}\sum_{i=1}^{n}(x_i - \bar{x})^4}{\left(\frac{1}{n}\sum_{i=1}^{n}(x_i - \bar{x})^2\right)^2} - 3 \qquad (12)$$

A total of 37 unique features for every path, as shown in Table 2, are generated. In order to provide the desired systematic visualization process (as shown in Fig. 2), the raw data of the mouse action is segmented through preprocessing, into different files. The data from these files are then used for subsequent data analysis processes. The raw data includes the captured page resolution, user-agent information, x-coordinates, y-coordinates, HTML objects, mouse events, time stamps, click delay (flight) as well as the URL. Summary of the overall features used in this study is presented in Table 2.

Table 2. Human behaviour attributes

Number	Features/human behavior attributes
F1	Number of the path
F2	Duration of the path
F3	Number of points in the path
F4–F6	Properties of scrolls (number of scrolls, scroll up and scroll down)
F7	Number of clicks in the path
F8	Number of movement in the path
F9–F16	Statistics of silent points (number of silent periods, mean, std. deviation, min, max, variance, skewness, and kurtosis)
F17	Flight of first click (duration between mouse down and mouse up)
F18	Flight of the last click
F19	Length of path
F20	Overall weight of the path
F21	Direction of the path
F22–F29	Statistics of angle of inclination (mean, std. deviation, min, max, variance, skewness, kurtosis, and mode)
F30–F37	Statistics of speed movement (mean, std. deviation, min, max, variance, skewness, kurtosis, and mode)

3.3   Visualization

To achieve the third design goal, it is necessary to read the stored data and visualize them. The developed tool accepts an input from a CSV file. The features and attributes of the corresponding file are loaded into the tool for visualization. The GUI offers the option to display an overview of the whole mouse action capture, as shown in Fig. 2. Furthermore, it is possible to choose a path directly in the drop-down menu to see the corresponding details. When a new path is selected and added, it creates a new internal frame in the main window frame. These internal windows are adjustable, resizable as well as closable, as shown in Fig. 3. From this, a comparison can be made among any number of paths. The layout of the internal path window in Fig. 3 is as followed. On the bottom right side is a zoomable area where the selected path is drawn from the recorded data. It is possible to zoom in and out on every drawn path, by scrolling the mouse wheel, to magnify or minimize individual points. For scroll events, it displays the scrolled number of pixels. Furthermore, on the bottom of the window, the GUI provides a table which displays the overview of the data. A tabular display of the individual features and values of each point in the path is also provided. The drawings of the paths are scaled based on the size of the window. The stored page resolution of the browser during the recording is also provided. This visualization process can be instrumental in the reconstruction of user-event which can be used to observe user activity. This can be particularly useful in tracing the action of a user in the event of insider misuse and investigation. In addition to the probability of attributing a user, the inclusion of the visualization process can be used to trace the exact path, within a specified period of an event.

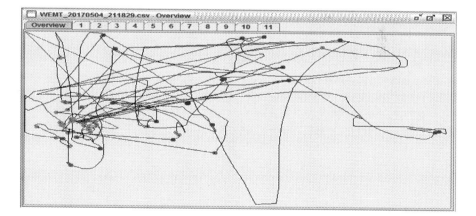

Fig. 2. Overview of visualization of all paths in a recording. Every colored dot displays a start and end point of a path. The bigger black dot (in the center) displays the start point of the whole recording. The blue points are displaying a click, red is for an expired session and green is for a movement. (Color figure online)

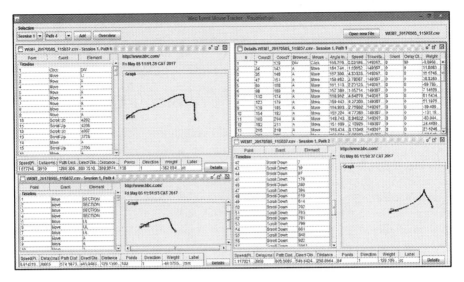

Fig. 3. Working space of the forensic-visualization tool with four open windows to compare movement paths of a user. Three (left and bottom right) displaying the overall path information and one (right top) displays a detailed table of the first path.

3.4   Experimental Set-up

To further validate the feasibility of the developed tool, an experimental process was set up in a computer laboratory. Eleven volunteers were recruited for this purpose. The laboratory comprises numerous workstations, each with the same configuration of hardware, software, and each operates a Deep Freeze enterprise software, which restores the workstation to a pristine state, upon workstation reboots. The forensic-tool developed for this research was installed on the workstation for three consecutive days. Initial evaluation of the capability of forensic-tool was assessed. Users were monitored for action taken and the resultant output from the forensic-tool was evaluated. The result showed consistency between the observation and the action of the users. Three users participated in the lab section, while the other eight users installed the forensic-tool on their personal computers. Each user was asked to freely surf the web using either a Chrome or Mozilla Firefox browser, based on a given list of news websites. The tool works on all operating systems. Free web surfing was encouraged so as to mimic, as nearly as possible, a real life browsing behavior. This is in contrast to a fully controlled experimental environment. A controlled environment is asserted to prevent the influence of extraneous variables. The notion of the introduction of extraneous variables, as suggested by [3], is deemed non-practicable in the behavioral analysis of human action. In practice, human actions are generally guided by self-interest and discretion which cannot be limited to a controlled environment. Using the behavioral features defined in Table 2, feature extraction was performed on the dataset from all users, followed by a pattern observation process. Summary of the data description is presented in Table 3. For each path, the feature summarized in Table 2 were extracted to generate individual datasets.

Table 3. Summary of the data

Users	Duration (min)	Number of instance (path)
1	30	31
2	90	158
3	60	67
4	120	173
5	90	147
6	150	407
7	150	434
8	150	259
9	250	309
10	150	321
11	90	977

The pattern identification mechanism for a user attribution process was carried out in two phases. In the first phase, pattern consistency; intra-user pattern consistencies, was observed for all users (excluding user-1, who had only one session of data) based on the daily activity, using a non-supervised machine learning method: the X-Means (an extension of K-means) clustering algorithm. In order to perform the cluster analysis, feature selection was carried out on the 37-features defined in Table 2. Based on this dimension reduction process, 8-base-features were observed to provide a significant discriminatory factor for the intra-user analysis. These include the duration, number of points, flight, length, and weight of path. Thereafter, inter-user variation (through dissimilarity in the pattern) observation based on a supervised classification process was carried out on the three laboratory users (hereinafter referred to as the Tier-2 dataset, using each user as the class). The study explored a nonlinear support vector machine (LibSVM), artificial neural network, C4.5 decision tree and RandomForest classifiers. These classifiers were selected due to their general usage in mouse dynamics studies [3, 18]. This exploration was carried out in the entire feature space as described in Table 2, with the assertion that such process can harness the semantic relation in the data, in addition to its potential to harness the syntactic relation in the data.

4   Results and Analysis

On the evaluation process, an optimization process was performed on the clustering algorithm. A Manhattan-distance (also referred to as the taxicab geometry) was used for the cluster optimization. X-means successfully generated a single cluster (0% error rate) for one user (user 3: U-3), while other users show significant intra-cluster similarity as shown in Table 4. The table shows the total number of observed cluster for each user. The number of the class represents the different dataset for each user.

Table 4. Result of intra-user similarity

User	U-2	U-3	U-4	U-5	U-6	U-7	U-8	U-9	U-10	U-11
No. of class	3	2	4	3	5	5	5	7	5	3
No. of observed cluster	2	1	2	2	2	2	2	2	2	2
Cluster similarity (%)	87	100	83	83	87	83	80	81	93	89

In order to study the inter-user dissimilarity, the supervised classifiers were applied to the laboratory users. The choice of the laboratory users was based on the uniform experimental condition across device and operating condition. RandomForest was subsequently observed to perform relatively better than the other explored classifiers on the Tier-2 dataset, extracted from the laboratory users. The true acceptance rate for the users are 0.935, 0.938 and 0.439 for users U-1, U-2 and U-3 respectively. Conversely, the false acceptance rate of 0.034, 0.361, and 0.035 was obtained for Users U-1, U-2 and U-3 respectively. Based on class distribution, the highest class prior probability of 53.81% and an average accuracy of 78.1% was obtained. The analysis was carried out on a 10-fold cross-validation process. The obtained result of the classification process falls below the European standard for commercial biometrics. However, this result shows a promising technique through which user attribution can be established.

5   Discussion

The result from the experimental process shows that the forensic-tool was able to capture every mouse action of each user. Furthermore, the visual representation shown in Fig. 3, presents a very flexible process of visualizing the mouse activity of a user. A graphical plot of the features can also be carried out on the user-interface of the tool. These characteristics further extend the tool in examining individual difference and similarity, at a higher abstraction. On a lower abstraction, the tools support the pre-processing and generation of mouse dynamics features. The features considered in this study attempt to expand the repository of mouse dynamics attributes. More specifically, the specific features considered include the path characteristics, flight duration, and the overall weight of the path.

These features were observed to significantly influence the observed accuracy of the classifiers. In terms of the behavioral characteristic feature, which can be adapted for user attribution, the path characteristics present a measurable and reliable feature. The result from the unsupervised learning process shows a very high probability of the existence of a unique behavioral signature for each user. Such signature could represent the principal component needed for user attribution based on mouse dynamics. The result of the unsupervised learning approach also debunks the assertion that an uncontrolled experimental environment is not suitable for user authentication research based on mouse dynamics. Based on the empirical assertion and fundamental assumption on variables that could induce experimental bias on mouse dynamics study, the current study heeded several recommendations from [18] on the extraneous variables that could influence mouse behavior.

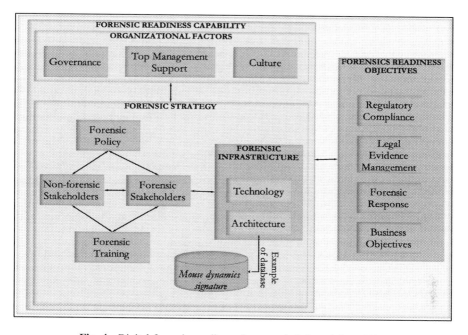

Fig. 4. Digital forensic readiness framework (adapted from [12])

This includes the type of mouse device, screen resolution, acceleration setting of a computer system, the perpetual delay caused by the load on the CPU, and properties of the surface area on which the mouse is placed. The psychological state of the user was not considered in this study. However, the users were not subjected to any experimental pressure. In addition, the study assumed that the list of the website used in this study will not inject any negative psychological episode on the respondents. To prevent data loss due to encryption protocols, the experimental websites considered in this study were all HTTP-based websites. This is because the HTTPS does not work with the developed JavaScript of the forensic-tool.

The application of the findings of this study in a digital forensic readiness framework falls within the architecture sub-module of the forensic infrastructure in Fig. 4, as asserted in [12]. A mouse dynamics signature database was introduced as an addition to the initial framework as shown in Fig. 4. The integration of the mouse dynamics signature database into the framework will complement other existing forensic architectures. This could include the installation of the forensic-tool on the existing hardware of an organization. The preparation of such contingency policy remains a viable complementary process to a postmortem forensic mechanism.

5.1 Limitation and Future Works

Given that the baseline for FAR and FRR are 0.001 and 1.00 respectively [3], it is obvious that the obtained accuracy based on the Tier-2 dataset is relatively low. This can be attributed to the relatively smaller sample size of respondents, shorter experimental duration, and smaller number of experimental sections. In terms of features, the study could integrate discriminative features such as double click, drag and drop, event thresholding, and other probable behavioral attributes. Considering that the HTTPS-based website is gaining wider adoption in typical client-server communication, the non-inclusion of an HTTPS server to capture a secure-web-page-response is one of the major limitations of this study. In defining the path delimiter, the study utilized a 10-s threshold. An adaptive threshold could be developed in future works. In terms of the development of behavioral signature and the eventual development of an updateable database for DFR, future works will explore modalities towards the extraction of unique behavioral fingerprints based on mouse action which can be adapted for user attribution. A reliable user attribution model will be considered in future works. Models that aim to establish a reliable mechanism for a user identification process is a critical component in this area of forensic analysis.

6   Conclusion

On a general note, mouse dynamics satisfy the underlying characteristics – reasonably permanent, easy to collect and easy to measure – of biometric modalities for user identification. Studies on biometric verification, whether on physiological or behavioral topics, require sufficient sample sizes for the effective evaluation of their parameters and of their performance. The tool developed in this study presents a step towards the actualization of the goal of establishing mouse dynamics research for user identification. This, in turn, will create a platform for an effective user-attribution process in the digital forensic analysis. The findings presented in this manuscript are part of an ongoing research which aims to provide a reliable model for the user attribution process based on mouse dynamics.

References

1. Bailey, K.O., Okolica, J.S., Peterson, G.L.: User identification and authentication using multi-modal behavioral biometrics. Comput. Secur. **43**, 77–89 (2014)
2. Chudá, D., Krátky, P., Tvarožek, J.: Mouse clicks can recognize web page visitors! In: Proceedings of 24th International Conference on World Wide Web, pp. 21–22 (2015)
3. Shen, C., Cai, Z., Guan, X., Du, Y., Maxion, R.A.: User authentication through mouse dynamics. IEEE Trans. Inf. Forensics Secur. **8**(1), 16–30 (2013)
4. Kasprowski, P., Harezlak, K.: Fusion of eye movement and mouse dynamics for reliable behavioral biometrics. Pattern Anal. Appl., 1–13 (2016). https://doi.org/10.1007/s10044-016-0568-5
5. Khalifa, A.A., Hassan, M.A. Khalid, T.A. Hamdoun, H.: Comparison between mixed binary classification and voting technique for active user authentication using mouse dynamics. In: Proceedings of - 2015 International Conference on Computing Control Networking, Electronics and Embedded Systems Engineering, ICCNEEE 2015, pp. 281–286 (2016)
6. Traore, I., Woungang, I., Obaidat, M.S., Nakkabi, Y., Lai, I.: Combining mouse and keystroke dynamics biometrics for risk-based authentication in web environments. In: Proceedings of 4th International Conference on Digital Home, ICDH 2012, pp. 138–145 (2012)
7. Traore, I., Woungang, I., Obaidat, M.S., Nakkabi, Y., Lai, I.: Online risk-based authentication using behavioral biometrics. Multimed. Tools Appl. **71**(2), 575–605 (2014)

8. Bevan, C., Fraser, D.S.: Different strokes for different folks? Revealing the physical characteristics of smartphone users from their swipe gestures. Int. J. Hum. Comput. Stud. **88**, 51–61 (2016)

9. Alzubaidi, A., Kalita, J.: Authentication of smartphone users using behavioral biometrics. IEEE Commun. Surv. Tutorials **18**(3), 1998–2026 (2016)

10. Olivier, M.S.: On metadata context in database forensics. Digit. Invest. **5**(3–4), 115–123 (2009)

11. Adeyemi, I.R., Razak, S.A., Azhan, N.A.N.: A review of current research in network forensic analysis. Int. J. Digit. Crime Forensics **5**(1), 1–26 (2013)

12. Elyas, M., Ahmad, A., Maynard, S.B., Lonie, A.: Digital forensic readiness: expert perspectives on a theoretical framework. Comput. Secur. **52**, 70–89 (2015)

13. Valjarevic, A., Venter, H.S.: Towards a digital forensic readiness framework for public key infrastructure systems. In: 2011 Information Security South Africa, pp. 1–10 (2011)

14. Anjomshoa, F., Aloqaily, M., Kantarci, B., Erol-Kantarci, M., Schuckers, S.: Social behaviometrics for personalized devices in the internet of things era. IEEE Access **5**, 12199–12213 (2017)

15. Alsultan, A., Warwick, K.: Keystroke dynamics authentication: a survey of free-text methods. Int. J. Comput. Sci. **10**(4), 1–10 (2013)

16. Pisani, P.H., Lorena, A.C.: A systematic review on keystroke dynamics. J. Brazilian Comput. Soc. **19**(4), 573–587 (2013)

17. Saevanee, H., Clarke, N., Furnell, S., Biscione, V.: Continuous user authentication using multi-modal biometrics. Comput. Secur. **53**, 234–246 (2015)

18. Jorgensen, Z., Yu, T.: On mouse dynamics as a behavioral biometric for authentication. In: Proceedings of the 6th ACM Symposium on Information, Computer and Communications Security - ASIACCS 2011, pp. 476–482 (2011)

19. Gamboa, H., Fred, A.: A behavioural biometric system based on human computer interaction. In: Proceedings of SPIE - International Society Optical Engineering, vol. 5404 (i), pp. 381–392 (2004)

20. Pusara, M., Brodley, C.E.: User re-authentication via mouse movements. In: Proceedings of 2004 ACM Workshop on Visualization and Data Mining for Computer Security, VizSECDMSEC 2004, pp. 1–8 (2004)

21. Gamboa, H., Fred, A.L.N., Jain, A.K.: Webbiometrics: user verification via web interaction. In: 2007 Biometrics Symposium on BSYM (2007)

22. Ahmed, A.A.E., Traore, I.: A new biometric technology based on mouse dynamics. IEEE Trans. Dependable Secur. Comput. **4**(3), 165–179 (2007)

23. Barske, D., Stander, A., Jordaan, J.: A digital forensic readiness framework for South African SME's. In: Proceedings of 2010 Information Security South Africa Conference ISSA 2010 (2010)

24. Bell Global Technologies, "RunJS - Run Javascript on Page Load."

25. Noe, R.: Execute JS

26. Sedlar, U., Bešter, J., Kos, A.: Tracking mouse movements for monitoring users' interaction with websites: implementation and applications. Elektrotehniski Vestnik/Electrotechnical Rev. **74**(1–2), 31–36 (2007)

27. HTTP access control (CORS)

28. Lakshminarayanan, K., Adkins, D., Perrig, A., Stoica, I.: Taming IP packet flooding attacks. ACM SIGCOMM Comput. Commun. Rev. **34**(1), 45–50 (2004)

29. Martín-Albo, D., Leiva, L.A., Huang, J., Plamondon, R.: Strokes of insight: user intent detection and kinematic compression of mouse cursor trails. Inf. Process. Manag. **52**, 989–1003 (2015)

30. Adeyemi, I.R., Razak, A.S., Salleh, M.: A psychographic framework for online user identification. In: International Symposium on Biometrics and Security Technologies (ISBAST), pp. 198–203 (2014)

Digital Forensics Tools I

Open Source Forensics for a Multi-platform Drone System

Thomas Edward Allen Barton and M. A. Hannan Bin Azhar(⊠)

Computing, Digital Forensics and Cybersecurity,
Canterbury Christ Church University, Canterbury, UK
{tbl150, hannan.azhar}@canterbury.ac.uk

Abstract. Drones or UAVs (Unmanned Air Vehicles) have a great potential to cause concerns over privacy, trespassing and safety. This is due to the increasing availability of drones and their capabilities of travelling large distances and taking high resolution photographs and videos. From a criminological perspective, drones are an ideal method of smuggling, physically removing the operator from the act. It is for this reason that drones are also being utilised as deadly weapons in conflict areas. The need for forensic research to successfully analyse captured drones is rising. The challenges that drones present include the need to interpret flight data and tackling the multi-platform nature of drone systems. This paper reports the extraction and interpretation of important artefacts found in the recorded flight logs on both the internal memory of the UAV and the controlling application, as well as analysis of media, logs and other important files for identifying artefacts. In addition, some basic scripts will be utilised to demonstrate the potential for developing fully fledged forensics tools applicable to other platforms. Tests of anti-forensics measures will also be reported.

Keywords: Drone forensics · Open source · Mobile forensics · DJI Phantom
Android · UAV · Anti-forensics

1 Introduction

Drone crime is a recent phenomenon. In the UK, there was a sharp rise in reported incidents between 2014 and 2015 [1]. The most widespread crime being committed is the transport of contraband, also known as smuggling [1, 2]. The capabilities of drones to carry items [3] and their remote operation makes drones ideal for this type of crime, which has become prolific in the UK and around the world [4]. The cost of even a high-end drone is far outweighed by the inflated value of the cargo [5, 6] meaning drones can be discarded after use. This type of crime has serious impact, and drones used in crime will need to be forensically analysed if caught or shot down. The potential for the misuse of drones to disrupt large scale operations as well as assist in major crime means the identification of suspects is of paramount importance in prevention of further crime. The vulnerability of many sensitive targets to a drone attack should not be ignored, again raising the need for forensic research to successfully analyse captured drones.

© ICST Institute for Computer Sciences, Social Informatics and Telecommunications Engineering 2018
P. Matoušek and M. Schmiedecker (Eds.): ICDF2C 2017, LNICST 216, pp. 83–96, 2018.
https://doi.org/10.1007/978-3-319-73697-6_6

Open Source techniques provide a number of advantages as they are flexible and meet guidelines on the admissibility of evidence [7]. This paper will cover the use of open source tools and development of some basic scripts to aid forensic analysis of a multi-platform drone system, which include not only the UAV itself but the accompanying mobile platform, application and controlling hardware. The UAV system chosen for analysis was the DJI Phantom 3 Professional (DJI) [8], a quadcopter drone with a variety of features and capabilities. Among commercially available drones, DJI has taken the largest market share of 36% [9] with its Phantom series setting the benchmark for professional drone use. The extensive capabilities of the Phantom include vision, GPS, automatic flight and homing, obstacle avoidance and long range control. These capabilities give the Phantom the potential to be used in various drone related crimes. The remainder of the paper is organised as follows: Sect. 2 describes literature reviews on crimes involving drones and in the area of drone forensic analysis, including techniques used for data extraction and interpretation. Section 3 discusses the methodology used to analyse the UAV and accompanying mobile platform. Section 4 reports the results of analysis, finally Sect. 5 concludes the paper.

2   Literature Review

Although drones are a relatively new technology, some literature exists on both the forensic analysis and their cybersecurity implications. Another technology that goes hand in hand with drones is cameras, implemented either as static recording devices, or for live streaming (sometimes known as vision). This raises a host of privacy concerns for organisations, as well as the public. Many different areas of airspace in the UK are designated no-fly zones [10] because they are considered sensitive areas – these include sites such as airports, military bases and power stations. The ability of drones to capture pictures and videos of operations in these sites presents a significant security threat. As well as the security of infrastructure, individual security may also be compromised. Of the reported incidents mentioned [1], many were simply concerns for public safety. As well as these general incidents, drones are also being used to aid traditional crime, a common example of which is burglary. Using drones, a burglar can survey a potential target site for entrances or exits and security features such as dogs, alarms and cameras in a process known as "casing" or keep an eye out for police [11]. Drones are being utilised as deadly weapons in the countries involved in conflicts [12]. A set of videos released by various forces and militants showed the use of commercially bought and homemade drones as bombers, hitting soft targets such as groups of exposed soldiers and vehicles with customised grenades and High Explosive Dual Purpose (HEDP) rounds [12]. These type of attacks are mostly performed with hovering-type drones, with modifications to add the capacity of dropping bombs [12].

Some important aspects of UAV forensic analysis were highlighted including establishing flight data and establishing ownership [13]. The identification of mobile devices, for comparison, is aided by the presence of artefacts such as account names and details whereas it is possible to operate a drone with little or no identifying artefacts left on it. The digital forensic investigator will also have to interpret recorded flight data. In order to successfully re-create the actions taken by the drone, the understanding of timestamped latitude, longitude and altitude measurements is required, as well as speed, battery level and other data from a host of on-board sensors. A drone system is comprised of a number of different hardware platforms, each containing different artefacts. Some of these component platforms are shown to have physically identifiable artefacts such as serial numbers printed on the casing, which can later be matched up to artefacts recovered using digital forensics [14]. Artefacts related to flight data were successfully recovered from various components of the DJI Phantom 2 Vision+, including the controller, mobile application and the UAV itself [15]. Analysis of recorded media such as photos and videos, stored on the UAV's removable SD card, showed they possessed Exchangeable Image Format (EXIF) metadata that included GPS readings. This can be used in the absence of flight logs, for example if the images were copied to a separate storage media or the UAV was damaged in some way. An analysis of the DJI Phantom 3 Standard version revealed multiple security vulnera-bilities [16], as well as establishing how the various components of the DJI Phantom 3 operate with each other. The controller, in this case, is essentially a range extender for sending commands to the UAV via 5 GHz radio signal. The smartphone running the DJI GO application connects to the controller via 2.4 GHz Wi-Fi or by USB con-nection, which provides access to a network created between the various components. Accessing this network may provide useful in acquiring data, where chip-off analysis is not available [16].

Open source and custom forensics tools provide some significant advantages over commercial toolkits, primarily the ability to be tested by the open source community, meeting what are known as the "daubert" guidelines for the admissibility of evidence provided by expert witnesses [7]. Furthermore, custom tools created by the forensic investigator to perform a specific job are extremely adaptable and, where successful, can be used again in other cases involving similar technology. The rising cost of commercial toolkits can be a barrier to use [17], which makes a stark comparison to the freedom of open source tools. However, commercial status does offer the advantage of support in the form of updates, bug reporting and additional documentation. While previously reported work [13–16] focussed on the extraction of automated flight plans and analysis of media, the investigation presented in this paper will primarily focus on the extraction and interpretation of wider range of important artefacts found both on the internal memory of the professional edition of the Phantom 3 and the controlling application with the use of open source tools. Anti-forensics measures will also be tested.

3 Methodology

The study reported in this paper focusses on the DJI Phantom 3 Professional Edition [8] and the accompanying mobile platform - a Motorola Moto G 3rd Generation, as shown in Tables 1 and 2. The choice of mobile platform in this case reflects the current state of the worldwide smartphone market, which is dominated by Android [18]. Another reason Android was chosen was its huge online developer community, which stems from its open source status. A custom community built version of Android, Cyano-genMod [19], was installed on the platform prior to analysis, which included features such as forensically sound rooting without extra modification. The scenario creation was performed before rooting took place. CyanogenMod is based on universal open-source Android software, tested to the same standards as stock operating systems [20]. A secondary platform - a Samsung Galaxy S4 Mini running a stock Android 4.4.4 operating system was tested alongside the main platform to ensure consistency between results, with the same version of the DJI GO application installed. The secondary platform was rooted using a rootkit, Kingo Root [21], which exploits weaknesses in the operating system - a method commonly used on Android systems where native rooting is not supported [22]. Upon examination, there was no noticeable difference in the data structures created by both applications on the internal storage media of the platforms.

Table 1. Drone.

Name	Price	Weight	Camera resolution	Range
DJI Phantom 3 Professional Edition	£699.99	1280 g	4K (12 Megapixels)	5 km

Table 2. Mobile platform.

Name	Model number	Android version	CyanogenMod version	Kernel version	Installed application
Motorola Moto G 3rd Generation	Moto G	5.1.1 (Lollipop)	12.1 (Osprey)	3.10.49-g55f6ac8	DJI GO v3.1.4
Samsung Galaxy S4 Mini	GT-I9195I	4.4.4 (Kitkat)	N/A	3.10.28-5334500	DJI GO v3.1.4

In order to test the devices and generate artefacts, a scenario must be created using the devices. This is a necessary and established part of forensic research [22]. A scenario, in a digital forensics context, is a simulation of a crime using the device to be tested. Because drones, as mentioned earlier, have a great potential to cause concerns over privacy, trespassing and safety, all tests of the devices were to follow legal guidelines on drone safety [10]. The location in which the flights were conducted was suitable for safely testing the capabilities of the drone away from congested areas, and possessed some useful features such as tall building structures and large open space. A chosen standard flight path, consisting of four waypoints within an approximate 150 m radius was established. A number of flights were conducted testing both the manual and automatic function of the drone.

The analysis performed on the UAV and the mobile platform was artefact-driven. Artefacts related to drones were divided into three categories relating to the identification of suspects, interpretation of flight data and the extraction of artefacts from recorded media. The main identification aspect was the method of control of the drone via a smartphone. The DJI Phantom uses a physical controller in conjunction with commands from the smartphone, transmitted to the drone over radio [8]. These methods of control leave footprints on the drone. Identifying artefacts such as MAC (Media Access Control) address, phone model, operating system etc. will be crucial in reducing a suspect pool in investigations.

Flight data was collected during flight via various sensors present in the drone platform including but not limited to GPS, altitude, speed and battery levels. These can reveal details about the flight of the drone that may prove crucial in an investigation, for example the "home" GPS co-ordinate is where the drone took off. Another example is in the event of a drone crash, as battery levels can be correlated with the time that the drone failed.

Media includes any photos or videos taken by the device's camera. The use of drones as bombers mentioned earlier [12] was all recorded via the drone's on-board camera in order to produce videos, and the capture and analysis of such a bombing drone would be able to reveal important intelligence. The DJI phantom is equipped with a high-end camera capable of high resolution photos and videos, making it suitable for this kind of activity.

Because the analysis performed comprised UAV systems, mobile devices, and removable storage, a variety of file systems and interfaces were encountered. Development environments for forensics tools include scripting tools for the Linux operating system such as Bash, Perl and Python, as well as compiled programming languages such as "C". A forensic workstation running Kali, a distribution of Linux, with several forensics and cybersecurity tools was used, as listed in Table 3.

Table 3. Forensic utilities.

Computer used	Operating system	Utilities
Toshiba Satellite L450D	Kali Linux Rolling Update	ls: Listing dd: Data Dump mount: Mount command dmesg: System Logging file: File signature identification script: Terminal recording feature arp: Address Resolution Protocol telnet: Remote Access uname: Version Identification cp: Copy cat: Print file contents bash: Scripting environment

3.1 Mobile Forensics

Mobile forensics was performed to analyse the data of the DJI GO application [23], which was installed via the Android app store. The test mobile platform was a Motorola Moto G 3rd Generation running a customised version of Android, CyanogenMod version 12.1 [19]. This operating system allows for extensive customisation including rooting of the device without needing to subvert operating system security. With the customised operating system, rooting was achieved simply by activating root requests from the developer settings of the phone. Rooting is necessary to acquire portions of the Android internal storage that are protected by the operating system [22], it is the most forensically sound way of acquiring data when chip-off analysis is not available.

After connecting the test platform to the forensic workstation via USB, access was established through an instance of Android Debug Bridge [24]. Running the command "ls/dev/block/bootdevice/by-name" gave a listing of the mounted partitions on the device, as shown in Fig. 1.

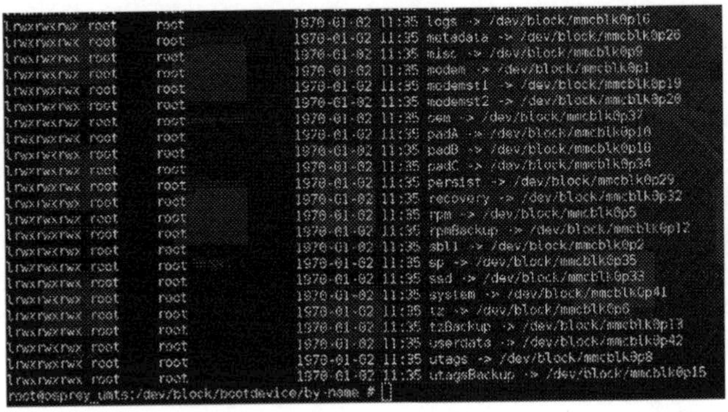

Fig. 1. Sample listing of mounted partitions on Android platform.

The mount point for the "userdata" partition, which contains all user-created data including application data, is shown as "/dev/block/mmcblk0p42". A forensic image of this partition was created using the "dd" command, as shown in Fig. 2. This is a type of physical acquisition, which creates an exact copy of the digital storage media. Before this could take place, a few conditions needed to be met. Firstly the ADB access needed to have root permissions, which was granted by an operating system root request. Secondly, the SD card used to store the image was formatted in the ExFAT (Extended FAT) file system, which has no restrictions on file sizes. Once completed, this created an image on a removable microSD card, which was copied to the forensic workstation for analysis.

Fig. 2. Forensic imaging of "mmcblk0p42" partition using "dd" command.

3.2   UAV

A number of flights were performed with the Phantom, as listed in Table 4. The source of this list is the practical log of flights taken on the day rather than data obtained from analysis of the UAV. Once the flights had been performed, the DJI was taken back to a forensics lab for analysis. The primary method of data storage for the DJI Phantom is the removable micro SD card slot. During the test flight, a 16 GB micro SD card was inserted, which was provided with the UAV itself. To analyse this media, the card was mounted to the forensic workstation and an image was created using the "dd" command. This is a forensically sound method of acquisition as the device does not need to be powered on. An initial check of the image using the Linux "file" command shows the card is formatted in the 32 bit File Allocation Table (FAT32) file system. The SD card's format is commonly found on many mass storage devices and it was analysed using various Linux utilities. The recorded media produced by the phantom stores some useful information, including GPS data, in the EXIF portion of the file. In order to interpret this data, the command line tool "exiftool" [25] was used. Data extracted from the UAV's mass storage devices was correlated with artefacts extracted from the DJI GO mobile application, to highlight links between the controlling application and the UAV.

Table 4. Flight record.

Flight	Start time	Waypoints	End time	Description, notes and recorded media
1	13:57	Travelled a short distance north of the home point before returning	13:18	Test flight for compass calibration
2	14:05	Waypoint 1: 14:06 Waypoint 2: 14:07 Waypoint 3: 14:12 Waypoint 4: 14:14	14:15	Manual flight, GPS assisted, 1 photo and one short video taken at each waypoint
3	14:17	Automatic reconnaissance flight Auto land (return to home) 14:22	14:22	Automatic flight, GPS assisted, using DJI's built-in Point Of Interest (POI) function, which makes the drone rotate around a specified point. Video was recorded the entire flight
4	14:34	(Same waypoints at flight 2, time not recorded due to operator concentrating on flight) Manual landing	14:37	In this flight, foil was attached to the drone covering the GPS module. The drone was operated completely manually independent of GPS. This simulated the intentional obfuscation of GPS signals as mentioned in related work [15, 16]

Along with the removable storage, the Phantom also has an internal storage media, a micro SD card, glued on to the centre board of the UAV [14]. To access this storage device, the UAV must be switched on and put into "Flight Data Mode" through the DJI GO application. The UAV was then connected to the forensic workstation via USB and the internal storage was mounted. Analysis of the file system using "fsstat" [26] showed the drive was formatted in FAT32, and a forensic image of the drive was acquired using the "dd" command. Upon examination, the drive contained a number of "FLYXXX.DAT" files - detailed flight logs, created by the Phantom's internal operating system and stored in a proprietary format [14]. These files were logically copied to a removable storage device for further analysis. There are many online services offering interpretation of these files, however uploading evidence to a third party server is not appropriate for a forensic investigation or intelligence purposes, so a tool designed to interpret and visualise these files, "CsvView" [27] was downloaded and installed to a separate machine running Windows, connected to the internet. The tool was established with a Google Maps API key, allowing it to download imagery from the Google Maps database.

4   Results

This section covers the key findings from the analysis described in Sect. 3. The results are broken down into three different areas of interest; the removable SD card used by the UAV, the internal storage of the UAV and the results of the mobile forensic analysis on the DJI GO application.

4.1   SD Card

The DJI Phantom micro SD card image acquired as described in Sect. 3.1 was mounted to the forensic workstation. Output from the "tree" [28] command lists the files and directories of this image. There are two directories, DCIM and MISC, as shown in Fig. 3. The DCIM directory contains a wealth of .JPG, .DNG and .MP4 files, all of which are common media file formats.

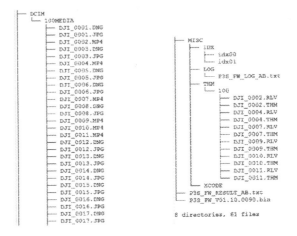

Fig. 3. Sample output of "tree" command.

The file found under the LOG directory was a firmware upgrade log for the UAV. It refers to the file "P3S_FW_v01.10.0090.bin", located on the root of the SD card, meaning that file is the firmware update itself. Other useful information in this log includes a version history of the firmware, up to the current version. The THM directory appears to contain thumbnails generated from each flight. To analyse the EXIF Data of the stored media files, "exiftool" [25] was run against the DCIM/100MEDIA directory. On initial inspection, GPS co-ordinates are stored under a "GPS Position" EXIF tag. To automate the process of extracting the GPS co-ordinates and to create a timestamped GPS flight log, a simple script was created, as shown in Fig. 4. The script executes "exiftool" on all files in the directory, formatting the GPS data to 6 decimal places. The output is then filtered to only contain the GPS Position and Create Date, which denotes when the picture or video was taken.

Fig. 4. Script to retrieve GPS data from media EXIF information.

4.2   Internal Storage

The files extracted from the internal storage of the DJI Phantom were analysed using the "CsvView" tool [27]. The DJI Phantom 3 Operating system begins recording flight data from the moment the UAV is switched on. This meant as flights 1–3 listed in Table 4 were performed in the same session of drone activity, the data for those flights were recorded in one file, "FLY012.DAT". After processing using "CsvView" [27], which converts the file from a ".DAT" to a ".csv" format, the flights were visualised using the "GeoPlayer" function, which utilised the Google Maps API Key mentioned in Sect. 3.2. A copy of this visualisation is shown in Fig. 5, with each flight and waypoints 1–4 and the point of interest (POI) highlighted. Because it is constantly recorded, the GPS data alone is not enough to distinguish between individual flights.

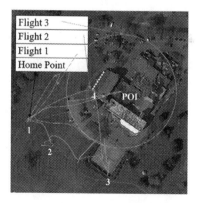

Fig. 5. Annotated visualisation of flights 1–3.

The DJI Phantom flight recorder produces a host of other artefacts. Plotting these artefacts against each other using the "CsvView" [27] tool provides a comprehensive understanding of the actions taken by the drone. Figure 6 shows the flight time (green), which remains constant under periods of non-activity, increasing in a linear function when the drone is in flight, as well as the barometric altitude (blue) and the total voltage level of the battery (purple) of the UAV. When compared with each other, it can be deduced that there was three distinct periods of movement and altitude changes by the drone, were interpreted as flights. The possible artefacts recoverable from these logs are extremely detailed, and are more than necessary to recreate a flight.

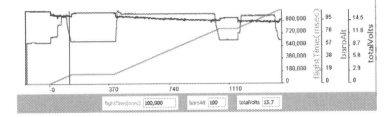

Fig. 6. Flight time, barometric altitude and battery voltage. (Color figure online)

The file "FLY014.DAT" file was identified as being the log for the Flight 4, listed in Table 4. The "GeoPlayer" visualisation for this flight showed that the GPS data recorded was mostly garbage data that had no relation to the actual flight, as shown in Fig. 7.

Fig. 7. Garbage GPS data from flight 4.

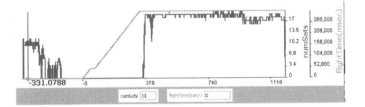

Fig. 8. GPS health plotted against flight time for flight 4.

According to the operator's previous experience, the recommended amount of GPS signals was about 11, but with the foil obstructing the unit, the Phantom struggled to receive enough GPS data to successfully triangulate a position. To confirm this was the case, the flight time and "numSats" (number of satellites) readings from the flight logs were compared, and showed that during flight, the "numSats" reading was 0, as shown in the time period (X-Axis) of 0 to 370 in Fig. 8. This is interpreted as a lack of available satellites for the UAV to receive data, which was true when the drone was in flight, as described by the flight time. The foil was removed after the flight due to fears of overheating the drone through obstruction of the cooling vents. The data shown in Figs. 7 and 8 confirms findings from related work [15] that the GPS can be obstructed simply by covering the module with aluminium foil. It is quite likely that in a crime scenario, this measure would be taken to prevent later forensic analysis of the flight path, or to evade no fly zones. In this case, investigators must instead rely on other data from the flight log. The DJI Phantom 3 Professional is equipped with accelerometers, which record the acceleration in an axis relative to the UAV in metres/second^2. Accelerometer measurements can be used to reconstruct a flight in 3D space, relative to an arbitrary home point. Inspection of the accelerometer readings showed a period of movement while the UAV was in flight. While it would be possible to perform analysis of this manually, the frequency of measurements taken by the Phantom makes it unreasonable, and it would be better to develop a tool to do this.

4.3 DJI GO Application

Artefacts from the DJI GO application [23] were located in different locations within the "userdata" partition of the Android test platform, which was acquired using methods described in Sect. 3.1. A list of these directories is shown in Table 5.

Table 5. Useful directories from the DJI GO application.

Path	Type of artefact	Description
/media/0/DJI/dji. pilot/LOG/CACHE	Flight data	Contains a number of logs relating to drone activity
/media/0/DJI/dji. pilot/LOG/CACHE/NFZ	Flight data	This is a log of activity relating to the DJI's built-in no fly zone function, and contains information such as GPS location
/media/0/DJI/dji. pilot/LOG/ERROR_POP_LOG	Flight data	An error log from the UAV
/media/0/DJI/dji. pilot/DJI_RECORD	Media	A number of video taken during flight named as a date in the format "YYYY_MM_DD_ hh_mm_ss" and stored with the "mp4" file extension. For each video file, there is also a corresponding text file, which contains GPS data, manufacturing information and capture dates
/media/0/DJI/dji. pilot/FlightRecord	Flight data, personally identifying information, serial number	Flight data relating to a number of flights. A string search revealed the presence of the "cccu phantom" string, which was the name assigned to the UAV during setup
/media/0/DJI/dji. pilot/CACHE_IMAGE	Media	Thumbnails of various images and videos taken during flight, seemingly random

The serial number for the UAV can be extracted from the contents of the DJI GO application and linked to track the specific device used in flight. The data reveals information about the UAV's internal system operations such as updates and errors. A log is also kept of instances when the UAV encountered a no fly zone (NFZ) during flight. Media is present as copies of videos captured during flight are locally stored by the application. Flight data files with the ".txt" extension were extracted from the "FlightRecord" directory. The flight record files extracted from the "FlightRecord" directory were analysed using the "CsvView" [27] tool for comparison to the ".DAT" flight logs extracted from the Phantom's internal storage. Upon inspection, the files were confirmed to be flight data stored in a similar format to the ".DAT" files, but with notable differences. Firstly, the resolution of the recorded data is much lower, with the DJI GO application flight records being between 1 Kb and 1 Mb, whereas the ".DAT" files from the UAV were much larger, often several hundred megabytes. Secondly, files were recorded per flight from take-off to landing rather than per session of activity, meaning it was clearer when distinguishing between flights. The ".txt" files also had noticeably more metadata than the ".DAT" files – including serial numbers of the UAV and the DJI smart battery, application version information and the operating system of the test platform, as shown in Fig. 9.

droneType	P3 Advanced
dateTime	2017/04/01 12:59:44.964
appVersion	3.1.4
batterySN	1589
aircraftSn	03Z1013321
appType	Android

Fig. 9. Metadata from DJI GO application flight log.

As well as the metadata shown in Fig. 9, several other streams of flight data relating to use of the DJI GO application were also available. The "flyCState" attribute described whether the Phantom was in manual or automatic mode. Figure 10 shows the distance of the UAV from the home point plotted against the "flyCState" attribute during the Flight 3.

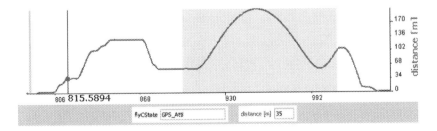

Fig. 10. Flight state plotted against distance from home point for flight 3.

The automatic POI function mentioned in Table 4 generated a clearly visible sine wave (Fig. 10) in the distance measurements during the time when the UAV was in automatic flight mode. This useful artefact identifies when the POI function has been used in a flight. While the GPS data for Flight 4 was also destroyed by the foil covering the GPS receiver, it was also possible to extract the GPS location of the controlling application. This is a crucial finding as it allows for the location of the operator at the time of flight. Anti-forensics measures to counteract this may include GPS spoofing on a software level on the mobile platform, which is possible with free applications available on app markets such as google play.

5 Conclusion

The results from the DJI Phantom 3 Professional show a number of successful methods to retrieve data from the UAV and controlling devices using open source tools. Artefacts present in the flight record data were used to identify key actions taken by the drone using some heuristics and pattern detection. Correlation of these and other artefacts extracted from the mobile platform were enough to establish a connection between the drone and the controlling application. With every drone system, there are many different artefacts spread across a number of devices, file systems, and networks. The forensic analysis of drones requires a correlation of these artefacts to retrieve the actions of the drone. The DJI phantom had an extraordinarily large amount of artefacts associated with it. This was due to having more sensors and a higher resolution of data capture, which stems from its status as a professional device. To recreate the actions of the drone, it was necessary to interpret flight data collected by the UAV. This involved interpreting the movements of the UAV in three dimensional space, as well as data from on-board sensors including accelerometer data and battery levels. A number of useful artefacts were found on the controlling application, and would be enough to identify a suspect.

Further work needs to be done in developing and exploring methods for analysing drone systems in the future, especially integrating the methods discussed in this paper into commercial forensics toolkits. The extraction of data from controlling applications on iOS devices should be explored for comparison to the Android mobile forensics methods demonstrated in this paper. Newer drones, such as the Phantom 4 and the Mavic, will also need to be analysed to explore the differences with previous versions.

References

1. Yeung, P.: Drone reports to UK police soar 352% in a year amid urgent calls for regulation, The Independent (2016). http://www.independent.co.uk/news/uk/home-news/drones-police-crime-reports-uk-england-safety-surveillance-a7155076.html. Accessed 7 Aug 2017
2. BBC news: big rise in drone smuggling incidents (2016). http://www.bbc.co.uk/news/uk-35641453. Accessed 7 Aug 2017
3. UAV Systems international: Tarot T-18 Ready to Fly Drone. https://uavsystemsinternational.com/product/tarot-t-18-ready-fly-drone/3. Accessed 7 Aug 2017

4. Noel, A.: Drone Carrying Three Kilos of Meth Crashes in Tijuana, Vice News (2015). https://news.vice.com/article/drone-carrying-three-kilos-of-meth-crashes-in-tijuana. Accessed 7 Aug 2017

5. Francis, D.: Want to Smuggle Drugs into Prison? Buy a Drone, The Cable - The Foreign Policy Group (2016). http://foreignpolicy.com/2015/08/04/want-to-smuggle-drugs-into-prison-buy-a-drone. Accessed 7 Aug 2017

6. Sullivan, J.P., Bunker, R.J.: Mexican Cartel Strategic Note No. 18: Narcodrones on the Border and Beyond. Small Wars J. (2016). http://smallwarsjournal.com/jrnl/art/mexican-cartel-strategic-note-no-18-narcodrones-on-the-border-and-beyond. Accessed 7 Aug 2017

7. Carrier, B.: Open source digital forensics tools: the legal argument, @stake research report. http://www.digital-evidence.org/papers/opensrc_legal.pdf. Accessed 7 Aug 2017

8. DJI Phantom 3 Professional. https://www.dji.com/phantom-3-pro. Accessed 7 Aug 2017

9. Glaser, A.: DJI is running away with the drone market, recode technology website. https://www.recode.net/2017/4/14/14690576/drone-market-share-growth-charts-dji-forecast. Accessed 7 Aug 2017

10. CAA: Flying Drones. https://www.caa.co.uk/Consumers/Guide-to-aviation/Airspace/Who-manages-UK-airspace-/. Accessed 7 Aug 2017

11. Barrett, D.: Burglars use drone helicopters to target homes, The Telegraph. http://www.telegraph.co.uk/news/uknews/crime/11613568/Burglars-use-drone-helicopters-to-identify-targe-homes.html. Accessed 7 Aug 2017

12. Waters, N.: Death From Above: The Drone Bombs of the Caliphate, Bellingcat open source intelligence. https://www.bellingcat.com/uncategorized/2017/02/10/death-drone-bombs-caliphate. Accessed 7 Aug 2017

13. Horsman, G.: Unmanned aerial vehicles: a preliminary analysis of forensic challenges. Digit. Invest. **16**, 1–11 (2016)

14. Kovar, D.: UAV (aka drone) Forensics, SANS DFIR summit (2015). https://www.sans.org/summit-archives/file/summit-archive-1492184184.pdf. Accessed 7 Aug 2017

15. Maarse, M., Sangers, L., van Ginkel, J., Pouw, M.: Digital forensics on a DJI Phantom 2 Vision+ UAV. MSc System and Network Engineering, University of Amsterdam (2016)

16. Trujano, F., Chan, B., Beams, G., Rivera, R.: Security Analysis of DJI Phantom 3 Standard, Massachusetts Institute of Technology (2016). https://courses.csail.mit.edu/6.857/2016/files/9.pdf. Accessed 7 Aug 2017

17. Huebner, E., Zanero, S.: The case for open source software in digital forensics. In: Huebner, E., Zanero, S. (eds.) Open Source Software for Digital Forensics, pp. 3–7. Springer, Heidelberg (2010). https://doi.org/10.1007/978-1-4419-5803-7_1

18. Woods, V., Meulen, R.V.D.: Gartner Says Worldwide Smartphone Sales Grew 3.9 Percent in First Quarter of 2016. http://www.gartner.com/newsroom/id/3323017. Accessed 7 Aug 2017

19. CyanogenMod android operating system. https://cyngn.com/. Accessed 7 Aug 2017

20. Karlsson, K.J.: Android anti-forensics at the operating system level. M.Sc. thesis, University of Glasgow (2012)

21. Kingo Root Tool. https://www.kingoapp.com. Accessed 7 Aug 2017

22. Barton, T., Azhar, M.H.B.: Forensic analysis of the recovery of Wickr's ephemeral data on Android platforms. In: The First International Conference on Cyber-Technologies and Cyber-Systems, pp. 35–40. IARIA (2016)

23. DJI GO application. http://www.dji.com/goapp. Accessed 7 Aug 2017

24. ADB tool – Android Debug Bridge tool. https://developer.android.com/studio/command-line/adb.html. Accessed 7 Aug 2017

25. Exiftool. http://www.sno.phy.queensu.ca/~phil/exiftool/. Accessed 7 Aug 2017

26. Sleuthkit – fsstat. https://www.sleuthkit.org/. Accessed 7 Aug 2017

27. CsvView tool. https://datfile.net/CsvView/downloads.html. Accessed 7 Aug 2017

28. The "tree" tool. http://www.easydos.com/tree.html. Accessed 7 Aug 2017

A Novel File Carving Algorithm
for EVTX Logs

Ming Xu[1,2(✉)], Jinkai Sun[1], Ning Zheng[1], Tong Qiao[2], Yiming Wu[2], Kai Shi[1],
Haidong Ge[1], and Tao Yang[3(✉)]

[1] Internet and Network Security Laboratory, School of Computer Science
and Technology, Hangzhou Dianzi University, Hangzhou, China
{mxu,152050160,nzheng,12084232,151050149}@hdu.edu.cn
[2] School of Cyberspace, Hangzhou Dianzi University, Hangzhou, China
{tong.qiao,ymwu}@hdu.edu.cn
[3] Key Lab of the Third Research Institute of the Ministry of Public Security,
Shanghai, China
yangtao@stars.org.cn

Abstract. The Microsoft Windows system provides very important
sources of forensic evidence. However, few attention has been paid to
the recovery of the deleted EVTX logs. Without using system metadata,
a novel carving algorithm of EVTX logs is proposed by analyzing the
characteristics and intrinsic structure. Firstly, we reassemble binary data
belonging to fragments of complete EVTX logs to reconstruct the deleted
logs. Secondly, extracting records for the corrupted logs can make the
algorithm robust through the special features of template and substitution array. Finally, some experiments are given to illustrate the effectiveness of the proposed algorithm. Moreover, when the logs are fragmented
or corrupted, our algorithm can still perform well.

Keywords: Windows forensics · Windows XML event logs
EVTX Files · File carving · Fragmented files

1 Introduction

Since log files generally link a certain event to the special time, they can provide
very important sources of forensic investigation. It is very easy for an internal
employee to steal or destroy the information of the company computers. During
committing illegal activities, a criminal possibly removes or hides traces after his
crime behavior. It makes operations untraceable with no digital evidence left.
Therefore, the technique which can help us to recover maliciously deleted logs
has received significant attention over the past few years [1].

As a replacement for the Windows event log (EVT) format, the Windows
XML event log (EVTX) format was first introduced in Vista for less storage
through binary XML technology. EVTX logs provide a great deal of basic and
valuable information such as name of the account, created time, record number

© ICST Institute for Computer Sciences, Social Informatics and Telecommunications Engineering 2018
P. Matoušek and M. Schmiedecker (Eds.): ICDF2C 2017, LNICST 216, pp. 97–105, 2018.
https://doi.org/10.1007/978-3-319-73697-6_7

and event ID which could be used to identify the specific kind of an event. For instance, event ID 4624 means that an account was logged on. It is confirmed that a criminal logged on a computer at a certain time associating with the included time and username.

Nevertheless, criminals are always expected to conceal their criminal records by deleting logs. Because of file fragmentation on actual file systems [2], it is too time consuming to use a brute-force approach dealing with each possible order without file system information. Thus we present a novel carving algorithm to extract deleted records and demonstrate the effectiveness of our proposed algorithm by comparing it with the commercial forensic software Encase[1].

2   Related Work

Several researchers have noted that logs of Windows contain a large amount of useful digital evidence [3,4]. Schuster first provides description about the newer EVTX format [5], and XML technology is adopted to parse Vista event log files [6]. For different Windows systems, Windows 8 event log format is introduced [7]. In addition, Do et al. present a Windows event forensic process for analyzing log files [8].

Moreover, researchers focus on caving contiguous files firstly [9,10]. For fragmented files, some carving algorithms based on file signature are proposed [11,12] and a novel framework is designed to resolve this problem [2,13]. Unfortunately, there has been relatively few papers published for file carving of the EVTX logs. Therefore, in this context, we propose a novel file carving algorithm to deal with this challenge.

3   Description of EVTX Logs

By investigating the characteristics and internal structure of EVTX Logs (see Fig. 1), we can smoothly establish our algorithm for realizing forensics.

3.1   File Header

Each log file contains a file header, which describes the basic information of the file. A file header occupies 4096 bytes space which is a complete cluster, but uses only 128 bytes actually. In our algorithm, the checksum which verifies integrity of the file header is gained through the CRC32 (Cyclic Redundancy Check) method to calculate the first 120 bytes of the file header. We use *magic string* "ElfFile" and *checksum* to find a integrated file header for marking the following chunk as the first chunk of the file.

---

[1] EnCase offers investigators the flexibility to collect critical evidence including text messages, call records, pictures, graphics, and much more.

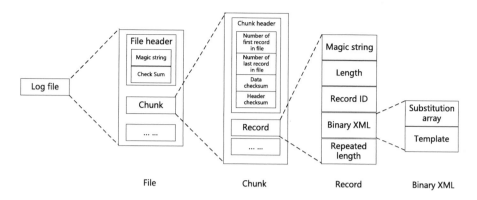

Fig. 1. File structure

3.2 Chunk Header

Each chunk consists of a smaller header and a series of event records. It starts with the *magic string* "ElfChnk", which helps to identify the chunk. Chunk header provides two different sets of counters for *record ID*[2], and for the same chunk it is safe to assume that *record ID* of the included record is in the range between *number of first record in file* and *number of last record in file*. It can contribute to determining whether a record belongs to the original chunk by the information of the chunk header.

Checksum is important for guaranteeing the integrity of the chunk. *Data checksum* is calculated for the CRC32 of all the records data belonging to this chunk. In addition, *header checksum* is the CRC32 of the first 120 bytes and bytes 128 to 512 of the chunk header. Therefore, we can use *header checksum* to confirm the integrity of the chunk header and *data checksum* to check whether the records of chunk are found completely.

3.3 Record

Each event record contains basic information. A fragment belongs to a record potentially for the existence of the *magic string* "**". *Length* and *repeated length* allow us to find a complete record.

The main content of the record is coded through the binary XML technology. Binary XML mainly involves two concepts: template and substitution array. Binary XML starts with a template which is transformed from a sequence of tokens and a template has some substitution tokens which are needed to be filled with the value of substitution array (see Fig. 2). Template is immediately followed by the substitution array. For each substitution, it lists size and data type (see Fig. 3), and uses actual value to fill into the corresponding substitution token to comprise complete plain text XML. For one chunk, most of records only

---

[2] Record ID is the same as record number.

have a reference of the template to reduce storage space. Probably a record in the fragment cannot be recovered for its dependence of the template. It is observed that the count of the substitution array is 18 or 20. Additionally, length and type should be followed by the hexadecimal value 0x00 [5]. Therefore we can locate the position of the substitution array, and even determine whether the record is complete by checking integrity of the substitution array.

```
<Event xmlns="http://schemas.microsoft.com/win/2004/08/events/event">
     <System>
     ...
     <EventID>substition 3, type 6</EventID>
     ...
     <EventRecordID>substition 10, type 10<EventRecordID>
     </System>
</Event>
```

The number of data(18 or 20)		
Length[0]	Type[0]	0x00
... ...		
Length[n-1]	Type[n-1]	0x00
Data[0]		
... ...		
Data[n-1]		

Fig. 2. Template with unfilled substitution array   **Fig. 3.** Substitution array

4   The Proposed Approach

In this section, it is proposed to introduce our algorithm showed in Fig. 4. The algorithm mainly includes three parts: pre-processing data, reassembling fragments and extracting corrupted records.

4.1   Data Pre-processing

In this stage, the fragments belonging to logs should be effectively classified with others. The fragmentation points which normally bring challenge in file carving can only be present at the boundary between two clusters [2]. Since the log data may be scattered in any part of the image, we need to locate all the fragments belonging to EVTX logs by using different *magic string* to finding the first cluster of the fragment. We recommend to use 4 KB cluster as the size of per scanning, since 4 KB cluster is default for all NTFS file systems since Windows NT 4.0.

Separate lists are designed base on the mentioned file structures. Each included element of the lists which can be regraded as the fragment will store corresponding binary data. Figure 5 illustrates the flowchart of data pre-processing, and these lists are as follows:

- File list (simply as $List_f$): in $List_f$, each $element_f$ as the start of file contains a file header, a chunk header and included records.
- Chunk list (simply as $List_c$): in $List_c$, each $element_c$ as an potential chunk contains a chunk header and included records.
- Record list (simply as $List_r$): in $List_r$, each $element_r$ is regarded as an assemblage of fragmented records.

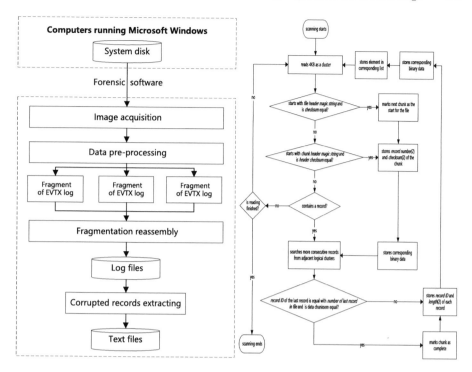

Fig. 4. Illustration of architecture

Fig. 5. The flowchart of data pre-processing

4.2 Fragmentation Reassembly

Before reassembly, we need to process the pinpointed fragments and reassemble them to reconstruct original files. Only the complete chunks can be combined into a valid log file, so we have to recover chunks belonging to the original file in the first step.

Afterwards, we generate log files by using complete chunks. Field *Channel* of the binary XML is used to determine whether a chunk belongs to the original file. It should be noted that the value of field *Channel* is not only stored in the substitution array but also in template. In order to acquire templates, we need to adopt XML technology to parse the complete chunks based on the previous research [5,6]. If one element cannot be used to reassemble finally, it will be added to *Broken list*.

For clarity, we introduce a discriminator for merging and a simplified algorithm is presented in Algorithm 1.

- Record ID: the *record ID* sequence of records in one chunk will be consistent and two adjacent chunks are supposed to have consecutive *record ID*.

– Channel: probably two logs have many same *record ID*, but different chunks from the same file will have the same value of the field *Channel* which can be used to reassemble chunks from the same log.
– Integrity of the substitution array: if *length* of the record which is to be connected is larger than 4 KB, the only way is to try all the situations of fragmentation to check the integrity of the substitution array. A simple instance uses Fig. 6 to illustrate it. If the size of uncertain data is 4 KB, we need to determine which cluster the potential 4 KB cluster is adjacent to the previous cluster or the next cluster by verifying the integrity of the substitution array.
– Checksum: we need to calculate the checksum of all the records data belonging to this chunk when finding the last record of the chunk.

Algorithm 1. Fragmentation Reassembly Algorithm

Input: $List_f$, $List_c$, $List_r$
Output: $Log\,files$, $Broken\,list$
for $element_f$, $element_c$ ∈ $List_f$, $List_c$ **do**
    for $element_r$ ∈ $List_r$ **do**
        $merge\,element_r\,into\,element_f$, $elment_r\,based\,on\,discriminator$
        if the last record of the chunk is found **then**
            $mark\,element_f$, $lement_c\,as\,complete$
        end if
    end for
end for
parse templates of the complete chunks
for $element_f$ ∈ $Complete\,list_f$ **do**
    for $element_c$ ∈ $Complete\,list_c$ **do**
        $merge\,element_c\,into\,list_f\,based\,on\,discriminator$
        generate a log file using corresponding binary data
    end for
end for
$Broken\,list$ ← $rest\,of\,elment$
return $Log\,files$, $Broken\,list$

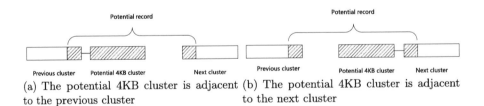

(a) The potential 4KB cluster is adjacent to the previous cluster
(b) The potential 4KB cluster is adjacent to the next cluster

Fig. 6. Reassembly of a record larger than 4 KB

4.3   Corrupted Records Extracting

Since EVTX log have three types of checksum to verify the integrity of a EVTX format file, any corruption results in that a log cannot be open by Windows. And a corrupted log file make its fragments not be merged. The only way to collect information of corrupted files is to match original templates and store generated plain text XML in other format files (e.g. text file). A warning is that this process may recover the incorrect records which are generated by Windows event logging service randomly.

Experimentally, the same template shared by different records in the same chunk must have only one *template id*. Only if the type of each substitution is compatible with template can the substitution array use value to fill into the corresponding substitution tokens. For each record in the *Broken list*, we consider a brute force approach to search its original template and write plain text XML into a text file.

5 Experiment and Evaluation

These experiments are designed to demonstrate the effectiveness of carving algorithm in dealing with the situation of unavailable file system metadata. In Windows, all computers event logs are normally found in: C : $Windows\backslash System32\backslash winevt\backslash Logs\backslash$. Due to the limitation of the public Windows images, we use our own 20 GB system disk images collected from three operating systems (Windows 7, Windows 8 and Windows 10). Note that, we use WinHex[3] to acquire the system disk image of computers for guaranteeing the reliability and integrity of raw data [14].

First of all, we save original files for calculating accuracy. We use regular deletion method to remove all the log files and make forensic images of system disk from each operation systems. The common evaluation method is to compare whether there exists the same record. First, all the records acquired from the original log files are to be gathered manually and analysed statistically. Then we use the same method in the recovered log files. Finally, by comparing the records from the original log files with recovered ones, we can determine whether the experimental result is effective or not.

We draw support from EnCase which is a widely-used commercial forensic software utilized by some law enforcement agencies. Unfortunately, no records are recovered by EnCase for the dependance of system metadata. Because of three types of verification in the EVTX format file, the recovered log files can guarantee their correctness. Zero-error carving strategy means that we only try to recover complete log files as far as possible, thus no error records will be recovered. Complete carving strategy means we also recover records from the log files which are overwritten or corrupted during deleting to write plain text XML into text files. Moreover, the precision rate might decrease with the increasement of recall rate. All things considered (see Table 1)[4], if there can exist error records, we recommend to use complete carving during investigation for better comprehensive evaluation.

---

[3] WinHex is a disk editor and a hex editor useful in data recovery and forensics.

[4] We use R/O(Recovered/original), PR(Precision rate), RR(Recall rate), F(F-value) and Time to evaluate the quality of results accurately.

Table 1. Results of different carving strategies

(a) After zero-error carving

System	R/O	PR	RR	F	Time
Win 10	15105/15248	100%	99.06%	99.53%	158s
Win 8	5124/6020	100%	85.11%	91.96%	159s
Win 7	4006/5210	100%	76.89%	86.94%	162s

(b) After complete carving

System	R/O	PR	RR	F	Time
Win 10	15292/15248	98.85%	99.13%	98.99%	160s
Win 8	5777/6020	100%	95.96%	97.94%	165s
Win 7	4842/5210	97.44%	90.57%	93.88%	171s

6   Summary

Since EVTX log files have tremendous forensic potential data in Windows forensic investigation, we present a carving algorithm for them without using the file system metadata in this paper. The traditional recovery method is highly dependent on file system metadata, thus the deleted files can not be recovered. By exploring the characteristics of Windows XML event log files, we design a caving algorithm to recover fragmented log files and extract corrupted records into text files. The numerical experiments reveal that our algorithm can perform well under the situation that log files are fragmented even corrupted.

Acknowledgment. This work is supported by the National Key R&D Plan of China under grant no. 2016YFB0800201, the Natural Science Foundation of China under grant no. 61070212 and 61572165, the State Key Program of Zhejiang Province Natural Science Foundation of China under grant no. LZ15F020003, the Key research and development plan project of Zhejiang Province under grant no. 2017C01065, the Key Lab of Information Network Security, Ministry of Public Security, under grant no. C16603.

References

1. Sharma, H., Sabharwal, N.: Investigating the implications of virtual forensics. In: 2012 International Conference on Advances in Engineering, Science and Management (ICAESM), pp. 617–620. IEEE (2012)
2. Garfinkel, S.L.: Carving contiguous and fragmented files with fast object validation. Digit. Invest. **4**, 2–12 (2007)
3. Murphey, R.: Automated windows event log forensics. Digit. Invest. **4**, 92–100 (2007)
4. Al-Nemrat, A., Ibrahim, N., Jahankhan, H.: Sufficiency of windows event log as evidence in digital forensics. University of East London, London
5. Schuster, A.: Introducing the Microsoft Vista event log file format. Digit. Invest. **4**, 65–72 (2007)
6. Xiaoyu, H., Shunxiang, W.: Vista event log file parsing based on XML technology. In: 4th International Conference on Computer Science & Education, ICCSE 2009, pp. 1186–1190. IEEE (2009)
7. Talebi, J., Dehghantanha, A., Mahmoud, R.: Introducing and analysis of the Windows 8 event log for forensic purposes. In: Garain, U., Shafait, F. (eds.) IWCF 2012/2014. LNCS, vol. 8915, pp. 145–162. Springer, Cham (2015). https://doi.org/10.1007/978-3-319-20125-2_13

8. Do, Q., Martini, B., Looi, J., Wang, Y., Choo, K.-K.: Windows event forensic process. In: Peterson, G., Shenoi, S. (eds.) DigitalForensics 2014. IAICT, vol. 433, pp. 87–100. Springer, Heidelberg (2014). https://doi.org/10.1007/978-3-662-44952-3_7

9. Mikus, N.: An analysis of disc carving techniques. Technical report, DTIC Document (2005)

10. Richard III, G.G., Roussev, V.: Scalpel: a frugal, high performance file carver. In: Refereed Proceedings of the Digital Forensic Research Workshop, DFRWS 2005, pp. 1–10, Astor Crowne Plaza, New Orleans, Louisiana, USA, August (2005)

11. Karresand, M., Shahmehri, N.: Reassembly of fragmented JPEG images containing restart markers. In: European Conference on Computer Network Defense, EC2ND 2008, pp. 25–32. IEEE (2008)

12. Na, G.-H., Shim, K.-S., Moon, K.-W., Kong, S.G., Kim, E.-S., Lee, J.: Frame-based recovery of corrupted video files using video codec specifications. IEEE Trans. Image Process. **23**(2), 517–526 (2014)

13. Cohen, M.I.: Advanced carving techniques. Digital Invest. **4**(3), 119–128 (2007)

14. Boddington, R., Hobbs, V., Mann, G.: Validating digital evidence for legal argument, p. 42 (2008)

Fuzzy System-Based Suspicious Pattern Detection in Mobile Forensic Evidence

Konstantia Barmpatsalou$^{(\boxtimes)}$, Tiago Cruz, Edmundo Monteiro, and Paulo Simoes

Pólo II-Pinhal de Marrocos, CISUC/DEI, University of Coimbra, 3030-290 Coimbra, Portugal
{konstantia,tjcruz,edmundo,psimoes}@dei.uc.pt

Abstract. Advances in Soft Computing have increased the probabilities of implementing mechanisms that are able to predict human behaviour. One of the fields that benefits more from the particular improvements are Digital Forensics. Criminal activity involving smartphones shows interesting behavioural variations that led the authors to create a technique that analyzes smartphone users' activity and recognizes potentially suspicious patterns according to predefined expert knowledge in actual use case scenarios by the use of fuzzy systems with different configurations.

Keywords: Mobile forensics · Fuzzy systems · Membership functions

1 Introduction

In the recent years, new Digital Forensic (DF) techniques emerged with the aid of Hard Computing (HC) [1]. However, activity driven by human behaviour is characterized by uncertainty [2] and renders them inefficient. Actions performed by individuals that are depicted in the digital fingerprint of a mobile device cannot be strictly characterized as innocent or guilty, but as entities that provoke different degrees of suspiciousness concerning specific criminal actions. This paper is the first part of a two-step approach aiming to create a semi-automated decision-making methodology for Mobile Forensic (MF) investigation purposes. Firstly, expert knowledge is used in order to create the ground truth and generate suspicious patterns concerning the outcome of user actions in data types retrieved during a forensic acquisition. Afterwards, the knowledge is diffused to the creation of fuzzy systems and their equivalent rules. Finally, the fuzzy system outputs are evaluated against the ground truth. However, the schema will be complete in the second part, which consists of the use and performance evaluation [3] of a Neuro-Fuzzy System (NFS) or a back-propagation neural network (NN) in comparison to the fuzzy systems and is the authors' future work.

The rest of the paper is presented in the following manner. Section 2 contains the related work in the field, while Sect. 3 presents the respective methodology the authors followed. Section 4 performs the results evaluation and Sect. 5 concludes the paper.

© ICST Institute for Computer Sciences, Social Informatics and Telecommunications Engineering 2018
P. Matoušek and M. Schmiedecker (Eds.): ICDF2C 2017, LNICST 216, pp. 106–114, 2018.
https://doi.org/10.1007/978-3-319-73697-6_8

2   Related Work

To the best of the authors' knowledge, noteworthy research has been conducted in the area of fuzzy and Neuro-Fuzzy data analysis for MF and similar disciplines, such as Intrusion Detection. Stoffel et al. [4] applied the fuzzy sets theory to evidence deriving from criminal activity in Switzerland and proved that their methodology is appropriate for "inferring expert-system-like rules from a forensic database" [4]. In order to detect *Denial of Service (DoS)* attacks in a computer network infrastructure, Kumar and Selvakumar [5] profited from the combination of the precise rule definition of fuzzy systems and the automatic rule acquisition of NNs. Automatic rule definition by a Neuro-Fuzzy system was also successful in cases of Android malware detection [6]. The next section describes the methodology the authors followed in order to develop the fuzzy systems for detecting suspicious patterns in mobile data.

3   Methodology

This section presents the proposed methodology concerning suspicious pattern detection from mobile datasets. The procedure consists of the construction of a use case scenario, the rule inference and the ground truth generation. Further details concerning the used datasets are provided and the fuzzy systems for the use case are configured.

3.1   Use Case Scenario

The authors used the FP 7 Project SALUS D2.3 publicly available deliverable [7] so as to determine a use case scenario with potential criminal activity occurrences. One of the use cases of the deliverable, public order demonstration or riot, was considered as the most suitable for the research purposes, due to the high probability of occurrence of unfortunate events involving mobile devices belonging to Protection and Disaster Relief (PPDR) officers. The case under examination concerns PPDR officers infiltrating the rioting forces and how this can be proved by their device seizure. The investigation authorities capture an image of the device at a given moment after the rioting incident, which is used as the base for further investigation. However, no assumptions can be made without the presence of expert knowledge, which is elaborated in detail below.

3.2   Expert Knowledge

The knowledge base encountered in the current paper is a hybrid compilation of incidents the use cases provided in the SALUS FP7 Project deliverables [7] and of on-field investigation practices provided by an officer of the *Greek Police Escort Teams Department (GPETD)*. The authors structured the rules of each fuzzy system present in the research. Due to space limitations, only the example of SMS data deriving from three devices will be presented. Another challenge that the authors faced was the lack or unavailability of actual evidence retrieved from devices involved in criminal activities. As a result, delinquent actions had to be simulated and injected in the datasets as standalone patterns. The a-priori expert knowledge served as a solid background for the rule generation, which is analyzed in the following subsection.

3.3 Rule Inference

Using the aforementioned expert knowledge, the authors created the respective rules from a combination of the available data and the investigation directives for the use case. For the scenario of the rioting infiltration by PPDR officers, the following setup was created. Sent SMS texts retrieved from a device of a potential infiltrator may have the following attributes. If officers are infiltrators, they will use their devices to communicate with their accomplices only in cases of extreme necessity. As a result, the rate with which a sent message will appear is going to be very low. Most of the accomplices may use one-time payphones, which are equipped with SIM modules from the same country the incidents occur. Thus, recipients with local numbers are considered more suspicious. Finally, messages exchanged right before or during rioting are very short in length. Consequently, the sent SMS pattern (very low appearance frequency–very short length–local country code source) is considered the most suspicious. Nonetheless, the rule inference procedure needs a functioning dataset that is able to fulfil the research requirements in size and content. The following subsection covers in detail the challenges the authors faced in the quest of a suitable data source.

3.4 Datasets and Ground Truth Generation

Due to the increased sensitivity of mobile device data, there are not many available sources of mobile device images. A more appropriate alternative was the "Device Analyzer Dataset" [8], a collection of real-time usage data from Android devices. Each dataset is a compilation of snapshots belonging to a certain device and contains lists of attributes such as call logs, SMS texts, network usage statistics, location data, etc., retrieved during a considerable period of time. All the information is stored in a Comma Separated Value (.csv) file and each row consists of the data type header, alongside with the existing data. Pre-processing is essential in order to separate the data types and adjust the information to the research needs. Adapted information from three different mobile devices, namely (Dev. 1, Dev. 2 and Dev. 3) is used for SMS data. The data are formatted in a three-column .csv file and each column represents one attribute; message length, receivers' appearance frequency and receivers' localization. Each row is a SMS text with its equivalent characteristics, which will from now on be referred to as a pattern. The SMS data type can be represented as follows:

$$\texttt{SMS}(\texttt{Appearance\_Frequency}, \texttt{Length}, \texttt{Country\_Source}) \qquad (1)$$

The next step is the generation of ground truth data, which included manual labelling for all the SMS patterns. Every tuple of attributes (see Eq. 1) corresponds to a suspiciousness numerical value in a scale from zero to one, where zero is the lowest and one is the highest value. Since the datasets were not originally created for DF analysis purposes and the existence of potentially suspicious patterns is unlikely, the authors injected the datasets with suspicious attribute combinations so as to have a complete view of the future system performance.

3.5   Fuzzy System Configuration

In order to proceed to the creation of the fuzzy systems, the authors followed the guidelines provided by Fuller [9]. One of the first factors to be taken into consideration is that all input and output variables should be described approximately or heuristically. Their fuzzy approximation is depicted in Table 1.

Table 1. Fuzzy variable ranges

Input variable	Fuzzy approximation	Numerical range
Length	VERY SHORT, SHORT, MEDIUM, LONG, VERY LONG	1–600 characters
Appearance frequency	VERY LOW, LOW, MEDIUM, HIGH, VERY HIGH	1–1100 appearances
Country source	FOREIGN, UNDEFINED, LOCAL	0, 1 and 2
Output variable	Fuzzy approximation	Numerical range
Suspiciousness	VERY LOW, LOW, MEDIUM, HIGH, VERY HIGH	0.15, 0.25, 0.50, 0.75, 1

The first column represents the variable, whereas the second shows the linguistic ranges attributed to it. The third column presents their numerical range. The rules in Subsect. 3.3 have to be represented in a formal manner and be placed in the appropriate system section so as to become structural elements of the rule base. An example of a rule concerning suspicious patterns is presented below. The rest of the rules are formed in a similar manner, with different variable values.

```
IF (Appearance == Very_Low) && (Length == Low) && (Country ==
    Local) THEN (Suspiciousness == Very_High)
```

Afterwards, the authors reviewed and verified the criteria for "readability and interpretability of the variables and the rules that are deriving from them" [10], as they were presented by Guillaume and Charnomordic [11]. While aiming to maintain a high degree of semantic cohesion, every fuzzy set should represent a well-defined and non-vague concept. The fuzzy sets and the value range of each variable have specific meanings (See Table 1). Additionally, each fuzzy variable should not exceed the 7 ± 2 range fields, which is defined as the threshold for human perception capabilities [10]. In the current paper, the maximum number of different value ranges is 5. There is no point within the system's universe of discourse that does not belong to at least one fuzzy set. Furthermore, a fuzzy set should be normal; in a fuzzy system $\overline{F}$, there should always exist at least one χ, the membership degree (height) of which should be equal to 1. Lastly, it is obligatory that "all fuzzy sets should overlap in a certain degree" [10]. After concluding the fuzzy system configuration phase, the system evaluation takes place.

4   Evaluation

The authors followed an evaluation methodology based on the comparison of the fuzzy systems' output and the ground truth values. With the ground truth considered the target and the fuzzy output being the feature variable, the fuzzy

Table 2. Evaluation metrics per membership function for the SMS Dev. 1 dataset

M.F	Algorithm	AUC	Accuracy	Precision	Recall	FPR
Triangular	kNN	0.583	0.267	0.811	0.267	0.175
	SVM	0.578	0.809	0.800	0.809	0.169
	Naive Bayes	0.567	0.805	0.649	0.805	0.174
	AdaBoost	**0.592**	**0.815**	**0.842**	**0.815**	**0.164**
	Random Forest	0.592	0.814	0.840	0.814	0.164
Trapezoidal	kNN	0.573	0.808	0.799	0.808	0.172
	SVM	0.573	0.808	0.799	0.806	0.172
	Naive Bayes	0.561	0.802	0.648	0.802	0.176
	AdaBoost	**0.574**	**0.808**	**0.846**	**0.808**	**0.171**
	Random Forest	**0.574**	**0.808**	**0.846**	**0.808**	**0.171**
Bell	kNN	0.923	0.951	0.951	0.9512	0.029
	SVM	0.748	0.824	0.825	0.824	0.102
	Naive Bayes	0.904	0.872	0.910	0.872	0.035
	AdaBoost	**0.974**	**0.981**	**0.981**	**0.981**	**0.009**
	Random Forest	0.945	0.963	0.964	0.963	0.021
Gauss	kNN	0.908	0.952	0.952	0.952	0.037
	SVM	0.858	0.864	0.889	0.864	0.058
	Naive Bayes	0.858	0.852	0.880	0.852	0.055
	AdaBoost	**0.925**	**0.960**	**0.961**	**0.960**	**0.030**
	Random Forest	0.915	0.956	0.956	0.956	0.032
Gauss2	kNN	0.924	0.961	0.961	0.961	0.0299
	SVM	0.884	0.871	0.903	0.871	0.0481
	Naive Bayes	0.882	0.865	0.893	0.865	0.0450
	AdaBoost	0.926	0.963	0.963	0.963	0.0305
	Random Forest	**0.931**	**0.963**	**0.963**	**0.963**	**0.0276**

output values of five systems configured with different membership functions (Triangular, Trapezoidal, Bell, Gauss and Gauss2) were classified into five different groups of suspiciousness using the *Nearest Neighbour, SVM, Naive Bayes, AdaBoost* and *Random Forest* classification techniques.

The confusion matrices were created and the following metrics were calculated in average for all the groups of suspiciousness; Area Under Curve (AUC) (higher positive-over-negative value ranking capability of a classifier), Accuracy (amount of correctly classified patterns over the total amount of patterns), Precision (ratio of True Positive (TP) values over the sum of TP and False Positives (FP)), Recall (TP rate or sensitivity, ratio of TP over the sum of TP and False Negative (FN) values) and False Positive Rate (FPR) (ratio of FP values over the sum of FP and True Negative (TN) values).

Table 2 contains the cumulative results for all the candidate membership functions and their respective metrics. After evaluating all the datasets (See Appendix A), the authors concluded that the Triangular and Trapezoidal membership functions perform worse than the rest of the other candidates under every classification algorithm. Moreover, the Bell membership function shows the best performance rates in every dataset. In the majority of the tests, AdaBoost showed the best performance rates. On the contrary, kNN, SVM and Naive Bayes performed poorly. Finally, the performance difference among the Bell, Gauss and Gauss2 membership function is very low and they can be considered as efficient alternatives. Figure 1 depicts the Receiver Operating Characteristic (ROC) Curves for two out of the five suspiciousness values of Table 1 (S = 0.75, S = 1) for the Dev. 3 dataset and the Bell membership function.

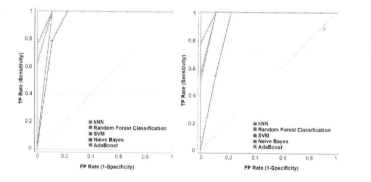

Fig. 1. ROC curves for the Dev. 3 dataset

5   Conclusions

The evaluation procedure was concluded successfully. The most appropriate parameters for the fuzzy systems were selected and the detection of potentially suspicious patterns was rather successful. Despite the satisfactory results, the aforementioned procedure revealed the need for a mechanism that will be able to optimize the parameters of a fuzzy system, so as to achieve the replacement of trial and error methods by automatic approaches. Moreover, accessing real data concerning the use case circumstances would be the best approach for evaluating the fuzzy systems' efficiency. The upcoming stage of the authors' work comprises the experimentation with different data types and the development of an appropriate NFS or back-propagation NN that will co-operate with the fuzzy systems and complete the current contribution.

Acknowledgments. This work was partially funded by the ATENA H2020 EU Project (H2020-DS-2015-1 Project 700581). We also thank the team of FP7 Project SALUS (Security and interoperability in next generation PPDR communication infrastructures) and the GEPTD officer Nikolaos Bouzis for the fruitful discussions, feedback and insights on in-field investigation practices.

A   SMS Datasets Evaluation Metrics

The appendix contains the analytical metrics for all the datasets tested in Sect. 4 as supplementary resources. Table 3 corresponds to the dataset of the second device (Dev. 2), whereas Table 4 refers to the dataset of the third device (Dev. 3).

Table 3. Evaluation metrics per membership function for the SMS Dev. 2 dataset

M.F.	Algorithm	AUC	Accuracy	Precision	Recall	FPR
Triangular	kNN	0.888	0.864	0.885	0.864	0.045
	SVM	0.875	0.822	0.840	0.822	0.052
	Naive Bayes	0.791	0.740	0.691	0.740	0.078
	AdaBoost	**0.897**	**0.850**	**0.870**	**0.850**	**0.043**
	Random Forest	0.890	0.867	0.888	0.867	0.045
Trapezoidal	**kNN**	**0.801**	**0.665**	**0.850**	**0.665**	**0.082**
	SVM	0.587	0.514	0.307	0.514	0.168
	Naive Bayes	0.727	0.684	0.606	0.684	0.107
	AdaBoost	0.742	0.704	0.647	0.704	0.102
	Random Forest	0.741	0.703	0.646	0.703	0.102
Bell	kNN	0.984	0.980	0.977	0.980	0.005
	SVM	0.976	0.968	0.966	0.968	0.008
	Naive Bayes	0.846	0.809	0.743	0.809	0.054
	AdaBoost	**0.998**	**0.997**	**0.997**	**0.997**	**0.001**
	Random Forest	0.991	0.989	0.986	0.989	0.004

(continued)

Table 3. (*continued*)

M.F.	Algorithm	AUC	Accuracy	Precision	Recall	FPR
Gauss	kNN	0.987	0.984	0.982	0.984	0.004
	SVM	0.980	0.972	0.9709	0.972	0.007
	Naive Bayes	0.850	0.815	0.746	0.815	0.052
	AdaBoost	**0.995**	**0.994**	**0.991**	**0.994**	**0.001**
	Random Forest	0.991	0.989	0.986	0.989	0.002
Gauss2	kNN	0.986	0.983	0.981	0.983	0.004
	SVM	0.988	0.984	0.982	0.984	0.003
	Naive Bayes	0.880	0.848	0.781	0.848	0.040
	AdaBoost	**0.989**	**0.986**	**0.983**	**0.986**	**0.003**
	Random Forest	0.988	0.984	0.982	0.984	0.003

Table 4. Evaluation metrics per membership function for the SMS Dev. 3 dataset

M.F.	Algorithm	AUC	Accuracy	Precision	Recall	FPR
Triangular	kNN	0.619	0.310	0.857	0.310	0.158
	SVM	0.611	0.582	0.508	0.582	0.159
	Naive Bayes	0.604	0.573	0.365	0.573	0.160
	AdaBoost	**0.617**	**0.591**	**0.651**	**0.591**	**0.156**
	Random Forest	0.617	0.590	0.610	0.590	0.157
Trapezoidal	kNN	0.608	0.294	0.571	0.294	0.143
	SVM	0.609	0.294	0.571	0.294	0.143
	Naive Bayes	0.600	0.571	0.365	0.571	0.162
	AdaBoost	**0.606**	**0.579**	**0.371**	**0.579**	**0.160**
	Random Forest	0.605	0.578	0.371	0.579	0.161
Bell	kNN	0.971	0.963	0.963	0.962	0.010
	SVM	0.937	0.906	0.922	0.906	0.025
	Naive Bayes	0.722	0.682	0.527	0.682	0.102
	AdaBoost	**0.990**	**0.986**	**0.986**	**0.986**	**0.004**
	Random Forest	0.983	0.978	0.978	0.978	0.033
Gauss	kNN	0.979	0.971	0.972	0.971	0.008
	SVM	0.940	0.909	0.975	0.975	0.025
	Naive Bayes	0.713	0.666	0.519	0.666	0.191
	AdaBoost	**0.990**	**0.986**	**0.986**	**0.986**	**0.006**
	Random Forest	0.981	0.975	0.975	0.975	0.006

(*continued*)

Table 4. (*continued*)

M.F.	Algorithm	AUC	Accuracy	Precision	Recall	FPR
Gauss2	**kNN**	**0.975**	**0.967**	**0.968**	**0.967**	**0.009**
	SVM	0.944	0.915	0.931	0.915	0.023
	Naive Bayes	0.716	0.671	0.521	0.671	0.108
	AdaBoost	0.949	0.920	0.935	0.920	0.022
	Random Forest	0.946	0.917	0.932	0.917	0.022

References

1. Barmpatsalou, K., Damopoulos, D., Kambourakis, G., Katos, V.: A critical review of 7 years of mobile device forensics. Digit. Invest. **10**(4), 323–349 (2013)
2. Gegov, A.: Fuzzy Networks for Complex Systems: A Modular Rule Base Approach, vol. 259. Springer, Heidelberg (2011). https://doi.org/10.1007/978-3-642-15600-7
3. Siddique, N., Adeli, H.: Computational Intelligence: Synergies of Fuzzy Logic, Neural Networks and Evolutionary Computing. Wiley, Hoboken (2013)
4. Stoffel, K., Cotofrei, P., Han, D: Fuzzy methods for forensic data analysis. In: 2010 International Conference of Soft Computing and Pattern Recognition, pp. 23–28 (2010)
5. Kumar, P.A.R., Selvakumar, S.: Detection of distributed denial of service attacks using an ensemble of adaptive and hybrid neuro-fuzzy systems. Comput. Commun. **36**(3), 303–319 (2013)
6. Shalaginov, A., Franke, K.: Automatic rule-mining for malware detection employing neuro-fuzzy approach. In: Norsk informasjons sikkerhets konferanse (NISK) (2013)
7. Nyanyo, A., Marques, H., Wickson, P., Brouwer, F., Blaha, M., Jelenc, D., Brouet, J., Junittila, K., Kolundzija, B.: Deliverable 2.3: SALUS use cases final. Technical report, SALUS Consortium (2014)
8. Wagner, D.T., Rice, A., Beresford, A.R.: Device analyzer: understanding smartphone usage. In: 10th International Conference on Mobile and Ubiquitous Systems: Computing, Networking, and Services, MOBIQUITOUS 2013, Tokyo, Japan (2013)
9. Fuller, R.: Neural Fuzzy Systems. Abo, Turku (1995)
10. de Lima, H.P., de Arruda Camargo, H.: A methodology for building fuzzy rule-based systems integrating expert and data knowledge. In: 2014 Brazilian Conference on Intelligent Systems, pp. 300–305 (2014)
11. Guillaume, S., Charnomordic, B.: Fuzzy inference systems: an integrated modeling environment for collaboration between expert knowledge and data using FISPRO. Expert Syst. Appl. **39**(10), 8744–8755 (2012)

Cyber Crime Investigation and Digital Forensics Triage

Digital Forensic Readiness in Critical Infrastructures: A Case of Substation Automation in the Power Sector

Asif Iqbal[1,2(✉)], Mathias Ekstedt[1], and Hanan Alobaidli[2]

[1] School of Electrical Engineering, KTH Royal Institute of Technology,
Stockholm, Sweden
asif.iqbal@ee.kth.se, mekstedt@kth.se
[2] Athena Labs, Dubai, UAE

Abstract. The proliferation of intelligent devices has provisioned more functionality in Critical Infrastructures. But the same automation also brings challenges when it comes to malicious activity, either internally or externally. One such challenge is the attribution of an attack and to ascertain who did what, when and how? Answers to these questions can only be found if the overall underlying infrastructure supports answering such queries. This study sheds light on the power sector specifically on smart grids to learn whether current setups support digital forensic investigations or no. We also address several challenges that arise in the process and a detailed look at the literature on the subject. To facilitate such a study our scope of work revolves around substation automation and devices called intelligent electronic devices (IEDs) in smart grids.

Keywords: Digital forensics · Forensic readiness · Substation automation
Smart grid · Forensic investigation · Critical infrastructures

1 Introduction

A critical infrastructure comprises of systems and assets, whether physical or virtual, that are so essential to a nation that any disruption of their services could have a serious impact on national security, economic well-being, public health or safety, or any combination thereof [1–3]. Our modern societies depend on critical infrastructures (CIs) to a great extent and sixteen such sectors of different critical infrastructures are defined by Department of Homeland Security [4]. For instance, several days long failure of power delivery in a large geographical area would not only lead to most business activity ceasing; it would also cause long-term damage to a range of industrial processes (e.g., animals dying in farms) and disrupt basic logistics that support our very living [5]. In the recent years, attacks on critical infrastructures and industrial control systems have become more frequent and more sophisticated [6]. State and non-state actors in today's volatile cyber arena are giving rise to increased cyber-attacks including those that target specifically critical infrastructure, like the recent attack on Ukrainian power grid [7] and the well-known Stuxnet [8, 26]. At the same time, the proliferation of computer tools

© ICST Institute for Computer Sciences, Social Informatics and Telecommunications Engineering 2018
P. Matoušek and M. Schmiedecker (Eds.): ICDF2C 2017, LNICST 216, pp. 117–129, 2018.
https://doi.org/10.1007/978-3-319-73697-6_9

and skills enabling individuals and teams to perform sophisticated cyber-attacks has been increasing, which leads to the attackers having to possess less skill and resources to launch a successful attack of a given sophistication compared to the past.

This paper zooms in onto investigative capabilities, through studying digital forensic readiness in critical infrastructures. Digital forensic readiness is the capability of an IT environment as a whole to determine whether or not an incriminating activity has taken place, using the remnants of different activities (e.g., state of systems, logs). While there have traditionally been many applications of digital forensics and forensic readiness within the domain of personal and enterprise IT, often used in law enforcement investigations; much less attention has been directed at applying digital forensics to critical infrastructures. As it is evident from the [9] that digital forensic readiness is of crucial importance but still it's quite at its infancy as far as critical information infrastructures are concerned. If we look through the published research as well as industry archives we see hints of other domains present in the literature but rarely anything to do with CIs. Here are a few examples that deal with network forensic readiness [10, 11].

2   SCADA System Architecture

There are different hardware components that create a (Supervisory Control And Data Acquisition) SCADA system. These components maybe considered as data sources in an investigation. Hence this section will mention some of the main components that might contain evidence in an investigation.

1. PLC (Programmable Logic Controller): A general control system that can function as a standalone system or participate in a network of PLCs. It has a flexible input and output facilities and it is programmed using techniques such as "Ladder logic". It is adapted to control manufacturing processes that require high reliability control and ease of programming such as assembly line and robotic devices.
2. RTU (Remote Terminal Unit): Typically used in SCADA systems as a communication hub where it collects data from sensors and actuators in substations and remote locations to a central system. It can also be used as a relay system for control commands.
3. IED (Intelligent Electronic Device): A term mostly used in power industry describing multifunction devices used for monitoring, protection and control. It is also used for upper level communication independently without the aid of other devices. It can receive data from sensors and power equipment's which can be used to issue control commands such as tripping circuit breakers if they sense voltage, current, or frequency anomalies, or raise/lower voltage levels in order to maintain the desired level.
4. HMI (Human Machine Interface): System engineers and operators utilize the HMI to interpret and visualize data received from the SCADA system through a graphical and/ or numerical presentation. It is also used to transfer algorithms, configure set points and adjust parameters of controllers. Depending on nature of the SCADA system controlled and monitored the HMI can be either a dedicated

hardware containing a control panel of switch and indicators to a software version either on a computer/ mobile application

5. Historian: A term used for a database management system that acquires and stores data sent to the control center. It is also used to create audit logs for all activities across a SCADA network. Hence it is considered important in any incident investigation

6. MTU (Master Terminal Unit): Is a central server that is sometimes referred to as SCADA server which is used to collect and process RTU/field devices data as well as issuing commands. It can provide a communication channel with these devices and it may be used to pre-process data before sending it to a historian. It also can provide a graphical representation of the information to be transferred and displayed on the HMI [12].

3   Related Work

According to the CESG Good Practice Guide No. 18, Forensic Readiness is defined as "The achievement of an appropriate level of capability by an organization in order for it to be able to collect, preserve, protect and analyze digital evidence so that this evidence can be effectively used in any legal matters, in disciplinary matters, in an employment tribunal or court of law" [9]. Implementing a forensic readiness system either specifically for digital forensics in general can provide several benefits such as [11]: Preparing for the potential need for digital evidence such as email communication, minimizing the cost of investigations, blocking the opportunity for malicious insiders to cover their tracks, reducing cost of regulatory or legal requirements for disclosure of data, showing due diligence, good corporate governance, and regulatory compliance.

Hence in the context of CI, it would be of paramount importance that we determine all such parameters that assist in such attribution to malicious activity as also defined in [13]. At the same time, digital forensics in critical infrastructure can provide benefits beyond capturing attackers. It can be useful in the context of troubleshooting, monitoring, recovery and the protection of sensitive data [14]. For example, it can be used to define and verify system monitoring requirements. This is done through determining logging conditions identifying errors and problems that can occur under failures or security breaches. It also identifies if this is done using software or hardware security equipment. It can also assist in the learning phase of advanced intrusion detection methods like anomaly detection, whitelisting and deep protocol behavior inspection [15].

3.1   Challenges to SCADA Forensics

According to a white paper by Enisa [16] with the security risks facing SCADA environment it becomes crucial to respond to critical incidents and be able to analyze and learn from what happened. The paper identified an incident analysis process based on good practices and recommendations for digital forensics. This process is divided into five stages which are: Examination, Identification, Collection, Analysis of evidence as well as Documentation of the process and results. Through these phases several challenges are faced by forensic investigators. This is divided into 3 categories of challenges: Data collection, Data Analysis and Operational.

Ahmed et al. [17] discussed some of the challenges faced while investigating a SCADA environment. The challenges mostly lay in the range of data acquisition. They stated that as per the sensitive nature of the SCADA environment that focuses on the availability of the services provided techniques such as live forensics would be needed. Nevertheless, this requires a prompt acquisition of the data as valuable information might be lost. At the same time, an important aspect of the forensic investigation process might be affected, this aspect is digital evidence integrity validity. As the data acquired from a live system that needs to be kept running methods such as creating hash value of the acquired image would be rendered apostolate. This is because data on the system will keep changing hence no two hash values will be the same.

Another challenge to the acquisition process may be resulted from the deterministic network traffic in SCADA environment, which might prevent forensic tools from operating properly. For example, a firewall might have strict rules that allow communication between specific SCADA components but disallow communication between the investigator's machine and SCADA components during data acquisition. Also, customized operating system kernels such as the one available in PatriotSCADA (firewall solution for SCADA networks) might affect the usability of acquisition tools. That is because tools such as DD might not run on customized kernels unless they are compatible with each other.

Other challenges include the unavailability of data to be acquired. For example, resource constrained devices such as RTU and PLC have limited resources hence data can have a limited life expectancy before being overwritten by other processes. Also logs in these devices might be considered inadequate for forensic investigation as they are geared toward process disturbances, not security breaches.

Ahmed et al. [17] also discussed some measures for forensic readiness in SCADA environment. They stated that forensic process can be improved in SCADA systems through preparedness and the selection of appropriate tools. The measure discussed was the creation of a data acquisition plan which consists of three steps. The first step is identifying the system environment; the second step is defining environment-specific requirements such as the impact of vendor solutions on OS. Finally, the third step is identification and collection of data such as activity and transaction logs.

They combined this with the need for data acquisition monitoring using tools such as EnCase CyberSecurity. This is needed in order to ensure that the acquisition process would not affect the availability of the SCADA system. They also recommended the use of lightweight data acquisition by using tools that have minimal impact so that adequate system resources are available for SCADA services to work properly.

Similar to the Enisa white paper [14] discusses investigation process of CI which starts with the identification of possible sources of evidence. They mention some of these sources which are engineering workstations, databases, historian, Human Management Interface (HMI), application server, Field devices like PLC, RTU, IED, firewall logs, web proxy cache and ARP tables. The second step is the preservation of the identified evidence, followed with data acquisition and data analysis.

Wu et al. [18] discussed a SCADA digital forensic process consisting of seven steps which are Identification and Preparation, Identifying data sources, Preservation,

Prioritizing and Collection of evidence, Examination Of the collected evidence, Analysis of the collected evidence, Reporting and Presentation, and finally Reviewing results. The paper also stated some challenges to the SCADA forensic investigation. These challenges are live forensics and integrity of data, lack of compatible forensic tools for field devices, lack of forensically sound storage, identifying data sources on SCADA systems, and finally increase of sophisticated attacks.

There were also other efforts by government organizations such as the Department of Homeland Security's the Control Systems Security Program to provide a guideline for the forensic investigation process [19].

Eden et al. [12] discussed a SCADA forensic incident response model consisting of four main stages: Prepare, Detect, Triage, and Respond. The model focuses on preparation before an incident occurs that would require a forensic investigation to happen. These stages are Prepare, Detect, Triage, and Respond. This paper also agreed with the SCADA forensic challenges mentioned in Ahmed et al. [17] work.

Figure 1 represents a mind map of the SCADA forensic challenges in relation to the discussed research.

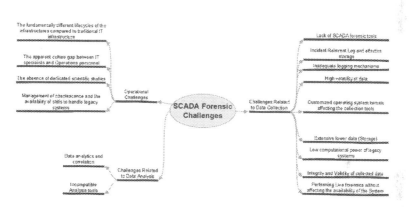

Fig. 1. Forensic challenges in SCADA environment [20]

3.2 SCADA Forensics Research

Some research such as the work done by Kilpatrick et al. [21] focused on network forensics in SCADA environment. The paper presented an architecture that is based on introducing forensic agents to the SCADA network. These agents are positioned on areas that will capture most of the network traffic in the SCADA network. The agents then forward the captured packets to a data warehouse using an isolated network in order to insure the integrity of the gathered information. The gathered information can also be used to incorporate mechanisms for monitoring process behavior, analyzing trends, and optimizing plant performance.

Valli [22] focused on exploit traceability during an investigation. The research presented a framework for producing verified signatures for Snort IDS using known and published vulnerabilities of SCADA and control systems. The research methodology consisted of five steps. The first step was the identification of vulnerabilities or traces at Black Hat, hacker, vendor, CERT or relevant cites. After identifying the possible vulnerabilities, a replication of the attack is designed through a script or a code base in order to ease the testing phase. These vulnerabilities are then studied from the networking perspective by analyzing the communication using modbus or DNP3 network protocols. Afterwards based on the gathered information a rule-set for Snort IDS is created. Finally, this ruleset is tested in an experimental environment.

Sohl et al. [23] discussed a set of vulnerabilities that can affect industrial control systems (ICS) as well as the fundamentals of forensic investigation in ICS with relation to these vulnerabilities. These vulnerabilities can be of low level in the control system such as stack overflow or heap overflow memory errors. Other discussed vulnerabilities were hardcoded credentials in control systems as well as vulnerabilities in Active X and cross site scripting (CSS) which can be used to attack system operators when visiting a malicious web site. An example of a SCADA system affected by the Active X vulnerability is MICROSYS PROMOTIC SCADA/HMI system before version 8.1.5 the vulnerability allows remote attackers to cause a denial of service via a crafted web page [24]. Another vulnerability to the MICROSYS PROMOTIC published is related to heap-based buffer overflow in versions before 8.3.11 which allows remote authenticated users to cause a denial of service via a malformed HTML document [25]. Sohl et al. [23] also discussed some of the possible evidence that an investigator will sought after while investigating an industrial control system. These evidences can be injected shellcode, rogue OS processes, additional malware code, code injected into the address space of existing OS processes, modifications to various kinds of data on the industrial control system, new client or server sockets, file creation and file access data. The author also discussed some forensic tools that can be used in control systems when suitable such as Linux LiME forensics tool for capturing volatile data along with Volatility Framework tool. Other tools discussed were FTK Imager, Dshell for network packet analysis. The authors stated that most of the tools are designed to work with general computing environment hence tools need to be designed to cope with specific interfaces, networking, and operating systems of control systems.

Nevertheless, most of the research focuses on the network element or the HMI of the SCADA environment but there isn't much discussion of the PLC or RTU devices regarding forensic investigation.

4 Discussion of the Related Work

As seen in the related work section there is variety of challenges that can affect the digital forensic investigation in SCADA systems. Most of these challenges are related to the fact that SCADA systems were designed at first with limited networking and security in mind. Most of the SCADA systems were isolated from the outside network such as the internet, but with the advancement in technology and the need for larger and faster processing they had to be connected. As a result, they became vulnerable to different attacks.

Also, SCADA system environment differ from traditional computing system with regard to the emphasis of availability. This emphasis proves to be one of the main challenges regarding digital forensics. The investigation process and technique needs to take this as a main consideration because if these systems went down the outcome maybe catastrophic to the country infrastructure. Hence traditional forensic techniques will not be suitable, but techniques such as live forensics will be of great value. Never the less more studies need to be done regarding live forensics techniques and tools that can be used in SCADA system.

Additionally, there are challenges related to the data created in the system, as it was mentioned above SCADA systems were not designed with security in mind. Hence data that can be gathered from sources such as logs may not cover all the needed aspects of the investigation. The logs mostly are designed to answer the system operator's needs not the security needs. Moreover, the issue of the limited logging capability in devices as well as limited storage makes a lot of the needed data to be highly volatile.

To overcome some of these challenges the research field discussed the possible investigation process. As per the author opinion the most comprehensive process were discussed in [12, 18]. The designed process paid a great attention toward the prepa- ration phase as it covers a challenge related to the limited knowledge of forensic investigators about the SCADA environment. Also these two processes shed light on the challenge of volatility of data sources by prioritizing which data sources are pro- viding the most valuable evidence in an investigation and acquiring the data accord- ingly. Never the less the process in [18] focused more in the investigation of the acquired evidence while the process in [12] introduced a detect phase that is related to identifying an attack and how it affected the system.

While in terms of other technical research in SCADA forensics filed the focus is on the network element or the HMI. There isn't much discussion of the PLC or RTU devices about the forensic investigation, some discussed that these devices don't have forensic capability or may not provide much data to the investigation. Having said that we consider these devices to be of value to the investigation and they should be studied and identify the possible evidence in these systems. Along with identifying the possible evidence the author believes that measures need to be implemented to make these devices provide more forensic evidence.

5   Case Studies

The aim of these case studies was to approach the problem of digital forensic readiness through an implementation point of view.

Substation automation refers to using data from intelligent electronic devices (IED), control and automation capabilities within the substation, and control commands from remote users to control power-system devices.

Figure 2 indicates our scope of work for this research as well as typical substation automation architecture.

5.1   Example 1: Digital Forensic Investigation of an IED Device

Transformer protection IED is a protection, control, and monitoring IED with extensive functional library, configuration possibilities and expandable hardware design to meet

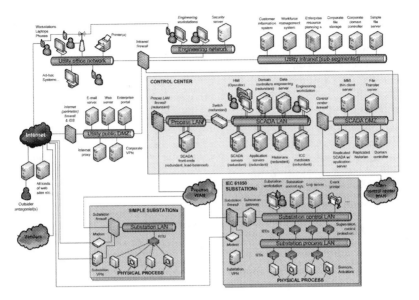

Fig. 2. A detailed SCADA network with a substation network

specific user requirements. It is usually used with a protection and Control IED manager. It helps manage protection and control equipment all the way from application and communication configuration to disturbance handling, including automatic disturbance reporting. The manager interacts with IEDs over fast and reliable TCP/IP protocols through LAN or WAN (rear communication port of the IED) or alternatively directly through the communication port at the front of the IED. It can read and write all configuration and setting parameters of an IED.

There are several elements of a substation automation and protection system. However, this use case will consider the interaction between only two of them. Measurements from a physical power system process are taken using Current Transformers (CTs) and Voltage Transformers (VTs). Those measurements are sampled using a device called Merging Unit (MU). MUs merge 4 voltage and 4 current samples per measurement point into a single IEC61850-9-2 Sampled Value (SV) packet which is then being distributed on an Ethernet based process bus using multicast.

The IED is implemented as a transformer differential function. Essentially, the function takes current measurements from both sides of a transformer and calculates the difference between the two. If this difference is greater than some predefined value, it disconnects the transformer from the grid by opening the corresponding breakers. The IED sends the IEC 61850-8-1 GOOSE messages to the I/O devices which oversee the opening of the transformer breakers.

Undesired opening of transformer breakers might have significant economical and societal consequences. Therefore, this use case attempts to demonstrate how operation of the power system can easily be disrupted by crafting GOOSE message packets. To simulate a power system process, operation of MUs and I/O devices, a real-time Opal-RT simulator is used. The simulator is connected to the IED via an Ethernet switch. Both IEC61850-9-2 SV packets and IEC 61850-8-1 GOOSE packets are sent via this switch. During a normal operation, the IED would send cyclic multicast GOOSE packets to the simulator with a Boolean value equal to False which corresponds to the closed state of the breaker. Conversely, when there is a fault in the system, IED would initially send avalanche of packets with Boolean value equal to True. This change in value would cause I/O devices to open the breakers and clear the fault.

However, if an attacker gains access to the network, it can craft the GOOSE messages which will cause the breakers to open regardless of the current state of the system. It should however be noted that, to craft the message, the structure and the content of the GOOSE message would have to be known, see Fig. 3.

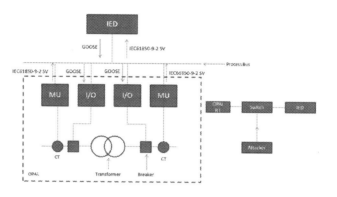

Fig. 3. IED attack example

5.2   Example 2: Digital Forensic Investigation of a Phasor Measurement Unit (PMU) Device

5.2.1   Introduction to PMU Device

Phasor Measurement Unit (PMU) is a device which measures the amplitude and phase of a power-grid voltage and/or current, relative to a known reference [27]. Synchrophasor technology uses PMUs to measure voltage and current waveforms and calculate phasors. Each measurement is time-stamped and thus synchronized against Coordinated Universal Time (UTC) using a time source such as the GPS [28]. PMU data is sampled between 30 to 120 samples per second which is fairly high enough, such that dynamics of the power-grid can be measured accurately.

Due to having high resolution data with accurate time-stamped information, Synchrophasors technology is being used for Wide-Area Monitoring System (WAMS), forensic event analysis and verification of grid model etc. [28].

5.2.2   Synchrophasor Network

As shown in Fig. 4, GPS receiver takes the timing signal from satellite. A substation clock interprets the GPS signal and converts into a protocol which is readable by PMUs. PMUs compute Synchrophasors using IEEE C37.118.2 standard [29] and streams data over Ethernet to Phasor Data Concentrator (PDC). PDC streams are sent via Wide Area Network (WAN) to a power system control center, where different monitoring, control and protection application utilize the PMU/PDC data.

5.2.3   Vulnerability of a PMU Device to Spoofing/Jamming Attacks

PMUs are vulnerable to cyber-attack because it uses TCP/IP and UDP/IP protocol which make it more susceptible to various attacks [30]. For example, modification attacks like malicious code injection, data fabrication attack in the form of data spoofing and jamming the input signals to the PMUs etc. [30–32]. A GPS signal which provides a time synchronization input to the PMUs, is one of the most vulnerable signals to a cyber-attack as shown in Fig. 4. An attack on GPS signal infects PMU data, which could adversely impact the performance of the power system applications which utilize the infected PMU data.

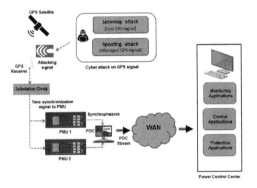

Fig. 4. Synchrophasor network

The impact of loss of time synchronization signal (in case of jamming attack) on synchrophasor based applications is investigated in [31]. As mentioned in [31], if PMU loses its GPS signal, this results in erroneous time-stamp calculations which lead to the wrong synchrophasors computations. This ultimately results in corrupted power system monitoring & control results.

In [32], the impact of time synchronization spoofing attacks on synchrophasor-based monitoring, protection and control applications has been extensively discussed. It was identified in [32] that the current PMUs lacks the functionalities to identify between authentic and spoofed time signals. This makes current PMU device to be highly vulnerable to cyber-attacks.

5.2.4   Digital Investigation of SEL-421 PMU

From [32], it can be concluded that, currently, PMU device is not smart enough to detect any cyber attacks on GPS signal (signal loss & data spoofing). In this paper, SEL-421 PMU device [33] is selected for a analysis in order to investigate the current shortcomings and limitations of this device for forensic analysis in case of any cyber attack. The data logs in a device are very important for its forensic analysis.

Figure 5(left) shows a snapshot of SEL-421 configuration software called SEL acSELerator QuickSet [34]. SEL-421 device is equipped with some nice data logging features. There are different triggers to capture data in the SEL-421 which are Relay Word bit TRIP assertions, SELOGIC® control equation ER (Event Report Trigger) and TRI command. The two main log sources we can consider as the connection log created using Terminal logging as well as the Sequential event Recorder (SER).

The connection log records all communications between the relay and the PC. On the other hand SER captures and time-tags state changes of Relay Word bit elements and relay conditions. These conditions include power-up, relay enable and disable, group changes, settings changes, memory overflow, diagnostic restarts, and SER auto-removal/ reinsertion. Figure 5(right) shows a snapshot about how to use data logging functionality in SEL-421 using its configuration software.

Fig. 5. Left: a snapshot from SEL-421 configuration software and Right: data logging functionality using SEL-421 configuration software [30]

The size of the event report length in SER affects the number of records available. With SEL-42 recorded events can range from 4 to 239 events before they get over-written again. Hence valuable information for an attack might be lost if it is not backed up. Moreover, the data logs available in SEL-421 device do not help in providing any notification or indication of any cyber attack. This leads us to a conclusion that current PMU technology is not forensically ready for digital investigation in case of any attacks.

6 Conclusions and Future Work

Having studied these devices for forensic purpose, it is evident that these devices are not forensic ready and there are no established methods that could be utilized to help in their forensic investigation.

As a future work, we intend to create a series of experiments in increasing complexity to measure the forensic readiness of SCADA controls. Following are the main points for the future work that we intend to perform:

- Development of a small suite of tools to extract and analyze the evidence from individual components of the SCADA network
- Creating a set of experiments with a base configuration to measure the forensic readiness of SCADA controls
- Using different configurations to measure the variance in results
- We'll document the experiments and their results, and based on the outcomes propose a set of recommendations to create a benchmark for SCADA forensic readiness.

Acknowledgment. This work has received funding from the Swedish Civil Contingencies Agency (MSB) through the research center Resilient Information and Control Systems (RICS).

References

1. U.S. General Accounting Office: Cyber security guidance is available, but more can be done to promote its use (2011). http://www.gao.gov/assets/590/587529.pdf
2. Alcaraz, C., Zeadally, S.: Critical infrastructure protection: requirements and challenges for the 21st century. Int. J. Crit. Infrastruct. Prot. **8**, 53–66 (2015)
3. U.S. Department of Homeland Security: What is critical infrastructure? (2016). https://www.dhs.gov/what-criticalinfrastructure
4. Critical infrastructure sectors (2016). https://www.dhs.gov/critical-infrastructure-sectors
5. KTH Royal Institute of Technology (2013). Viking: https://www.kth.se/en/ees/omskolan/organisation/avdelningar/ics/research/cc/proj/v/viking-1.407871
6. Trend Micro Incorporated: Report on cybersecurity and critical infrastructure in the americas (2015). http://www.trendmicro.com/cloudcontent/us/pdfs/securityintelligence/reports/critical-infrastructures-west-hemisphere.pdf
7. SANS ICS: Analysis of the cyber attack on the Ukrainian power grid (2016). https://ics.sans.org/media/E-ISAC_SANS_Ukraine_DUC_5.pdf
8. Langner, R.: Stuxnet: dissecting a cyberwarfare weapon. IEEE Secur. Priv. **9**(3), 49–51 (2011)
9. CESG National Technical Authority for Information Assurance: Good practice guide: Forensic readiness (2015). https://www.cesg.gov.uk/content/files/guidancefiles/Forensic%20Readiness%20(Good%20Practice%20Guide%2018)1.2.pdf
10. Ammann, R.: Network forensic readiness: a bottom-up approach for IPv6 networks. Ph.D. dissertation, Auckland University of Technology (2012)
11. Sule, D.: Importance of forensic readiness (2014). http://www.isaca.org/Journal/archives/2014/Volume-1/Pages/JOnline-Importance-of-Forensic-Readiness.aspx
12. Eden, P., Blyth, A., Burnap, P., Cherdantseva, Y., Jones, K., Soulsby, H., Stoddart, K.: A cyber forensic taxonomy for SCADA systems in critical infrastructure. In: Rome, E., Theocharidou, M., Wolthusen, S. (eds.) CRITIS 2015. LNCS, vol. 9578, pp. 27–39. Springer, Cham (2016). https://doi.org/10.1007/978-3-319-33331-1_3
13. Cook, A., Nicholson, A., Janicke, H., Maglaras, L.A., Smith, R.: Attribution of cyber attacks on industrial control systems. EAI Endorsed Trans. Indust. Netw. Intellig. Syst. **3**(7), e3 (2016). https://doi.org/10.4108/eai.21-4-2016.151158
14. van der Knijff, R.M.: Control systems/SCADA forensics, what's the difference? Digit. Invest. **11**(3), 160–174 (2014). https://doi.org/10.1016/j.diin.2014.06.007. ISSN 1742-2876
15. Etalle, S., Gregory, C., Bolzoni, D., Zambon, E.: Self-configuring deep protocol network whitelisting. Security Matters (2013). http://www.secmatters.com/sites/www.secmatters.com/files/documents/whitepaper_ics_EU.Pdf

16. Pauna, A., May, J., Tryfonas, T.: Can we learn from SCADA security incidents? – ENISA, 09 October 2013. https://www.enisa.europa.eu/publications/can-we-learn-from-scada-security-incidents
17. Ahmed, I., Obermeier, S., Naedele, M., Richard III, G.G.: SCADA systems: challenges for forensic investigators. Computer **45**(12), 44–51 (2012). https://doi.org/10.1109/mc.2012.325
18. Wu, T., Pagna Disso, J.F., Jones, K., Campos, A.: Towards a SCADA forensics architecture. In: Proceedings of the 1st International Symposium for ICS & SCADA Cyber Security Research, pp. 12–21 (2013)
19. Fabro, M., Cornelius, E.: Recommended practice: creating cyber forensics plans for control systems. DHS Control Systems Security Program (2008). https://ics-cert.us-cert.gov/sites/default/files/recommended_practices/Forensics_RP.pdf. Accessed 15 May 2017
20. Iqbal, A.: [Extended Abstract] Digital Forensic Readiness in Critical Infrastructures: Exploring substation automation in the power sector. Stockholm (2017). http://urn.kb.se/resolve?urn=urn:nbn:se:kth:diva-209689
21. Kilpatrick, T., Gonzalez, J., Chandia, R., Papa, M., Shenoi, S.: An architecture for SCADA network forensics. In: Olivier, M.S., Shenoi, S. (eds.) DigitalForensics 2006. IAIC, vol. 222, pp. 273–285. Springer, Boston, MA (2006). https://doi.org/10.1007/0-387-36891-4_22
22. Valli, C.: SCADA forensics with Snort IDS. In: Proceedings of the 2009 International Conference Security and Management (SAM 2009), pp. 618–621. CSREA Press (2009)
23. Sohl, E., Fielding, C., Hanlon, T., Rrushi, J., Farhangi, H., Howey, C., Carmichael, K., Dabell, J.: A field study of digital forensics of intrusions in the electrical power grid. In: Proceedings of the First ACM Workshop on Cyber-Physical Systems-Security and/or PrivaCy (CPS-SPC 2015), pp. 113–122. ACM, New York (2015)
24. CVE Details, Security Vulnerabilities, Promotic. https://www.cvedetails.com/vulnerability-list/vendor_id-649/product_id-22225/Microsys-Promotic.html
25. Hunt, R., Slay, J.: Achieving critical infrastructure protection through the interaction of computer security and network forensics. In: 2010 Eighth Annual International Conference on Privacy Security and Trust (PST), pp. 23–30. IEEE (2010)
26. Langner, R.: Robust Control System Networks: How to Achieve Reliable Control after Stuxnet. Momentum Press, New York (2011)
27. IEEE C37.118.1-2011: IEEE Standard for Synchrophasor Measurement for Power Systems
28. NASPI Technical Report: Time Synchronization in the Electric Power System, USA, March 2017. https://www.naspi.org/sites/default/files/reference_documents/tstf_electric_power_system_report_pnnl_26331_march_2017_0.pdf
29. IEEE Standard for Synchrophasor Data Transfer for Power Systems. In: IEEE Std C37.118.2-2011 (Revision of IEEE Std C37.118-2005), pp. 1–53, 28 December 2011
30. Beasley, C., Zhong, X., Deng, J., Brooks, R., Venayagamoorthy, G.K.: A survey of electric power synchrophasor network cyber security. In: IEEE PES Innovative Smart Grid Technologies, Europe, Istanbul, pp. 1–5 (2014)
31. Almas, M.S., Vanfretti, L.: Impact of time-synchronization signal loss on PMU-based WAMPAC applications. In: 2016 IEEE Power and Energy Society General Meeting (PESGM), Boston, MA, pp. 1–5 (2016)
32. Almas, M.S., Vanfretti, L., Singh, R.S., Jonsdottir, G.M.: Vulnerability of synchrophasor-based WAMPAC applications' to time synchronization spoofing. IEEE Trans. Smart Grid **8**(99), 1 (2017)
33. SEL: Protection Relays by Schweitzer Engineering Laboratories. https://selinc.com/products/421/
34. SEL-5030 acSELerator QuickSet Software. https://selinc.com/products/5030/

A Visualization Scheme for Network Forensics Based on Attribute Oriented Induction Based Frequent Item Mining and Hyper Graph

Jianguo Jiang[1], Jiuming Chen[1,2], Kim-Kwang Raymond Choo[3],
Chao Liu[1], Kunying Liu[1], and Min Yu[1,2(✉)]

[1] Institute of Information Engineering,
Chinese Academy of Sciences, Beijing, China
yumin@iie.ac.cn
[2] School of Cyber Security, University of Chinese Academy of Sciences,
Beijing, China
[3] Department of Information Systems and Cyber Security,
University of Texas at San Antonio, San Antonio, TX, USA

Abstract. Visualizing massive network traffic flows or security logs can facilitate network forensics, such as in the detection of anomalies. However, existing visualization methods do not generally scale well, or are not suited for dealing with large datasets. Thus, in this paper, we propose a visualization scheme, where an attribute-oriented induction-based frequent-item mining algorithm (AOI-FIM) is used to extract attack patterns hidden in a large dataset. Also, we leverage the hypergraph to display multi-attribute associations of the extracted patterns. An interaction module designed to facilitate forensics analyst in fetching event information from the database and identifying unknown attack patterns is also presented. We then demonstrate the utility of our approach (i.e. using both frequent item mining and hypergraphs to deal with visualization problems in network forensics).

Keywords: Visualization · Big data analysis · Network forensic · Hypergraph

1 Introduction

In our increasingly Internet-connected society (e.g. smart cities and smart grids), the capability to identify, mitigate and respond to a cyber security incident effectively and efficiently is crucial to organizational and national security. Existing security products include those that enforce policies and generate situational intelligence [1, 2]. However, existing solutions are generally not designed to deal with the increasing volume, variety, velocity and veracity of data generated by existing security solutions [3].

Thus, in this paper, a visualization analysis scheme based on attribute oriented induction based frequent item mining and hyper graph is proposed. The choice of attribute oriented induction based frequent item mining algorithm and hyper graph is as follows. In network attacks, for example, using frequent item mining algorithm only allows us to extract records whose attributes meet the frequent character. In a host scan attack, however, the destination port number may varies. Thus, we use attribute

© ICST Institute for Computer Sciences, Social Informatics and Telecommunications Engineering 2018
P. Matoušek and M. Schmiedecker (Eds.): ICDF2C 2017, LNICST 216, pp. 130–143, 2018.
https://doi.org/10.1007/978-3-319-73697-6_10

oriented induction based frequent item mining algorithm instead of only frequent item mining (FIM) algorithm to process network traffic data and security logs. This allows us to effectively filter out the redundant data and discover interesting patterns hidden in the data. In addition, several commonly seen attacks have a one-to-many relationship, which could be visualized and distinguished [7] Thus, using hyper graph, we can clearly display multi-attribute associations and the specific attack event information. In our scheme, we also include an interaction module for the forensics analyst to manual analyze the visualized event and obtain the original information of these events.

Our scheme is designed to handle both network flow data and security logs, and therefore, a forensic analyst can easily understand the behavior of hosts or users from the visualization graph when an attack occurs. Specifically, our scheme allows the forensic analyst to identify new anomaly and attack patterns using the graph visualization and the interaction module. The scheme can deal with big dataset using attribute oriented induction based frequent item mining, where multi-attribute relationship of parameters such as source IP, destination IP address, port number, and time, can be explored to provide in-depth information about malicious cyber incidents or events.

The remaining of this paper is structured as follows. In the next section, we review related literature. In Sects. 3 and 4, we describe our visualization scheme and demonstrate the utility of our scheme using real-world dataset, respectively. Finally, we conclude our paper in Sect. 5.

2   Related Work

Many approaches designed to handle and display complex data in networks have been proposed in the literature. Such approaches facilitate humans in recognizing abnormal events in the network [4–7]. Parallel coordinate, a commonly used visualization method proposed by Inselberg [8], displays multi-dimensional data. Specifically, in a parallel coordinate, each vertical axis represents a different attribute and the lines display the associations between two coordinates. There are a number of published parallel coordinate based visualization schemes and tools, such as NFSight [9], VisFlowConnect [10], and PCAV [11].

There are several other visualization tools, such as Nfsen [12], FlowScan [13], FloVis [14], NFlowVis [15] and Fluxoscope [16], which use a range of visualization methods (e.g. histograms, pie charts, scatterplots, heavy hitter lists, and tree maps). A key limitation in parallel coordinate based approaches and several other visualization approaches is that the lines they use in the graph can only indicate associations between two linked parameters. However, these approaches cannot visualize multi-attribute associations. In addition, the parallel coordinate approach cannot display the quantitative characteristics.

Krasser and Conti [17] used parallel coordinate for real time and forensic data analysis. Their approach displays both malicious and non-malicious network activities, but the approach does not scale well to deal with big dataset. The plane coordinate diagram, another popular approach used in the literature, can only represent the association between two attributes.

The hyper graph approach, however, can effectively display the association between the multi-attributes and facilitate a forensic analyst to reconstruct the event [18]. For example, Glatz et al. [19] proposed a hyper graph based approach to display traffic flow data. While the proposed approach in [19] visualizes dominant patterns of network traffic, the authors did not explain how their approach can be used to distinguish attacks features (i.e. a visualizing approach, rather than a visualizing analysis method). Unlike existing approaches, in this paper, we first analyze the "one-to-many relationship" in popular attack patterns that allows us to distinguish between the attacks. We then add an interaction module in our visualization scheme so that a forensics analyst can easily interact with the database and the hyper graph to discover unknown attack patterns.

There have also been efforts to using signature based methods, such as hash function, to handle the traffic flow data and mining interesting patterns [20]. However, these methods need to know the characteristics in advance and these methods' efficiency is limited when dealing with big dataset. Therefore, in our research, we use attribute oriented induction based frequent item mining algorithm to extract attack patterns hidden in the data. Frequent item mining algorithm is widely used in the field of data mining, but to the best our knowledge, our work is the first to leverage both hyper graph and frequent item mining to network forensic visualization.

3 Proposed Network Forensic Visualization Scheme

The complex and noisy network traffic and security logs can be simplified using visualization techniques or tools, which allows network forensic analysts to have an in-depth insight into the network and the activities (e.g. attack event information). For example, using visualization, we can deduce some new or unknown attacks in the network; thus, enabling unknown attack(s) to be detected. Key challenges in security visualization include data volume and the correlating methods. In order to mitigate existing limitations, we propose a data extraction method based on a frequent item mining algorithm to reduce the volume of the noisy data set. Specifically, we propose a hypergraph based method that allows the correlation of several parameters such as source address, destination address, source port, destination port, packet length and time.

3.1 Attack Features

There is no one size fits all visualization method, but we can design the graph on a case-by-case basis to fulfill specific needs. There are mainly four attack types, namely: scan attacks, denial of service attacks, worm attacks and other attacks (e.g. botnet facilitated attacks). In order to design an effective visual method for most popular attacks, their features must be considered. For example, these popular attacks have one common characteristics, which is "one–to–many relationship" between network attacker and victim/victim machine(s) [7]. The characteristics can inform the design of detection algorithm for maximal accuracy.

Network scanning attack is generally (one of) the first step(s) in an attack, such as a host or port scan to probe and identify vulnerable host(s) in the network and available service(s) of the target(s) host for exploitation. In both scanning processes, there is a "one to many relationship", in the sense of one attack host with one or many victim hosts and many ports.

Denial of service (DoS) and distributed denial of service (DDoS) attacks are another popular type of attack, seeking to exhaust and overwhelm the target network's bandwidth and computational resources. Similarly, such attackers have a "one-to-many relationship".

Worm is a self-propagating code whose propagation process is similar to botnet attack. After detecting the vulnerable machines in the network, an infected host may propagate the worm code to one or more target hosts. Therefore, we have a "one-to-many relationship" between the source infected host and the target hosts. Similar relationship is in botnet attacks, where the attacker propagates the malicious code to an infected host, and builds a relationship between controller and infected client hosts.

Attackers may also change or hide the parameters and find new vulnerability(ies) to increase the possibility of success and reduce the probability of detection. Such efforts will compound the challenges in detection. Thus, we need to identify avenues that can be used to effectively mitigate such efforts. One such avenue is in their (common) characteristics, as discussed above.

In this remaining section, we will show how to extract and display the characteristic, and when combined with the use of AOI-FIM algorithm and hyper graph, facilitates forensics analysis.

3.2   Attack Parameters

When an attack occurs, there are many logs (e.g. security device logs, system logs, web server application logs and network logs) containing information related to the event and could be used to reconstruct the event. For example, network flow data and security logs are two main sources in network forensics. In this paper, we use network flow data and security logs to collect the data for the following analysis. There are many parameters within flow data and network security logs, such as IP, port, time and alert type. We need to choose parameters that will be helpful to visualize the "one-to-many" relationship and distinguish the type of attacks for forensics analysis.

Firstly, the source IP address and the destination IP address are selected as parameters, which could be used to specify the victim and attacker. Secondly, Internet worms and botnet attacks may choose one or more ports to propagate the malicious code. Therefore, the port number is another parameter to be considered. Thirdly, network scanning and DDoS attacks generally make use of packets without payload or with fixed length such as 40 or 48, but Internet worms and botnet attacks generally have a fixed length payload of more than 48 (i.e. due to the malicious payload). Thus, we can use the packet length parameter to distinguish between different types of attacks. Finally, to distinguish one flow or multiple flows with the same value, we add the time of the flow to display the quantity characteristic of the network flow.

The following is a sample of a normalized record analyzed using the proposed visualization scheme. The SIP represents the source IP, and DIP represents the destination IP address. The SPort and DPort represent the source and destination port number of the flow data, respectively. The pSize represents the packet size when the data is flow data. The alert type represents the type of alert from a security log.

{SIP: x.x.x.x, DIP: y.y.y.y, SPort: t, DPort: p, time: xx-xx-xx, pSize: m, Alert Type: IRC}

3.3   AOI-FIM Algorithm

Analyzing network packets, logs and systems events for forensics has always been a challenge, due to the large data volume. Thus, we apply frequent item set mining algorithm to extract patterns hidden within the data, and visualize them using hyper graph to show the relationship between each parameter.

Frequent item set mining algorithm, a process that extracts patterns from transactions, is one of the most used methods to create association rules. Let $I = \{i_i ..., i_n\}$ be a set of parameters and the sum of parameters is n, and $D = \{t_{1...} t_m\}$ be a set of transactions, where the sum of transactions is m [21]. Each transaction t_i contains the subset of parameters in I. A frequent item set is a transaction that appears at least s transactions in D. The parameter s determines the threshold size of frequent item sets. The parameter k determines the minimum number of parameters in each frequent item. In our context, we use network flow and security logs as transactions, and the parameters consist of source IP, destination IP, etc. The frequent item sets are a set of some traffic parameters which frequently appear in the data, such as {SrcIP = a.a.a.a, Sport = x, DestIP = b.b.b.b, DestPort = y}. The result of the frequent item mining process is a collection of the IP, port, and other parameters in the flow data attributes and security logs.

For a port scan attack, the port may be various and there is a frequent pattern between the varied port number and source IP. Using the traditional FIM algorithm, the various port numbers may not be detected as a single port does not occur frequently. In addition, directly using only a conventional FIM algorithm (e.g. Apriori) does not allow us to distinguish the types of attack automatically. Although many popular attacks meet "one-to-many" relationship, the frequent distribution of data cannot be extracted directly by many classical frequent mining items algorithms. To merge some records with multiple port numbers or multiple IP address into one frequent pattern, we apply the attribute oriented induction method [22] into the frequent item mining algorithm (AOI-FIM), which improves the detection precision.

Attribute oriented induction (AOI) algorithm is a useful method for knowledge discovery in relational database, which uses a machine learning paradigm such as learning-from-examples to extract generalized data from original data records [23]. The attribute-oriented concept tree ascension for generalization is the key to the AOI method, which can reduce the computational complexity of the database. Figure 1 is an example application of the AOI concept tree.

In this paper, we use the AOI method to redesign the FIM algorithm so that it can extract some specific and unknown attack patterns. Using the AOI method, the AOI-FIM algorithm can promptly extract attack patterns from normalized records that have a "one-to-many" relationship. For some special frequent item set that meets the threshold requirement of frequent pattern but the value distribute of the parameters may vary, we use 'Vary' to merge the items and represent the distributed frequent pattern of the special parameter.

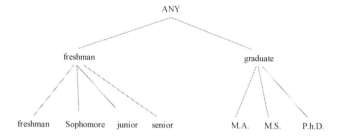

Fig. 1. A sample concept tree of AOI method

The attribute oriented induction based mining algorithm [24] can be used to generalize some records with a different parameter value into one frequent item set when the generated patterns meet the frequent rule. In the next subsection, we explain how the hypergraph theory can be used to visualize the frequent item sets for forensic investigations.

3.4   Hyper Graph

Existing network security log visualization approaches generally use parallel coordinates to represent the relationship between the network parameters. However, parallel coordinate cannot correlate the relationship between multiple attributes, or reflect the quantitative characteristics of various transactions. To overcome these limitations, we use hypergraph [25] to reflect the multi-attribute associations within the frequent item sets. Hypergraph also allows us to distinguish some specific attacks based on the displayed characteristics.

Mathematically, a hypergraph is a generalization of a graph, where an edge can connect any number of vertices [26]. Formally, a hypergraph H is a pair H = (X, E), where X is a set of elements, called nodes or vertices, and E is a set of non-empty subsets of X called hyper edges or links. In this paper, the nodes or vertices represent the parameters consisting frequent item sets and each hyper edge represents a frequent item set extracted from the flow data and security logs.

To display the quantitative characteristics of data, we add a circle to each hyper edge and the circles is varied based on the size of frequent item sets. We display the number within the circle node to represent the quantity characteristic within the frequent item set. In this paper, we seek to automatically extract the one-to-many relationship and find the hyper edges that are potentially associated with an attack.

Figure 2 shows some typical hyper edges that represent some popular attacks. Attacks that have a "one-to-many relationship" can be easily visualized and distinguished using hypergraph. What's more, the combination of some different frequent items which meet one-to-many relationship can also infer some specific attacks such as botnets and Trojans. To display some frequents patterns with different parameter values, we use the attribute oriented induction based frequent item mining algorithm (AOI-FIM) to extract the attack patterns, and "Vary" to represent the parameter whose distribution of values is dispersed but the parameter and other frequent item sets have a one-to-many relationship. For example, we use a port-fixed DDoS attack as an example, and the graph shows that in this example, three distributed hosts are attacking target hosts y_1. y_2. y_3. y_4 via n ports. We use "Vary" to represent the multiple source hosts in the hyper graph to show the induced frequent quantitative relation.

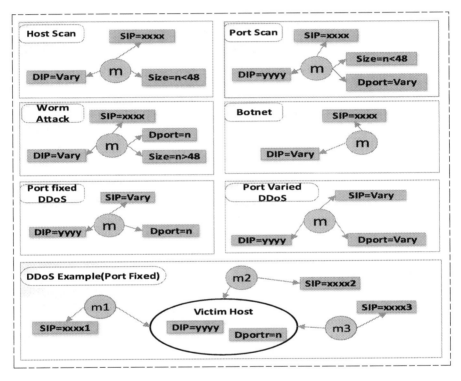

Fig. 2. Attack pattern visualized by hyper graph

3.5   Visualization System for Network Forensic

In order to automate the data correlation and displaying of event information for forensic investigation, we design a system based on frequent item mining algorithm and hyper graph. The architecture of the system is presented in Fig. 3, where the system consists of data collection, data pre-process, frequent item set mining, attack detection, hypergraph visualization, and manual inspection.

The system also has five main modules, namely: a collection module, analysis module, visualizer module, data store module and forensics interaction module. The collection module receives network traffic flow data and security logs using some sensor routes and security devices. It extracts parameters such as IP, port from the data set. The collection module stores the raw data into database that can be used in subsequent forensic investigation. The analyzer module uses the frequent item mining algorithm to extract the association rules and detect attacks. The visualization module uses hypergraph to display the frequent item set and attack information. According to the attack information within the hypergraph, forensic investigators can use the interaction module to manually correlate the event and extract original event information from the database for in-depth analysis.

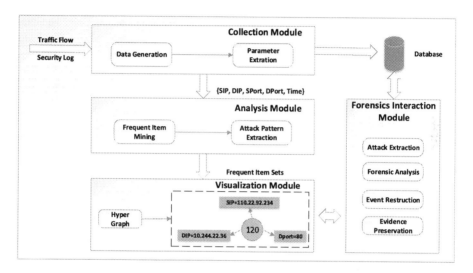

Fig. 3. Proposed visualization system architecture

4   Evaluation

In this section, we extract and display the one-to-many relationship from the flow data and security logs using two different data sets, namely: a local network traffic flow data and the VAST 2012 [27] data set. We implement the visualization system so that it could extract and display the characteristic automatically. We firstly collect the raw data in CSV format, and filter out the other parameters to retain IP, Port and alert type data. Then, we implement the AOI based FIM processing program using the Java language, which extracts the one-to-many relationship from the data set and build the frequent item set for the visualization. After that, we build the hypergraph for these frequent item sets and design a specific hypergraph template for each popular attack described in Sect. 3.4. We also assign values for these templates and display them based on the frequent item set extracted by the preceding step. For each frequent item set that represents the characteristic of an attack, we design a link for the raw data so that the forensic analysts can carry out detailed inspection.

We will now describe the experiments on both data sets. Specifically, the local network traffic flow data set consists of traffic data collected over a total of seven days in the local network. The VAST data set is from the VAST contest, which has a variety of visualization tasks and data source for researchers to analyze each year. In this paper, we use the VAST 2012 data set to show the effectiveness on firewall and IDS logs. In this particular data set, the context is a virtual international bank's network of nearly 5,000 hosts, and the data set contains log information of IDS and firewalls in its network over a period of time.

4.1 VAST Firewall and IDS Logs

The logs in the VAST data set are in csv format. For the pre-processing, we first transform them into normalized format records, which consist of source IP address, source Port number, destination IP address, destination Port number, alert type and timestamp information. We then filter the firewall logs by manually building a white list according to the BOM network configurations and operation policies. As IDS already filter the logs based on suspected attacks, we label them as anomalies. There are a total of 17,530 records after pre-processing. Then, we extract the necessary parameters from the records.

We extract the one-to-many relationship within the records using the attribute oriented induction based frequent item mining algorithm. The frequent items are presented in Table 1, where each frequent item extracted from the records represent a suspected attack that has a one-to-many relationship.

Table 1. Frequent item mining result for VAST data set.

Frequent item sets	Frequency
SIP = Varied, DIP = 10.32.5.57, type = IRC-Malware Infection SIP = {172.23.231.69-80, 172.23.127.100-120}	696
SIP = 10.32.5.57, DIP = Varied, Sport = 6667, type = IRC-Authorization DIP = {172.23.231.69-80, 172.23.127.100-120}	1464
SIP = Varied, DIP = 10.32.5.57, type = Attempted Information SIP = {172.23.231.69-80, 172.23.127.100-120}	687
SIP = Varied, DIP = 172.23.0.1, type = Misc-activity SIP = {172.23.236.8, 172.23.234.58, 172.23.234.4, 172.231.69}	466

We visualize the frequent item sets using hypergraph – see Fig. 4. We compare the frequent item with the hypergraph template and display them using a hyper edge. The first frequent item and the second meet the Botnet template, and the third frequent item meets the DDoS attack template. From the first and second frequent item sets, we determine that the two main malicious attacks are Botnet behavior and some illegal connections. We also locate a large number of IRC connections from different hosts to IP address 10.32.5.57. These hosts include 172.23.231.69-172.23.231.80, 172.23. 127.100-172.23.127.120, which suggest that most of the hosts are infected via the IRC traffic. The second frequent item shows that the host 10.32.5.57 replies to the infected hosts with IRC authorization messages; thus, indicting a potential Botnet attack. We also found a number of attempted information alerts between 10.32.5.57 and the infected hosts, which suggest a need for further forensic investigation to determine whether data has been exfiltrated.

From the last frequent item, 172.23.0.1 is determined to be the external interface at the firewall, and there have been a number of attempted connections. This suggests the presence of potential DDoS attack or remote services.

Forensic investigators can use the forensic interaction module to fetch and analyze the original data for further investigation.

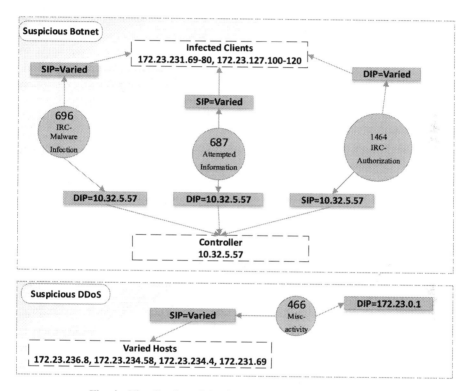

Fig. 4. Visualization of the frequent items using hyper graph

4.2 Local Network Traffic

In order to evaluate the performance of our visualization scheme on the traffic flow data, we collect the flow data from an internal monitoring environment. The environment would generate an alarm in the event of a suspected attack, as well as retaining the flow data of the alert event. We collect 1096 alert data and fetch their flow data to build the records. After pre-processing, the formatted log information is obtained from the data set, which includes 1,096 records. The association rules mining algorithm is used to process the log to extract the attack patterns hidden in the data. We choose the support threshold to be 5%. The frequent item sets are presented in Table 2:

Table 2. Frequent item mining result for local network traffic

Frequent item sets	Frequency
SIP = 193.169.244.73, DIP = 114.255.165.142, Sport = Varied Sport = {80, 443, 5430}	226
SIP = 114.255.165.142, DIP = 193.169.244.73	107
SIP = 221.130.179.36, DIP = 202.106.90.2, SPort = 8888	54

We will now use hypergraph to visualize the above frequent items sets. We use circular nodes and hyper edges with some property rectangles to represent a frequent item with a one-to-many relationship. We identify their quantity characteristics in circular nodes. The rectangle nodes are linked to a circular node indicating the relationship between an associated rule and its attributes. Figure 5 shows the malicious attack patterns extracted by the scheme visualized using hyper graph.

In Fig. 5, SIP denotes the source IP address, and DIP denotes the destination IP address. SPort denotes the source port used by the source host, and DPort denotes the destination port. The number represents the occurrences of a frequent item with a one-to-many relationship. The following information can be found from the visualization results.

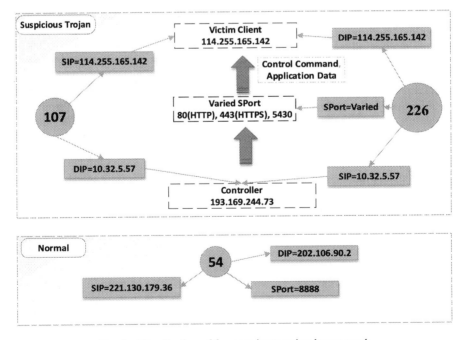

Fig. 5. Visualization of frequent items using hyper graph

(1) Host with IP address 114.255.165.142 connects to host with IP address 193.169.244.73 several times, and the former is an internal host and the latter is an external host.

(2) The external host with IP address 193.169.244.73 mainly connects through ports 80,443 and 5430 with the internal target host 114.255.165.242.

(3) There are a large number of connections between IP addresses 221.130.179.36 and IP 202.106.90.2 via port 8888. Both the source host and destination host are determined to be internal hosts. A large number of connections without a corresponding large data transportation may indicate a specific business need of the network.

From the above findings (1) and (2), forensic investigators can easily determine the malicious connections between internal host 114.255.165.142 and external host 193.169.244.73 and that this is most probably a Trojan attack. The external host continually sends information to the internal infected host via ports 80, 443 and 5430. Both port numbers 80 and 443 are often used for HTTP and HTTPS communication, which could indicate that the controller host sent some commands or some application data to the target host. The event can then be reconstructed based on the attack pattern and original traffic data using the forensic interaction module.

5 Conclusion and Future Work

Network forensics and forensic visualization will be increasingly important in our networked society. Extracting and analyzing anomaly and damage from large scale network data remains a key challenge in network forensics. In order to extract attack patterns hidden in large volume traffic data and security logs and visualize the multi-attribute associations within the attack events, we designed a visualization scheme based on AOI-FIM and hyper graph. Using two real-world data sets, we demonstrated the effectiveness of our proposed scheme in distinguishing attacks and obtaining event-relevant information.

Although frequent item mining based algorithms can be used on big dataset, the processing speed will be affected by significant increases in the data volume. Therefore, future research includes extending our proposed approach to improve the processing speed, and consequently improve the efficiency of network forensics. In addition, research on automated classification and distinguishing methods to extract unknown attacks such as 0-day attacks will be on the agenda.

Acknowledgment. This work is supported by National Natural Science Foundation of China (No. 91646120, 61402124, 61572469, 61402022) and Key Lab of Information Network Security, Ministry of Public Security (No. C17614).

References

1. Zuech, R., Khoshgoftaar, T.M., Wald, R.: Intrusion detection and big heterogeneous data: a survey. J. Big Data **2**(1), 3 (2015)
2. Bhatt, S., Manadhata, P.K., Zomlot, L.: The operational role of security information and event management systems. IEEE Secur. Priv. **12**(5), 35–41 (2014)
3. Cardenas, A.A., Manadhata, P.K., Rajan, S.P.: Big data analytics for security. Secur. Priv. IEEE **11**(6), 74–76 (2013)
4. Tassone, C., Martini, B., Choo, K.K.R.: Forensic visualization: survey and future research directions. In: Contemporary Digital Forensic Investigations of Cloud & Mobile Applications, pp. 163–184 (2017)
5. Tassone, C.F., Martini, B., Choo, K.R.: Visualizing digital forensic datasets: a proof of concept. J. Forensic Sci. (2017)
6. Quick, D., Choo, K.K.R.: Big forensic data management in heterogeneous distributed systems: quick analysis of multimedia forensic data. Softw. Pract. Exp. **47**(8), 1095–1109 (2016)
7. Choi, H., Lee, H., Kim, H.: Fast detection and visualization of network attacks on parallel coordinates. Comput. Secur. **28**(5), 276–288 (2009)
8. Inselberg, A.: Multidimensional detective. In: IEEE Symposium on IEEE Information Visualization, Proceedings, pp. 100–107 (1997)
9. Berthier, R., et al.: Nfsight: NetFlow-based network awareness tool. In: International Conference on Large Installation System Administration USENIX Association, pp. 1–8 (2010)
10. Yin, X., et al.: VisFlowConnect: NetFlow visualizations of link relationships for security situational awareness. ACM Workshop on Visualization and Data Mining for Computer Security, pp. 26–34. ACM (2004)
11. Choi, H., Lee, H.: PCAV: internet attack visualization on parallel coordinates. In: Qing, S., Mao, W., López, J., Wang, G. (eds.) ICICS 2005. LNCS, vol. 3783, pp. 454–466. Springer, Heidelberg (2005). https://doi.org/10.1007/11602897_38
12. Krmíček, V., Čeleda, P., Novotný, J.: NfSen plugin supporting the virtual network monitoring. Virtual networks; monitoring; NetFlow, NfSen (2010)
13. Plonka, D.: FlowScan: a network traffic flow reporting and visualization tool. In: Usenix Conference on System Administration USENIX Association, pp. 305–318 (2000)
14. Taylor, T., et al.: FloVis: flow visualization system. In: Cybersecurity Applications & Technology IEEE Conference for Homeland Security, CATCH 2009, pp. 186–198 (2009)
15. Fischer, F., Mansmann, F., Keim, D.A., Pietzko, S., Waldvogel, M.: Large-scale network monitoring for visual analysis of attacks. In: Goodall, J.R., Conti, G., Ma, K.-L. (eds.) VizSec 2008. LNCS, vol. 5210, pp. 111–118. Springer, Heidelberg (2008). https://doi.org/10.1007/978-3-540-85933-8_11
16. Leinen, S.: Fluxoscope a system for flow-based accounting (2000)
17. Promrit, N., Mingkhwan, A.: Traffic flow classification and visualization for network forensic analysis. In: IEEE International Confrence on Advanced Information Networking and Applications. IEEE, pp. 358–364 (2015)
18. Yang, W., Wang, G., Bhuiyan, M.Z.A., Choo, K.-K.R.: Hypergraph partitioning for social networks based on information entropy modularity. J. Netw. Comput. Appl. **86**, 59–71 (2017)
19. Glatz, E., et al.: Visualizing big network traffic data using frequent pattern mining and hypergraphs. Computing **96**(1), 27–38 (2014)
20. Hirsch, C., et al.: Traffic flow densities in large transport networks (2016)

21. Borgelt, C.: Frequent item set mining. Wiley Interdisc. Rev. Data Min. Knowl. Discov. **2**(6), 437–456 (2012)
22. Cai, Y., Cercone, N., Han, J.: Attribute-oriented induction in relational databases. Knowl. Discovery Databases **15**(7), 1328–1337 (1989)
23. Han, J., Cai, Y., Cercone, N.: Knowledge discovery in databases: an attribute-oriented approach. In: International Conference on Very Large Data Bases. Morgan Kaufmann Publishers Inc. 547–559 (1992)
24. Warnars, S.: Mining frequent pattern with attribute oriented induction high level emerging pattern (AOI-HEP). In: International Conference on Information and Communication Technology IEEE, pp. 149–154 (2014)
25. Guzzo, A., Pugliese, A., Rullo, A., Saccà, D.: Intrusion detection with hypergraph-based attack models. In: Croitoru, M., Rudolph, S., Woltran, S., Gonzales, C. (eds.) GKR 2013. LNCS (LNAI), vol. 8323, pp. 58–73. Springer, Cham (2014). https://doi.org/10.1007/978-3-319-04534-4_5
26. Zhou, D., Huang, J.: Learning with hypergraphs: clustering, classification, and embedding. In: International Conference on Neural Information Processing Systems. MIT Press, pp. 1601–1608 (2006)
27. Cook, K., et al.: VAST challenge 2012: visual analytics for big data. In: 2012 IEEE Conference on Visual Analytics Science and Technology (VAST), 251–255. IEEE (2012)

Expediting MRSH-v2 Approximate Matching with Hierarchical Bloom Filter Trees

David Lillis[1]([⊠]), Frank Breitinger[2], and Mark Scanlon[1]

[1] Forensics and Security Research Group, School of Computer Science,
University College Dublin, Dublin, Ireland
{david.lillis,mark.scanlon}@ucd.ie
[2] Cyber Forensics Research and Education Group,
Tagliatela College of Engineering, ECECS,
University of New Haven, West Haven, CT, USA
fbreitinger@newhaven.edu

Abstract. Perhaps the most common task encountered by digital forensic investigators consists of searching through a seized device for pertinent data. Frequently, an investigator will be in possession of a collection of "known-illegal" files (e.g. a collection of child pornographic images) and will seek to find whether copies of these are stored on the seized drive. Traditional hash matching techniques can efficiently find files that precisely match. However, these will fail in the case of merged files, embedded files, partial files, or if a file has been changed in any way.

In recent years, approximate matching algorithms have shown significant promise in the detection of files that have a high bytewise similarity. This paper focuses on MRSH-v2. A number of experiments were conducted using Hierarchical Bloom Filter Trees to dramatically reduce the quantity of pairwise comparisons that must be made between known-illegal files and files on the seized disk. The experiments demonstrate substantial speed gains over the original MRSH-v2, while maintaining effectiveness.

Keywords: Approximate matching · Hierarchical bloom filter trees · MRSH-v2

1 Introduction

Current digital forensic process models are surprisingly arduous, inefficient, and expensive. Coupled with the sheer volume of digital forensic investigations facing law enforcement agencies worldwide, this has resulted in significant evidence backlogs becoming commonplace [22], frequently reaching 18–24 months [9] and exceeding 4 years in extreme cases [14]. The backlogs have grown due to a number of factors including the volume of cases requiring analysis, the number of devices per case, the volume of data on each device, and the limited availability of skilled experts [16]. Automated techniques are in continuous development to aid investigators, but due to the sensitive nature of this work, the ultimate inferences and decisions will always be made by skilled human experts [12].

© ICST Institute for Computer Sciences, Social Informatics and Telecommunications Engineering 2018
P. Matoušek and M. Schmiedecker (Eds.): ICDF2C 2017, LNICST 216, pp. 144–157, 2018.
https://doi.org/10.1007/978-3-319-73697-6_11

Perhaps the most common (and most time-consuming) task facing digital investigators involves examination of seized suspect devices to determine if pertinent evidence is contained therein. Often, this examination requires significant manual, expert data processing and analysis during the acquisition and analysis phases of an investigation. A number of techniques have been created or are in development to expedite/automate parts of the typical digital forensic process. These include triage [17], distributed processing [20], Digital Forensics as a Service (DFaaS) [1], workflow management and automation [3,10]. While these techniques can help to alleviate the backlog, the premise behind many of them involves evidence discovery based on exact matching of hash values (e.g., MD5, SHA1). Typically, this requires a set of hashes of known incriminating/pertinent content. The hash of each artefact from a suspect device is then compared against this set. This approach falls short against basic counter-forensic techniques (e.g., content editing, content embedding, data transformation).

Approximate matching (often referred to as "fuzzy hashing") is one technique used to aid in the discovery of these obfuscated files [6]. A number of approximate matching algorithms have been developed including ssdeep [13], sdhash [18], and MRSH-v2 [4]. This paper focuses specifically on MRSH-v2. This algorithm operates by generating a "similarity digest" for each file, represented as Bloom filters [2]. An all-against-all pairwise comparison is then required to determine if files from a set of desired content is present in a corpus of unanalysed content. Thus, MRSH-v2 does not exhibit strong scalability for use with larger datasets.

This paper presents an improvement in the runtime efficiency of approximate matching techniques, primarily through the implementation of a Hierarchical Bloom Filter Tree (HBFT). Additionally, it examines some of the tunable parameters of the algorithm to gauge their effect on the required running time. A number of experiments were conducted, which indicated a substantial reduction in the running time, in addition to which the final experiment achieved a 100% recall rate for identical files and also for files that have a MRSH-v2 similarity above a reasonable threshold of 40%.

Section 2 outlines the prior work that has been conducted in the area of approximate matching. The operation of MRSH-v2 is discussed in Sect. 3. HBFTs are introduced in Sect. 4. Section 5 presents the series of experiments designed to evaluate the effectiveness of the HBFT approach, and finally Sect. 6 concludes the paper and outlines directions for further work.

2 Background: Approximate Matching

Bytewise approximate matching for digital forensics gained popularity in 2006 when [13] presented context-triggered piecewise hashing (CTPH) including an implementation called ssdeep. It was at that time referred to as "fuzzy hashing". Later, this term converted to "similarity hashing" (most likely due to sdhash which stands for "similarity digest hash" [18]). In 2014, the National Institute of Standards and Technology (NIST) developed Special Publication 800-168, which outlines the definition and technology for these kinds of algorithms [6].

In addition to the prominent aforementioned implementations, there are several others. MinHash [8] and SimHash [21] are ideas on how to detect/identify small changes (up to several bytes), but were not designed to compare hard disk images with each other. In 2014, Oliver presented an algorithm named TLSH, which is premised on locality sensitivity hashing (LSH) [15]. There are significantly more algorithms, but to explain all of them would be beyond the scope of this paper; a good summary is provided by Harichandran et al. [11].

While these algorithms have great capabilities, they suffer one significant drawback, which we call the "database lookup problem". In comparison to traditional hash values which can be sorted and have a lookup complexity of $O(1)$ (hashmap) or $O(log(n))$ (binary tree; where n is the number of entries in the database), looking up a similarity digest usually requires an all-against-all comparison $(O(n^2))$ to identify all matches. To overcome this drawback, Breitinger et al. [5] presented a new idea that overcomes the lookup complexity (it is approximately $O(1)$) but at the cost of inaccuracy. More specifically, the method allows item vs. set queries, resulting in the answer either being "yes, the queried item is in the set" or "no, it is not"; one cannot say against which item it matches.

As a means of addressing these drawbacks, Breitinger et al. [7] presented a further article where they offered a theoretical solution to the lookup problem, based on a tree of Bloom filters. However, an implementation (and thus a validation) has not been conducted to date. We refer to this as a Hierarchical Bloom Filter Tree (HBFT). The focus of the present work is the empirical evaluation of this approach, so as to demonstrate its effectiveness and to investigate some practical factors that affect its performance.

3   The MRSH-v2 Algorithm

The work in this paper is intended to improve upon the performance of the MRSH-v2 algorithm. Therefore, it is important to firstly outline its operation in informal terms, which will aid the discussion later. A more detailed, formal description of the algorithm can be found in [4]. The primary goal of MRSH-v2 is to compress any byte sequence and output a similarity digest. Similarity digests are created in a way that they can be compared with each other, which will result in a similarity score. Each similarity digest is a collection of Bloom filters [2].

To create the similarity digest, MRSH-v2 splits an input into chunks (also known as "subhashes") of approximately 160 bytes. These chunks are hashed using FNV (a fast non-cryptographic hash function), which is used to set 5 bits of the Bloom filter. To divide the input into chunks, it uses a window of 7 bytes, which slides through the input byte-by-byte. The content of the window is processed and whenever it hits a certain value (based on a modulus operation), the end of a chunk is identified. Thus, the actual size of each chunk varies. Each Bloom filter has a specific capacity. Once this has been reached, any further chunks are inserted into a new Bloom filter that is appended to the digest. Approximate matching occurs by comparing similarity digests against one another. To compare two file sets, an all-against-all pairwise comparison is required.

Extending the file-against-set comparison outlined in [5], an alternative strategy to combat this is to use a hierarchical Bloom filter tree (HBFT) [7]. It is intended to achieve speed benefits over a pairwise comparison while supporting the identification of specific matching files. The primary contribution of this paper is to investigate the factors that affect the runtime performance of this approach, compared to the classic pairwise approach.

4   Hierarchical Bloom Filter Trees (HBFT)

In a Hierarchical Bloom Filter Tree (HBFT), the root node of the tree is a Bloom filter that represents the entire collection. When searching for a file, if a match is found at the root of the tree, its child nodes can then be searched. Although this structure is inspired by a classic binary search tree, a match at a particular node in a HBFT does not indicate whether the search should continue in the left or right subtree. Instead, both child nodes need to be searched, with the search path ending when a leaf node is reached or a node does not match.

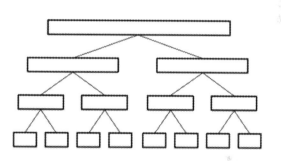

Fig. 1. Hierarchical Bloom Filter Tree (HBFT) structure.

The tree layout is shown in Fig. 1. Each level in the tree is allocated an equal amount of memory. Thus each Bloom filter occupies half the memory of its parent, and also represents a file set that is half the size of its parent. The expected false positive rates will be approximately equal at all levels in the tree.

When a collection is being modelled as a HBFT, each file is inserted into the Bloom filter at some leaf node in the tree, and also into its ancestor nodes. The mechanism of inserting a file into a Bloom filter is the same as for the single Bloom filter approach from [5], which is also very similar to the approach taken by the classic MRSH-v2 algorithm outlined in Sect. 3. The key difference is that instead of creating a similarity digest of potentially multiple small Bloom filters for an individual file, each subhash is used to set 5 bits of the larger Bloom filter within a tree node that usually relates to multiple files.

Depending on the design of the tree, a leaf node may represent multiple files. Thus a search that reaches a leaf node will still require a pairwise comparison with each file in this subset, using MRSH-v2. However, given that most searches will reach only a subset of the root nodes, the number of pairwise comparisons required for each file is greatly reduced.

The process to check if a file matches a Bloom filter node is similar to the process of inserting a file into the tree. However, instead of inserting each hash into the node, its subhashes are instead checked against the Bloom filter to see if they are contained in it. If a specific number of consecutive hashes are contained in the node, this is considered to be a match. The number of consecutive hashes is configurable as a parameter named `min_run`. The first experiment in this paper (discussed in Sect. 5.2) explores the effects of altering this value.

In the construction of a HBFT, memory constraints will have a strong influence on the design of the tree. In practical situations, a typical workstation is unlikely (at present) to have access to over 16 GiB of main memory. Thus trade-offs in the design of the tree are likely. Larger Bloom filters have lower false positive rates (assuming the quantity of data is constant), but lead to shallower trees (thus potentially increasing the number of pairwise comparisons required).

5   Experiments

As part of this work, a number of experiments were conducted to examine the factors that affect the performance of the HBFT structure. In each case, a HBFT was used to model the contents of a dataset. Files from another dataset were then searched for in the tree, and the results reported. Because the speed of execution is of paramount importance, and because the original `MRSH-v2` implementation was written in C, the HBFT implementation used for these experiments was also written in that language. The source code has been made available (at http://github.com/ishnid/mrsh-hbft) under the Apache 2.0 licence.

The workstation used for the experiments contains a quad-core Intel Core i7 2.67 GHz processor, 12 GiB of RAM and uses a solid state drive for storage. The operating system is Ubuntu Linux 16.04 LTS. The primary constraint this system imposes on the design of experiments is that of the memory that is available for storing the HBFTs. For all experiments, the maximum amount of memory made available for the HBFT was 10 GiB. The size of the individual Bloom filters within the trees then depended on the number of nodes in the tree (which in turn depends on the number of leaf nodes).

For each experiment, the number of leaf nodes (n) is specified in advance, from which the total number of nodes can be computed (since this is a binary tree). Given the upper total memory limit (u, in bytes), and that the size of each Bloom filter should be a power of two (per [5]), it is possible to calculate the maximum possible size of each Bloom filter. Because all levels in the tree are allocated the same amount of memory, the size of the root Bloom filter in bytes (r) is given by:

$$r = 2^{\lfloor log_2(u/(log_2(n)+1)) \rfloor} \tag{1}$$

The size of the other nodes in bytes is then $\frac{r}{2^d}$ where d is the depth of the node in the tree (i.e. the size of a Bloom filter is half the size of its parent).

The ultimate goal of the experiments is to demonstrate that the HBFT approach can improve the running time of an investigation over the all-against-all comparison approach of `MRSH-v2` without suffering a degradation in effectiveness. It achieves this by narrowing the search space so that each file that is searched for need only be compared against a subset of the dataset.

Using a HBFT, the final outcome will be a set of similarity scores. This score is calculated by using `MRSH-v2` to compare the search file with all files contained in any leaves that are reached during the search. Therefore, the HBFT approach will not identify a file as being similar if `MRSH-v2` does not also do so.

In these experiments, the similarity scores generated by `MRSH-v2` are considered to be ground truth. Evaluating the degree to which this agrees with the opinion of a human judge, or how it compares with other algorithms, is outside the scope of this paper. The primary difference between the outputs is that the HBFT may fail to identify files that `MRSH-v2` considers to be similar (i.e. false negatives) due to an appropriate leaf node not being reached.

Therefore the primary metric used, aside from running time, is recall: the proportion of known-similar (or known-identical) files for which the HBFT search reaches the appropriate leaf node.

5.1   Datasets

Two datasets were used as the basis for the experiments conducted in this paper:

– The **t5** dataset [19] is frequently used for approximate matching experimentation. It consists of 4,457 files (approximately 1.8 GiB) taken from US government websites. It includes plain text files, HTML pages, PDFs, Microsoft Office documents and image files.
– The **win7** dataset is a fresh installation of a Windows 7 operating system, with default options selected during installation. It consists of 48,384 files (excluding symbolic links and zero-byte files) and occupies approximately 10 GiB.

The first two experiments use one or both of these datasets directly. The final experiment includes some modifications, as outlined in Sect. 5.2.

5.2   Experiment Overview

The following sections present three experiments that were conducted to evaluate the HBFT approach. Section 5.2 compares the **t5** dataset with itself. This is intended to find whether the HBFT approach is effective in finding identical files, and to investigate the effect of varying certain parameters when designing and searching a HBFT. It also aims to demonstrate the extent to which the number of pairwise comparisons required can be reduced by using this technique.

Section 5.2 uses disjoint corpora of different sizes (**t5** and **win7**). In a typical investigation, there may be a large difference between the size of the collection of search files and a seized hard disk. This experiment aims to investigate whether it is preferable to use the tree to model the smaller or the larger corpus.

Finally, Sect. 5.2 uses overlapping corpora where a number of files have been planted on the disk image. These files are identical to, or similar to, files in the search corpus. This experiment demonstrates that using a HBFT is substantially faster than the pairwise approach.

Experiment 1: t5 vs. t5. For the initial experiment, the HBFT was constructed to represent the t5 corpus. All files from t5 were also used for searching. Thus every file searched for is also located in the tree and should be found. Conducting an all-against-all pairwise comparison using MRSH-v2 required a total of 19,864,849 comparisons, which took 319 s.

To construct the tree, the smallest number of leaf nodes was 32. Following this, the number of leaf nodes was doubled each time (maintaining a balanced tree). The exception was that 4,457 leaf nodes were used for the final run, thereby representing a single file from the corpus in each leaf.

The aims of this experiment were:

1. Evaluate the effectiveness of the HBFT approach for exact matching (i.e. finding identical files) using recall.
2. Identify an appropriate value for MRSH-v2's min_run parameter.
3. Investigate the relationship between the size of the tree and the time taken to build and search the tree.
4. Investigate the relationship between the size of the tree and the number of pairwise comparisons that are required to calculate a similarity score.

Table 1. Effect of min_run on recall: identical files.

min_run	Recall
4	100%
6	99.96%
8	99.93%

When running the experiment, it became apparent that the first two aims are linked. Table 1 shows the recall associated with three values of min_run: 4, 6 and 8. Using a min_run value of 4 resulted in full recall. However, increasing min_run to 6 or 8 resulted in a small number of files being omitted. When min_run is set to 8, three files are not found in the tree. This indicates the dangers inherent in requiring longer matching runs. The files in question are 000462.text, 001774.html, 003225.html. These files are 6.5 KiB, 6.6 KiB and 4.5 KiB in size respectively. Although each chunk is approximately 160 bytes, this changes depending on the file content. While these are relatively small files, they are not the smallest in the corpus. This shows that even when the file is large enough to contain 8 chunks of the average size, a min_run requirement of

8 successive matches may still not be possible. Similarly, using 6 as the min_run value results in two files being missed.

It should be acknowledged that if the aim is solely to identify identical files, then existing hash-based techniques will take less time and yield more reliable results. Intuitively, however, a system that is intended to find similar files should also find identical files. While the chunk size of 160 bytes will always fail to match very small files, it is desirable to find matches when file sizes are larger.

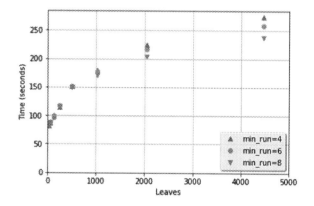

Fig. 2. Effect of varying number of leaf nodes on time taken: t5 vs. t5

Figure 2 shows the time taken to build the tree and search for all files. As the number of leaf nodes in the tree increases, so too does the time taken to search the tree. Higher values of min_run use slightly less time, due to the fact that it is more difficult for a search to descend to a lower level when more matches are required to do so. However, as the recall for these higher values is lower, 4 was used as the min_run value for further experiments.

The times shown here relate only to building the tree and searching for files within it, and does not include the time for the pairwise comparisons at the leaves. Therefore, although using 32 leaf nodes results in the shortest search time (due to the shallower tree), it would require a most comparisons, as each leaf node represents $\frac{1}{32}$ of the entire corpus. As an illustration, using a tree with 32 leaf nodes and min_run value of 4 requires 8,538,193 pairwise comparisons after searching the tree. A similar tree with 4,457 leaves requires 617,860 comparisons.

One issue that is important to note is that the time required to perform a full pairwise comparison is 319 s. However, for the largest trees, 274 s were required to build and search the tree, before any comparisons were conducted. Thus, for a relatively small collection such as this, the use of the tree is unlikely to provide benefits in terms of time.

Figure 3 plots the number of leaf nodes against the total number of comparisons required to complete the investigation. As the size of corpora increases, so does the number of pairwise comparisons required by MRSH-v2. Thus reducing

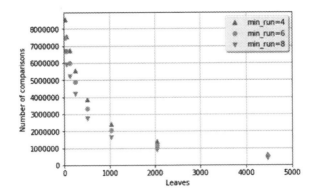

Fig. 3. Effect of varying number of leaf nodes on number of comparisons: t5 vs. t5

this search space is the primary function of the tree. Larger trees tend to result in a smaller number of comparisons. For the largest tree (with 4,457 leaves), the min_run value does not have a material effect on the number of comparisons required. This implies that although searches tend to reach deeper into the tree (hence the longer running time), they do not reach substantially more leaves.

From this experiment, it can be concluded that using a min_run value of 4 is desirable in order to find exact matches. This causes the time taken to search to be slightly longer, while having a negligible impact on the number of pairwise comparisons required afterwards.

Experiment 2: t5 vs. win7 and win7 vs. t5. The second experiment was designed to operate with larger dataset sizes. t5 was used as a proxy for a set of known-illegal files, and win7 was used to represent a seized disk.

The aims of this experiment were:

1. Investigate whether the HBFT should represent the smaller or larger corpus.
2. Measure the effect on overall running time of using a HBFT.

The experiment was first run by building a tree to represent t5 and then searching for the files contained in win7. The number of leaf nodes in this tree was varied in the same way as in Experiment 1. Then this was repeated by inserting win7 into a tree and searching for the files from t5. Again the number of leaf nodes was doubled every time, with the exception that the largest tree contained one leaf node for every file in the collection (i.e. 48,384 leaves).

The time taken to build and search the trees are shown in Figs. 4 and 5. Figure 4 shows the results when the tree represents t5, with the time subdivided into the time spent building the tree and the time spent searching for all the files from win7. The total time is relatively consistent for this type of tree. This is unsurprising in the context of disjoint corpora. Most files will not match, so many searches will end at the root node, or at an otherwise shallow depth.

Figure 5 shows results when the tree models win7. With only 32 leaf nodes, both experimental runs take approximately the same total time. Due to its size,

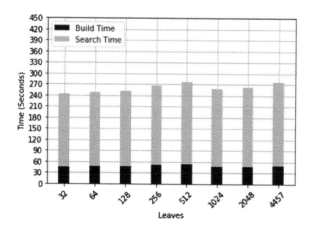

Fig. 4. Time to search for win7 in a t5 tree.

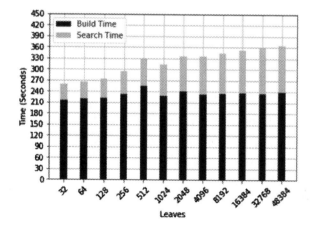

Fig. 5. Time to search for t5 in a win7 tree.

the build time for the win7 tree is substantially longer than for t5. The search time exhibits a generally upward trend as the number of leaf nodes increases. This is because of the hardware constraints associated with the realistic setup. Because memory footprint is constrained, a tree with 48,384 leaf nodes will contain Bloom filters that are much smaller than for trees with fewer nodes. In this experiment, leaves are 8 KiB in size, with a root node of 512 MiB.

Overall, the total time taken is less when the tree represents the smaller dataset. Again, the total number of pairwise comparisons decreases as the number of leaves increases. Both approaches yield a similar quantity of necessary comparisons for their largest tree (i.e. with the most leaf nodes). The tree modelling t5 requires 98,260 comparisons whereas the one modelling win7 requires 101,386. This, combined with the lower build and search time suggests that the preferred approach should be to use the smaller corpus to construct the

HBFT. Memory is an additional consideration. Using a HBFT to model the larger dataset requires the similarity hashes of all its files to be cached at the leaves. This requires a greater memory footprint than for the smaller collection, thus reducing the amount of memory available to store the HBFT itself.

Following these observations, the experiment was repeated once more. The tree modelled t5 with 4,457 leaves and win7 was searched for. The total running time, including pairwise comparisons, was 1,094 s. In comparison, the time taken to perform a full pairwise comparison using MRSH-v2 is 2,858 s.

Experiment 3: Planted Evidence. The final experiment involved overlapping datasets, constructed as follows:

- A set of simulated "known-illegal" files: 4,000 files from t5.
- A simulated seized hard disk: the win7 image, plus 140 files from t5, as follows:
    - 100 files that are contained within the 4,000 "illegal" files.
    - 40 files that themselves are not contained within the "illegal" files, but that have a high similarity with files in the corpus, according to MRSH-v2. 10 of these files have a similarity of 80% or higher, 10 have a similarity between 60% and 79% (inclusive), 10 have a similarity between 40% and 59% (inclusive) and 10 have a similarity between 20% and 39% (inclusive).

The aims of this third experiment were:

1. Evaluate the time taken to perform a full search, compared with MRSH-v2.
2. Evaluate the success of the approach in finding the 100 "illegal" files that are included verbatim in the hard disk image, and the 40 files from the image that are similar to "illegal" files, according to MRSH-v2.

For the first aim, the primary metric is the time taken for the entire process to run, comprising the time to build the tree, the time to search the tree and the time required to conduct the pairwise comparisons at the leaves. In evaluating the latter aim, recall is used. Here, "recall" refers to the percentage of the 100 identical files that are successfully identified, and "similar recall" refers to the percentage of the 40 similar files that are successfully found. A file is considered to have been found if the search for the file it is similar or identical to reaches the leaf node that contains it, yielding a pairwise comparison.

The total running time for MRSH-v2 was 2,592 s. The running times of the HBFT approach are shown in Fig. 6. The smaller collection of 4,000 "illegal" files was used to construct the tree and then searches were conducted for all of the files in the larger corpus. The "Search Time" includes the time spent searching the tree and the time to perform the comparisons at the leaves.

As expected, the maximum number of leaf nodes resulted in the fastest run time. This configuration also yielded the maximum reduction in the number of pairwise comparisons required, without substantially adding to the time required to build and search the tree. The remainder of this analysis focuses on this scenario, where the tree has 4,000 leaf nodes.

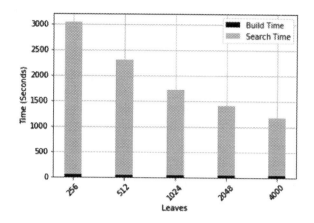

Fig. 6. Time to search for planted evidence (including pairwise comparisons).

The total time was 1,182 s (a 54% reduction in the time required for an all-against-all pairwise comparison). Due to the lack of scalability of the pairwise approach, this difference is likely to be even more pronounced for larger datasets.

Table 2. Similar recall for planted evidence experiment.

MRSH-v2 similarity	Files planted	Files found	Similar recall
80%–100%	10	10	100%
60%–79%	10	10	100%
40%–59%	10	10	100%
20%–39%	10	8	80%
Overall	40	38	95%

In terms of effectiveness, all 100 files that were common to the two corpora were successfully found. The similar recall is shown in Table 2. All files with a MRSH-v2 similarity of 40% or greater with a file in the "illegal" set were successfully identified. Two files with a lower similarity (25% and 26%) were not found. This yields an overall similar recall score of 95% for all 40 files.

This is an encouraging result, indicating that the HBFT approach is extremely effective at finding files that are similar above a reasonable threshold of 40% and exhibits full recall for identical files. Thus it can be concluded that the HBFT data structure is a viable alternative to all-against-all comparisons in terms of effectiveness, while achieving substantial speed gains.

6   Conclusions and Future Work

This paper aimed to investigate the effectiveness of using a Hierarchical Bloom Filter Tree (HBFT) data structure to improve upon the all-against-all pairwise comparison approach used by MRSH-v2. A number of experiments were conducted with the aim of improving the speed of the process. Additionally, it was important that files that should be found were not omitted.

The first experiment found that while HBFTs with more leaf nodes take longer to build and search, they reduce the number of pairwise comparisons required by the greatest degree. It also suggested the use of a min_run value of 4, as higher values resulted in imperfect recall for identical files.

The results of the second experiment indicated that when using corpora of different sizes, it is preferable to build the tree to model the smaller collection and then search for the files that are contained the larger corpus.

For the final experiment, a Windows 7 image was augmented by the addition of a number of files that were identical to those being searched for, and a further group that were similar. The HBFT approach yielded a recall level of 100% for the identical files and of 95% for the similar files, when using mrsh-v2 as ground truth. On examining the two files that were not found, it was noted that these had a relatively low similarity to the search files (25% and 26% respectively), with all files with a higher similarity score being identified successfully. The run time for this experiment was 54% of the time required for a pairwise comparison.

These experiments lead to the conclusion that the HBFT approach is a highly promising technique. Due the poor scalability of the traditional all-against-all approach, it can be inferred that this performance improvement will be even more pronounced as datasets become larger.

Given the promising results of the experiments presented in this paper, further work is planned. Currently, when building the tree, files are allocated to leaf nodes in a round-robin fashion. For trees with multiple files represented at each leaf, it may be possible that a more optimised allocation mechanism could be used for this (e.g. to allocate similar files to the same leaf node). Additionally, the current model also uses balanced trees, with the result that all successful searches reach the same depth in the tree. In some circumstances, an unbalanced tree may be preferable so as to shorten some more common searches.

References

1. van Baar, R., van Beek, H., van Eijk, E.: Digital forensics as a service: a game changer. Digit. Invest. **11**(Supplement 1), S54–S62 (2014). https://doi.org/10.1016/j.diin.2014.03.007
2. Bloom, B.H.: Space/time trade-offs in hash coding with allowable errors. Commun. ACM **13**(7), 422–426 (1970)
3. de Braekt, R.I., Le-Khac, N.A., Farina, J., Scanlon, M., Kechadi, T.: Increasing digital investigator availability through efficient workflow management and automation. In: 2016 4th International Symposium on Digital Forensic and Security (ISDFS), pp. 68–73 (2016). https://doi.org/10.1109/ISDFS.2016.7473520
4. Breitinger, F., Baier, H.: Similarity preserving hashing: eligible properties and a new algorithm MRSH-v2. In: Rogers, M., Seigfried-Spellar, K.C. (eds.) ICDF2C 2012. LNICST, vol. 114, pp. 167–182. Springer, Heidelberg (2013). https://doi.org/10.1007/978-3-642-39891-9_11

5. Breitinger, F., Baier, H., White, D.: On the database lookup problem of approximate matching. Digit. Invest. **11**, S1–S9 (2014). https://doi.org/10.1016/j.diin.2014.03.001
6. Breitinger, F., Guttman, B., McCarrin, M., Roussev, V., White, D.: Approximate matching: definition and terminology. NIST Spec. Publ. **800**, 168 (2014)
7. Breitinger, F., Rathgeb, C., Baier, H.: An efficient similarity digests database lookup - a logarithmic divide & conquer approach. J. Digit. Forensics Secur. Law **9**(2), 155–166 (2014)
8. Broder, A.Z.: On the resemblance and containment of documents. In: Compression and Complexity of Sequences 1997, Proceedings, pp. 21–29. IEEE (1997). https://doi.org/10.1109/SEQUEN.1997.666900
9. Casey, E., Ferraro, M., Nguyen, L.: Investigation delayed is justice denied: proposals for expediting forensic examinations of digital evidence. J. Forensic Sci. **54**(6), 1353–1364 (2009)
10. Gupta, J.N., Kalaimannan, E., Yoo, S.M.: A heuristic for maximizing investigation effectiveness of digital forensic cases involving multiple investigators. Comput. Oper. Res. **69**, 1–9 (2016). https://doi.org/10.1016/j.cor.2015.11.003
11. Harichandran, V.S., Breitinger, F., Baggili, I.: Bytewise approximate matching: the good, the bad, and the unknown. J. Digit. Forensics Secur. Law: JDFSL **11**(2), 59 (2016)
12. James, J.I., Gladyshev, P.: Automated inference of past action instances in digital investigations. Int. J. Inf. Secur. **14**(3), 249–261 (2015). https://doi.org/10.1007/s10207-014-0249-6
13. Kornblum, J.: Identifying identical files using context triggered piecewise hashing. Digit. Invest. **3**, 91–97 (2006). https://doi.org/10.1016/j.diin.2006.06.015
14. Lillis, D., Becker, B., O'Sullivan, T., Scanlon, M.: Current challenges and future research areas for digital forensic investigation. In: 11th ADFSL Conference on Digital Forensics, Security and Law (CDFSL 2016), ADFSL, Daytona Beach, FL, USA (2016). https://doi.org/10.13140/RG.2.2.34898.76489
15. Oliver, J., Cheng, C., Chen, Y.: TLSH-a locality sensitive hash. In: Cybercrime and Trustworthy Computing Workshop (CTC), 2013 Fourth, pp. 7–13. IEEE (2013). https://doi.org/10.1109/CTC.2013.9
16. Quick, D., Choo, K.K.R.: Impacts of increasing volume of digital forensic data: a survey and future research challenges. Digit. Invest. **11**(4), 273–294 (2014). https://doi.org/10.1016/j.diin.2014.09.002
17. Rogers, M.K., Goldman, J., Mislan, R., Wedge, T., Debrota, S.: Computer forensics field triage process model. J. Digit. Forensics Secur. Law **1**(2), 19–38 (2006)
18. Roussev, V.: Data fingerprinting with similarity digests. In: Chow, K.P., Shenoi, S. (eds.) IFIP International Conference on Digital Forensics. IFIP AICT, vol. 337, pp. 207–226. Springer, Heidelberg (2010). https://doi.org/10.1007/978-3-642-15506-2_15
19. Roussev, V.: An evaluation of forensic similarity hashes. Digit. Invest. **8**, S34–S41 (2011)
20. Roussev, V., Richard III, G.G.: Breaking the performance wall: the case for distributed digital forensics. In: Proceedings of the 2004 Digital Forensics Research Workshop, vol. 94 (2004)
21. Sadowski, C., Levin, G.: Simhash: hash-based similarity detection. Technical report, Google (2007)
22. Scanlon, M.: Battling the digital forensic backlog through data deduplication. In: Proceedings of the 6th IEEE International Conference on Innovative Computing Technologies (INTECH 2016). IEEE, Dublin (2016)

Approxis: A Fast, Robust, Lightweight and Approximate Disassembler Considered in the Field of Memory Forensics

Lorenz Liebler[(✉)] and Harald Baier

da/sec - Biometrics and Internet Security Research Group,
University of Applied Sciences, Darmstadt, Germany
{lorenz.liebler,harald.baier}@h-da.de

Abstract. The discipline of detecting known and unknown code structures in large sets of data is a challenging task. An example could be the examination of memory dumps of an infected system. Memory forensic frameworks rely on system relevant information and the examination of structures which are located within a dump itself. With the constant increasing size of used memory, the creation of additional methods of data reduction (similar to those in disk forensics) are eligible. In the field of disk forensics, approximate matching algorithms are well known. However, in the field of memory forensics, the application of those algorithms is impractical. In this paper we introduce `approxis`: an approximate disassembler. In contrary to other disassemblers our approach does not rely on an internal disassembler engine, as the system is based on a compressed set of ground truth x86 and x86-64 assemblies. Our first prototype shows a good computational performance and is able to detect code in large sets of raw data. Additionally, our current implementation is able to differentiate between architectures while disassembling. Summarized, `approxis` is the first attempt to interface approximate matching with the field of memory forensics.

Keywords: Approximate disassembly · Approximate matching
Disassembly · Binary analysis · Memory forensics

1 Introduction

Detecting known malicious code in memory is a challenging task. This is mainly due to two reasons: first, malware authors tend to obfuscate their code by tampering it for each instance. Second, code in memory differs from persistent code because of changes performed by the memory loader (e.g., the security feature *Address Space Layout Randomization (ASLR)* makes it impossible to predict the final state of an executable right before run time). Hence an approach to identify malicious code within a memory forensics investigation by comparing code fragments in its untampered shape (e.g., as an image on disk) to its memory loaded representation (e.g., a module with variable code) is a non-trivial task.

© ICST Institute for Computer Sciences, Social Informatics and Telecommunications Engineering 2018
P. Matoušek and M. Schmiedecker (Eds.): ICDF2C 2017, LNICST 216, pp. 158–172, 2018.
https://doi.org/10.1007/978-3-319-73697-6_12

Memory forensic tools like volatility use system related structures to extract loaded executables and to list executed processes on a system. The classical approach to identify loaded malware is performed with the help of signatures, static byte sequences or by the examination of access protections. White et al. [10] formulate requirements of investigating a memory image and postulate that methods of data reduction (similar to those in disk forensics) are eligible. In the field of disk forensics approximate matching algorithms (a.k.a. similarity hashing or fuzzy hashing) represent a robust and fast instrument to differentiate between known and unknown data fragments [3,6]. However, White et al. [10] claim that approximate matching algorithms are not suitable in the course of memory forensics, as code in memory always differs to on disk.

In this paper we argue that the concept of approximate matching may be transferred from post-mortem or network forensics to the field of memory forensics. We differentiate between two stages of research to succeed. First, a technical component is needed, which acquires portions of code in different domains and extracts these fragments out of vast amounts of unknown data. Second, the acquired code fragments must be comparable. As the existing approaches in the field of memory forensics try to solve both issues at once by creating a stack of dependencies and accepting limitations of applicability [8,10], our approach focuses on the technical component first and introduces an interface to transfer the overall problem of code detection into the domain of approximate matching.

Our main contribution of this paper is the technical acquisition component approxis: a lightweight, robust, fast and approximate disassembler as a prerequisite for memory-based approximate matching. The goal of approxis is to build a technical component for the usage in digital forensics, however, approxis may be used in different fields like real-time systems, too. Its functionality is comparable to a basic length-disassembler approach with additional features.

Our approach is unaware of the full instruction encoding scheme of x86 or x86-64 platforms: by the usage of 4.2 GiB precompiled ELF (Executable and Linking Format) files and its corresponding ground truth assembly structure obtained by [1], we build up a decision tree of byte instructions. Each path of the tree represents the decoding process of a byte sequence to its corresponding instruction length. We use the opcode and mnemonic frequencies to assist the disassembling process and to differentiate between code and non-code byte sequences. The overall goal of approxis is not to reach the accuracy of professional disassemblers, but to outreach the capabilities of a simple length disassembler.

We evaluate our approach in different fields of application. First, we show the promising disassembling accuracy of approxis compared to objdump, a widely distributed and often used linear disassembler. Second, our approach is able to distinguish between code and data. Third, we demonstrate the capabilities to identify interleaved segments of code within large sets of raw binary data. Our current implementation introduces the possibility to determine the architecture of code during the process of disassembling. Finally, we demonstrate the computational performance of approxis by the application on a raw memory image.

It is important to outline the conditions and the operational field of `approxis`, as our approach should not be considered in the well known domains of binary analysis. Thus, even if the final evaluation of `approxis` could seem to be incomplete to the reader, we argue that the extensive introduction of our approach in the field of memory forensics is important to understand the following design decisions. Additionally, it is somewhat negligible and deceptive to compare our approach to other disassemblers. However, our current implementation of `approxis` is designed for processing large portions of raw memory dumps, so a straight comparison with other disassemblers is not always valid.

The remainder of this paper is organized as follows: In Sect. 2 we give an overview of related work. We introduce key features of existing research and describe instances of different disassemblers. In Sect. 3 we define central requirements which should be fulfilled by `approxis`. In Sect. 4 we briefly introduce the x86 decoding scheme and the challenges of disassembling. We also introduce the results of analyzing our ground truth assemblies obtained by [1], which build the foundation for our code detection and approximate disassembling approach. In Sect. 5 we introduce `approxis` and its functionality. In Sect. 6 we present our assessment and experimental results. Finally, Sect. 7 concludes this paper.

2 Related Work

Researches discussed different approaches for the application of cryptographic hash functions on memory fragments. Existing work addresses the problem of identifying known code by hashing normalized portions of code in memory. A short survey of existing approaches was given by [10]. In [8] offsets of variable code fragments were used to normalize and hash executables on a page level. A database of hash templates was created which consists of hash values and its corresponding offsets. These hash templates are applied on the physical address space. The comparison between each template and each page lead to a complexity of $O(n * m)$ for a comparison of n templates against m memory pages.

The authors of [10] extended the approach and tried to improve the naive all-against-all comparison introduced by [8]. Therefore, they applied the hashes on virtual memory pages and used structures in memory to identify a process. By identifying a process, the lookup of a corresponding hash template could be performed efficiently. Before creating the hash values, the introduced approaches convert a present executable from disk to its state in memory and normalize it. The conversion of disk stored image files to a virtual loaded module was accomplished with the help of a virtual Windows PE Loader [10]. The identification of variable offsets by imitating the loading process of an executable seems legit. A normalization based on previously disassembling a present sequence of bytes in memory was not mentioned by the authors.

Recent research of linear disassemblers has shown the significant underestimation of linear disassembly and the dualism in the stance on disassembly in literature [1]. A more exotic form are the so called length-disassemblers, which could be understood as a limited subset of linear disassemblers. A length-disassembler only extracts the lengths of an instruction. Beside the classical linear and recursive disassemblers, the authors of [7] introduced an experimental approach of fast and approximate disassembly. The approach is based on the statistically examination of the most frequent occurred mnemonics. A set of extracted sequences of mnemonics have been used to create a lookup table of predominant bigrams. With the help of this table, a fuzzy 32 bit decoding scheme was proposed, which showed decent results.

As already introduced, approximate matching algorithms can be used to detect similarities among objects, but also to detect embedded objects or fragment of objects [3,6]. Investigators can use it to differ between non-relevant and relevant fragments in large sets of suspicious data. In the course of memory forensics this approach would obviously struggle with volatile instruction operands and updated byte-sequences. Current approximate matching techniques constantly evolve, e.g. by the integration of better lookup strategies like Cuckoo Filters [5].

The problem of identifying code structures in large sets of binary data could be misleadingly compared with the problem of identifying interleaved data within code sections of a single executable [9]. The major goals of our approach are the fast identification and the approximate disassembly of code fragments.

3   Requirements of Approximate Disassembling

In this section we introduce and explain four essential requirements for our research: *lightweight*, *robustness*, *speed* and *versatility*. These requirements should be understood as superior and long term goals in the context of applying approximate matching to the field of memory forensics. They have to be respected in this research and beyond this work. To be able to better describe the fundamental requirements, we first introduce the central goals of this publication. As the application of approximate matching algorithms to portions of memory seems unfeasible due to a unpredictable representation of code in memory, we suggest a process of normalization after approximate disassembling portions of code in large sets of raw and mixed data. As this work addresses the step of identifying and disassembling code in data, we define four major goals:

1. Detect sequences of code in a vast amount of different shaped raw data.
2. Extract sequences of instruction-related bytes with little overhead.
3. Make a statement about the confidence of the code detection process.
4. Determine additional information, like the architecture of the code.

These practical goals describe the motivation of this work, where the following requirements describe the bounding conditions to achieve those goals. The defined requirements are discussed by recalling some central properties of the introduced competing approaches and by considering the mentioned goals.

The first requirement *lightweight* aims to reduce the stack of dependencies of the target system with a focus on the instruction set and the loader traces. In contrast to existing approaches, we propose a normalization based on previously disassembling code in different states of an executable. We consider this approach significant more lightweight than imitating loader traces with the help of a self-constructed virtual loader. A disassembler is therefore less interleaved to record the changes of a memory loader to an image file.

Previous work to detect known fragments of code (e.g., the approach introduced by [10]) relies on the correct identification of a running process. This offers new degrees of bypassing and obfuscation to the malware author, e.g., by unlinking Virtual Address Descriptor (VAD) nodes using Direct Kernel Object Manipulation [4]. Our second requirement *robustness* means to identify a code fragment without process structures and being thus more robust against obfuscation compared to competing approaches.

Our third requirement is *speed*, which is a central requirement adopted from the field of approximate matching. In our current stage of research the detection and extraction of code from a vast amount of data has to be done with good computational performance. As we are interested in an approximate disassembler, we trade computational performance more important than accuracy of the disassembled code. However, the degree of disassembling should enable further normalization or the reduction of code representation.

Most of the introduced systems in Sect. 2 are limited to x86 systems. A more *versatile* approach is desirable, which is not dependent on an a-priori knowledge of the architecture of the target system. The requirement *versatility* means that the disassembler works reliably for different target architectures.

4   Background and Fundamentals

In this section we introduce the basic fundamentals of our approach for the introduction of `approxis`. We briefly introduce the target x86 system. Afterwards, we introduce the set of ground truth assembly files in a detailed way.

4.1   Disassembling

We first give a short introduction to the x86 encoding scheme and the fundamentals of disassembling. Disassemblers are used to transform machine code into a human readable representation. In the field of binary analysis and reverse engineering the demands and requirements of a disassembler engine are clearly identified. With the x86 instruction set these tools have to deal with variable-length and unaligned instruction encodings. Additional, executables sections could be interleaved by code and data sequences. As the authors of [9] already described, this system design trades simplicity for brevity and speed. Summarized, the process of disassembly in general is undecidable [1,9]. As could be seen in Fig. 1 the x86 instructions are defined by sequences of mandatory and non-mandatory bytes. The `Reg` field of the `ModR/M` byte is sometimes used as an additional opcode extension field. Prefix bytes could additionally change the overall instruction length. For further details we refer to the Intel Instruction manual[1].

---

[1] https://software.intel.com/en-us/articles/intel-sdm.

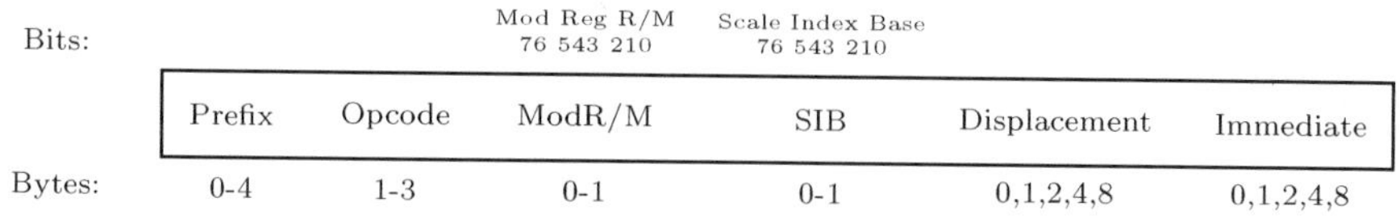

Bits:			Mod Reg R/M 76 543 210	Scale Index Base 76 543 210		
	Prefix	Opcode	ModR/M	SIB	Displacement	Immediate
Bytes:	0-4	1-3	0-1	0-1	0,1,2,4,8	0,1,2,4,8

Fig. 1. x86 machine instruction format

The core of this research is to approximate disassemble a vast amount of unknown data. This desire clearly stays in conflict with the goal of classical disassembler engines, where computational performance is often understood as a secondary goal. We ignore recursive traversal, as this would implicate an impractical layer of computational overhead. The development and the maintenance process of disassemblers is somewhat cumbersome and tedious. Even the lookup tables of a simple length-disassembler have to be maintained.

4.2 Mnemonic Frequency Analysis

We analyzed the opcode and mnemonic distribution of a set of ELF binaries, namely a dataset containing 521 different binaries obtained by [1]. As we focus on the acquisition of byte sequences which rely to code only, we extracted the .text section of each binary file. It should be mentioned that the following distribution analysis is nothing new [2,7]. However, existing distribution analysis of mnemonics often rely on malware, which could be biased. We used the ground truth of assemblies to determine the distribution of mnemonics and extracted the bigrams of mnemonics (see Table 1). We splitted the set of assemblies by its architecture and determined the *total* amount of unigrams and bigrams. The column of *distinct* values describes the set of all occurring mnemonics. The columns *max*, *mean* and *min* describe the assignment of the *total* amount of instructions to each *distinct* unigram or bigram. For example, the most frequently occurred mnemonic in the case of 32 bit binaries represents 33.25% of all instructions.

Table 1. Overview of unigram and bigram mnemonic counts.

	32 bit (200 files)				64 bit (321 files)			
	Total	Distinct	Max	Mean	Total	Distinct	Max	Mean
Unigrams	35.232k	322	11.714k	1531	61.441k	436	21.627k	1859
Bigrams	35.232k	11632	5.889k	17	61.441k	16059	10.360k	28

The frequency of occurrence of all bigrams are extracted, the probability p of each bigram is saved as logarithmic odds (logit). We further denote the absolute values of logits as λ (see Eq. 1). Similar to [7] we want to avoid computational underflow by multiplication of probabilities.

$$\lambda = \left| \ln \frac{p}{1-p} \right| \tag{1}$$

4.3   Byte Tree Analysis

The former subsection revisits the frequencies of most frequently occurred mnemonics. In a next step we analyze the byte frequencies on a instruction base. We have to deal with a vast amount of overlapping byte sequences and non-relevant operand information. To refine our demands, the overall goal of `approxis` is not do establish a high-accuracy disassembler, but to identify instruction offsets and a predominant mnemonic. We extract all bytes of an instruction and insert them in a database structured as tree. Each node of the tree represents a byte and stores a reference to all its corresponding children, the subsequent instruction bytes (see Fig. 2).

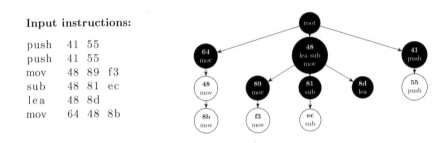

Input instructions:

```
push   41 55
push   41 55
mov    48 89 f3
sub    48 81 ec
lea    48 8d
mov    64 48 8b
```

Fig. 2. Oversimplified bytetree example after inserting several instructions.

As an example we inspect the byte sequence 488d and its subsequent bytes after inserting our ground truth into the tree. In listing 1 we can see the complete output of a single node. We should mention that the amount of the child nodes was shortened for a better representation ❷. We also save auxiliary information like the amount of counted bytes for a current node ❶, the counts of all corresponding mnemonics ❸❺ and the counts of different occurring instruction lengths ❸❹. Each node maintains different formats and could possibly lead to redundant information. This structure represents an intermediate state needed for the following steps of data analysis, post processing and tree reduction.

Listing 1: Inspecting a node of lea (48 8d) instruction

```
1  Current node:  ['48,8d']; Count: 1334022 ❶
2  Child nodes:   [83,aa,04,87,2d,8b,0c,8f,93, ... ,69,7d,6d,71,75,48] ❷
3  { 3:669k, 2:11k, 4:273k, 7:207k, 6:172k}
4  { 2:{lea:11k}, 3:{lea:669k}, 4:{lea:273k}, 6:{lea:172k}, 7:{lea:207k}} ❸
5  [[3, 669k], [4, 273k], [7, 207k], [6, 172k], [2, 11k]] ❹
6  (lea', 1334k) ❺
```

After inserting the whole ground truth into the tree we perform an additional step of reduction. Every node which represents a single length and a single mnemonic was transformed to a leaf node. So we cropped all subsequent child nodes of the current node, which doesn't affect the instruction mnemonic. The reduced shape of the tree is highlighted black in Fig. 2. The impact of reduction could be seen in Table 2.

Table 2. Comparison of original and reduced bytetree.

Platform	Input bytes	Original tree			Reduced tree		
		Nodes	Height	Size	Nodes	Height	Size
64 bit	253.535.572	12.773.078	15	445M	87.224	10	7.5M
32 bit	123.221.439	5.871.232	15	206M	35.211	9	3.0M

5 Approach

The observation of the preceding section lead the deduction of our approach, which is based on the introduced bytetree and mnemonic frequency analysis.

5.1 Disassembling

We argue that length-disassemblers could be assumed to be very fast and lightweight. Though, even a simple length-disassembler needs to respect a lot of basic operations and needs to be maintained for different target architectures. The disassembler library distorm[2] is based on a trie structure and conceptional similar to our approach. It outperforms other disassemblers with its instruction lookup complexity of $O(1)$. However, the engine still respects instruction sets on a bit granularity and performs a detailed decoding. As we trade computational speed more important than accuracy, approxis will stay on a byte granularity level. We consult the previously gained learnings of the mnemonic analysis to improve our process of length disassembling. It should be clear and fair to mention that existing disassemblers aren't designed for our field of application. Processing a large amount of raw data is out of the scope of classical disassemblers. As existing length-disassembler engines reduce the amount of needed decoding mechanisms to a minimum, we introduce an approach to resolve a corresponding mnemonic without respecting any provided opcode maps. Hence, comparing the computational speed of approxis with other disassemblers seems less meaningful.

Bytetree Disassembling. To address the introduced requirement *lightweight* (see Sect. 3), approxis does not depend on the integration of a specific disassembler engine. The process of disassembling is mainly realized with the already introduced bytetree. We implemented our first prototype of approxis in the language C and used a reduced bytetree to generate cascades of switch statements. These statements are used to sequentially process the input instructions and to perform the translation into a corresponding length and mnemonic. The information of the bytetree nodes have been reduced to a minimum core. We only store the amount of counted visited bytes per node and the lengths. Nodes with more than one mnemonic are reduced to a single representative, which is the predominant and most counted mnemonic of the specific node.

---

[2] https://github.com/gdabah/distorm.

The performance of the bytetree was evaluated by a set of 1318 64 bit binaries. The disassemblies obtained by the bytetree have been compared to the disassemblies obtained by objdump. Determining the correct offsets is important to build a solid foundation for further normalization. Thus, it is important to measure the amount of correctly disassembled instruction offsets compared to the set of true instruction offsets. We disassembled all binaries of an *Ubuntu LTS 16.04 x86_64* and extracted the .text sections. The determined instruction offsets by objdump build our ground truth of *relevant offsets* θ_{rl}. We measured the performance of our bytetree disassembler by verifying all *retrieved offsets* θ_{rt} against our set of *relevant offsets*. An overview of fairly good performance is shown in Table 3 (row bt-dis). We denote the performance in values of precision and recall, where

$$\text{precision} = \frac{|\{\theta_{rl}\} \cap \{\theta_{rt}\}|}{|\{\theta_{rt}\}|} \quad \text{and} \quad \text{recall} = \frac{|\{\theta_{rl}\} \cap \{\theta_{rt}\}|}{|\{\theta_{rl}\}|}.$$

Table 3. Precision and recall of approxis.

Approach	Precision				Recall			
	Max	Min	Mean (geo./ari.)		Max	Min	Mean (geo./ari.)	
bt-dis	100%	84.40%	99.50%	99.51%	100%	92.40%	99.80%	99.80%
bta-dis	100%	91.49%	99.76%	99.76%	100%	93.62%	99.84%	99.84%

We examined the binary with the lowest precision (i.e., 84.40%), namely xvminitoppm, which converts a XV thumbnail picture to PPM. Extracting a bunch of false positives underlines our assumption: even with a reliable vast amount of ground truth files, the integration of all instructions is impossible. In case of xvminitoppm a lot of overlong Multi Media Extension (MMX) instructions are implemented, which are not present in the bytetree.

Assisted Length Disassembling. Disassembling a unknown binary, with unknown instruction bytes could lead to ambiguous decision paths within the bytetree. Namely, an unknown sequence of input bytes would lead to an exit of the tree structure at a non-leaf node, with multiple remaining lengths and mnemonics. An example in Fig. 3 could not be clearly disassembled with the tree from Fig. 2. To detect those outliers and to extend approxis with other features, we integrate our results from Sect. 4. In detail, we use the logarithmic odds of mnemonic bigrams to assist the process of disassembling and to identify reasonable instruction lengths, which could not be resolved by the bytetree itself. As the authors of [7] proposed a disassembler based on a set of logarithmic odds only, we argue that the descent performance of this approach is not sufficient.

As the process of bytetree based disassembling is straightforward, the integration of the absolute logit value λ has not yet been described. We consider

λ as a *value of confidence* if two disassembled and subsequent instructions are plausible or not. So it is more likely that a sequence of instructions is in fact meaningful as long as λ remains small. In contrast, a high value of λ illustrates two subsequent instructions, which are not common at all. We limit the range of the absolute logit λ, where $0 \leq \lambda \leq 100$. This *value of confidence* could be used differently to cope with the goals and requirements in Sect. 3. We first focus on assisting our process of disassembling by resolving plausible instruction lengths. Summarized, we use λ to determine the most plausible offset of a byte sequence, which is not known by our bytetree. The following steps describe the process of assisted disassembling in detail:

1. We use a table of **confidence values** λ_i to evaluate the transition between two instruction sequences denoted by its mnemonic. If a lookup of a subsequent mnemonic pair fails, the action gets penalized with an exorbitant high value. Every retrieved λ_i has to be under a selected threshold τ. We repeat the disassembling with all stored length values of a current node until an offset fulfills the threshold. If none of the length values returns a λ_i under the threshold τ, we select the most common length of the current node.
2. All byte sequences with an unknown byte at **offset zero**, i.e. a byte which is not present in the first level of the bytetree, are penalized by the system. As bytes, which are not present on the first level of the bytetree after processing a fairly large amount of ground truth files, are expected to be not common.
3. A simple **running length counter** keeps track of subsequently repeating confidence values, as these indicate a significant lack of variance, often occurring in large fragments of zero byte sequences or random padding sequences. These non-relevant byte sequences are additionally penalized.

Figure 3 illustrates the process of offset determination. We repeated the process of disassembling the set of 1318 64 bit ELF binaries with assisted length-disassembling. The obtained results in Table 3 (row `bta-dis`) show a significant improvement in the case of precision.

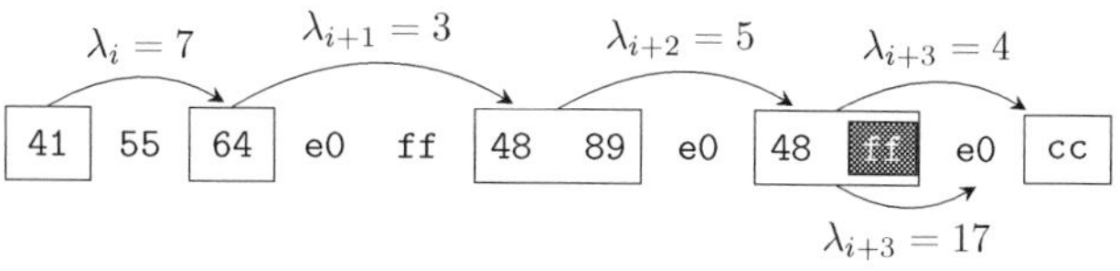

Fig. 3. Selecting certain offsets with a predefined threshold $\tau = 16$.

5.2   Code and Architecture Detection

Beside supporting the process of determining unknown instruction offsets during disassembling, we use the value of confidence to realize two goals: detect code sequences in data and discriminate the architecture of code.

Code Detection. The current implementation of `approxis` could differ between code and non-code fragments in unknown sequences of bytes. As shown in the previous subsection, the value of confidence λ_i is determined for two subsequent instructions to enhance the disassembling process. We use a sliding window approach to consider those values over sequences of subsequent instructions. More formally, we define a *windowed confidence value* ω_x in Eq. 2 as the average of all λ_i within a sliding window, with a predefined size n at offset x. Penalized values overwrite a local value λ_i and thus influence ω_x. The value of ω should be interpreted as a value of confidence over time. A rising value ω underlines the presence of large data fragments. A short rising peak of λ indicates the presence of short and interleaved data. A mid-ranged value of ω indicates the loose presence of instructions or the presence of non-common instructions.

$$\omega_x = \frac{\sum_{i=x}^{n+x} \lambda_i}{n} \tag{2}$$

Architecture Detection. We created a bytetree and a lookup table of λ_i for each architecture of our ground truth. Thus, switching the mode of operation could be realized by simply changing the references of the used bytetree and lookup-table. Mid-ranged values of ω could indicate uncommon sequences of instructions, which we will show later. Large sections of mid-range ω values could also indicate the presence of alternative architectures. We will demonstrate that these variances are significant for different architectures. Sections of code are normally within a range from 1 (high confidence) to 17 (low confidence).

6   Assessment and Experimental Results

In this section we evaluate `approxis` in different fields of application. These assessments focus on the detection of code in different areas of application.

Code Detection: The following evaluation addresses our defined requirement of *robustness* (see Sect. 3). To evaluate the code detection performance in the field of binary analysis, we first examined a randomly selected ELF binary. The result in Fig. 4 illustrates the capabilities of `approxis` to differentiate code from data. Figure 4a shows the initial reduction of confidence by the header. Figure 4b shows that the `.text` section is clearly distinguishable and introduced by the `.plt` section, which is not filled with common sequences of instructions.

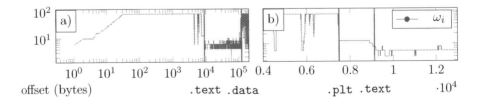

Fig. 4. `approxis` applied on `zip` (64 bit); value of ω_i with cutoff set to 100;

We extracted from a set of 792 ELF binaries the file offsets of different sections with the help of `objdump`. The offsets θ of the sections `.plt`, `.text` and `.data` define points of transition between code and data in each file. To evaluate the code detection performance we inspected the average local value of confidence λ_i for κ preceding and κ subsequent instructions at an offset θ. A transition τ_d from code to data or τ_c from data to code at offset θ is recognized by `approxis`, if the average local confidence differs by a threshold δ (see formula 3). In the case of transitions between `.plt` and `.text` we lowered the threshold from $\delta = 30$ to $\delta = 5$. The ratio of all correctly registered transitions is shown in Table 4.

$$\tau_c = \tau_d = \begin{cases} 1, & \text{if } \left| \dfrac{\sum_{i=\theta-\kappa}^{\theta} \lambda_i}{n} - \dfrac{\sum_{i=\theta}^{\theta+\kappa} \lambda_i}{n} \right| > \delta \\ 0, & \text{otherwise} \end{cases} \tag{3}$$

Table 4. Ratio of correctly detected transitions.

Arch	# files	# transition	Detected
x86-64	400	1200	99 %
x86	392	1176	92 %

Architecture Detection. The following evaluation addresses our defined requirement of *versatility* (see Sect. 3). To illustrate the detection process of `approxis` for code fragments of different types, an image with random bytes was generated. Within the random byte sequences we inserted several non-overlapping binaries at predefined offsets. In detail, we inserted a 32 bit (i.e., ELF 64-bit LSB, dynam. linked, stripped) and a 64 bit (i.e., ELF 32-bit LSB, dynam. linked, stripped) version of four different binaries: `wget`, `curl`, `info` and `cut`. As introduced in Sect. 5, `approxis` currently relies on two different bytetrees and mnemonic lookup-tables. By applying both versions on our pathological image, we visualize the changing values of confidence (see Fig. 5a, b).

Similar to the analysis of data and code transitions, we examined the architecture discrimination with the help of 400 randomly selected ELF binaries for each architecture. We extracted the `.text` section of each binary and disassembled them with `approxis` in 64 bit and 32 bit mode. We determined the average of all ω_x for the whole `.text` section of each binary, denoted as $\bar{\omega}$. The distribution of $\bar{\omega}$ for each binary is illustrated in Fig. 6 and outlines the capabilities of `approxis` to discriminate a present architecture.

Computational Performance. The following evaluation addresses our defined requirement of *speed* (see Sect. 3). The execution time of `approxis` was tested on a machine with an `Intel(R) Core(TM) i5-3570K CPU @ 3.40 GHz` with 16 GiB DDR3 RAM (1333 MHz) and 6 MiB L3 cache. The implementation was done in C and compiled with optimization set to `-O3`. As we focus on a possible

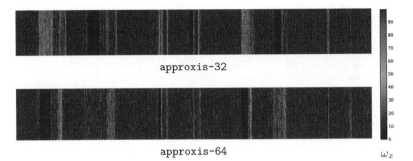

Fig. 5. Comparison of code detection for x86 and x86-64 binaries.

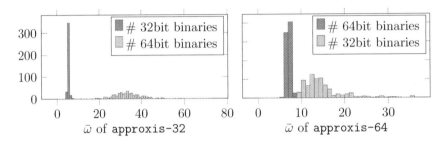

Fig. 6. Architecture detection of `approxis` with a selected bin size of one.

integration in existing approximate matching techniques, we only measured the
computation time of the disassembling process and ignored the loading process
to memory. It should be mentioned that the current prototype doesn't focus on
performance optimization or parallelization. We created three images with a size
of 2 GiB each to evaluate the runtime performance. As we already mentioned
in Sect. 5.1, the comparison of `approxis` with other disassemblers is somewhat
misleading. As `approxis` outreaches the capabilities of length-disassemblers, but
is not able to completely decode x86 instructions, the comparison of those disassemblers should not be understood as a comparison of competing approaches. We
applied each disassembler in different modes and optimized our implementation
of the distorm engine by removing unnecessary printouts and buffers. Table 5
outlines that the execution time of `approxis` relies on the processed input.

Table 5. Execution time of `approxis` and distorm with different input data.

Execution time				Description
Approxis		Distorm		Disassembler
32	64	32	64	Mode
29.084 s	21.936 s	1 m 20.770 s	1 m 7.772 s	Concatenated set of 64 bit binaries from /usr/bin
27.859 s	31.918 s	1 m 43.999 s	1 m 43.046 s	Raw memory dump acquired with LiME[a]
1 m 15.521 s	1 m 44.990 s	1 m 58.278 s	1 m 56.192 s	Random sequences of bytes generated with /dev/urandom

[a]https://github.com/504ensicslabs/lime

7   Conclusion

In this paper, we demonstrated a first approach to detect, discriminate and approximate disassemble code fragments within vast amount of data. In contrast to previous work, `approxis` revisits the analysis of raw memory with less prerequisites and dependencies. Our approach is a first step to fill the gap between state of the art high level memory examination (e.g., by the usage of volatility) and methods of data reduction similar to those in disk forensics. Our results show the capabilities of `approxis` to differentiate between code and data during the process of disassembling. By maintaining a value of confidence throughout the process of disassembling, we can reliably distinguish between different architectures and switch the used bytetree to obtain a better degree of accuracy. The current implementation shows also a good computational speed.

A next step should be the extraction of features, which are used in a context of approximate matching. Possible methods of subversion (e.g. anti-disassembling) should be considered. A process of exact and inexact matching of code is eligible to consider metamorphic structures and to damp variances in detected code. The approach could be transferred to other domains (e.g. embedded systems).

Acknowledgement. This work was supported by the German Federal Ministry of Education and Research (BMBF) as well as by the Hessen State Ministry for Higher Education, Research and the Arts (HMWK) within CRISP (crisp-da.de).

References

1. Andriesse, D., Chen, X., van der Veen, V., Slowinska, A., Bos, H.: An in-depth analysis of disassembly on full-scale x86/x64 binaries. In: USENIX Security Symposium (2016)
2. Bilar, D.: Statistical structures: fingerprinting malware for classification and analysis. In: Proceedings of Black Hat Federal 2006 (2006)
3. Breitinger, F., Baier, H.: Similarity preserving hashing: eligible properties and a new algorithm MRSH-v2. In: Rogers, M., Seigfried-Spellar, K.C. (eds.) ICDF2C 2012. LNICST, vol. 114, pp. 167–182. Springer, Heidelberg (2013). https://doi.org/10.1007/978-3-642-39891-9_11
4. Dolan-Gavitt, B.: The VAD tree: a process-eye view of physical memory. Digit. Invest. **4**, 62–64 (2007)
5. Gupta, V., Breitinger, F.: How cuckoo filter can improve existing approximate matching techniques. In: James, J.I., Breitinger, F. (eds.) ICDF2C 2015. LNICST, vol. 157, pp. 39–52. Springer, Cham (2015). https://doi.org/10.1007/978-3-319-25512-5_4
6. Roussev, V., Richard, G.G., Marziale, L.: Multi-resolution similarity hashing. Digit. Invest. **4**, 105–113 (2007)
7. Radhakrishnan, D.: Approximate disassembly. Master's Projects. 155 (2010). http://scholarworks.sjsu.edu/etd_projects/155/
8. Walters, A., Matheny, B., White, D.: Using hashing to improve volatile memory forensic analysis. In: American Acadaemy of Forensic Sciences Annual Meeting (2008)

9. Wartell, R., Zhou, Y., Hamlen, K.W., Kantarcioglu, M., Thuraisingham, B.: Differentiating code from data in x86 binaries. In: Gunopulos, D., Hofmann, T., Malerba, D., Vazirgiannis, M. (eds.) ECML PKDD 2011. LNCS (LNAI), vol. 6913, pp. 522–536. Springer, Heidelberg (2011). https://doi.org/10.1007/978-3-642-23808-6_34
10. White, A., Schatz, B., Foo, E.: Integrity verification of user space code. Digit. Invest. **10**, S59–S68 (2013)

Digital Forensics Tools Testing
and Validation

Memory Forensics and the Macintosh OS X Operating System

Charles B. Leopard[✉], Neil C. Rowe, and Michael R. McCarrin

U.S. Naval Postgraduate School, Monterey, CA 93940, USA
cbleopard@gmail.com, {ncrowe,mrmccarr}@nps.edu

Abstract. Memory acquisition is essential to defeat anti-forensic operating system features and investigate clever cyberattacks that leave little or no evidence on physical storage media. The forensic community has developed tools to acquire physical memory from Apple's Macintosh computers, but they have not much been tested. This work in progress tested three major OS X memory-acquisition tools. Although all tools tested could capture system memory in most cases, the open-source tool OSXPmem bettered its proprietary counterparts in reliability and support for memory configurations and versions of the OS X operating system.

Keywords: Digital forensics · Acquisition · Main memory · Apple · Macintosh OSX · Testing · MacQuisition · OSXPMem · RECON · Reserved area

1 Introduction

Recent Macintosh OS X operating systems incorporate many recent anti-forensic features, most notably cloud storage and encryption. Users can fully encrypt many things including whole operating system volumes, making it impossible to recover forensic evidence in a reasonable time frame without passwords. Because of this, forensics on the main memory of such systems is increasingly valuable. Memory forensics can recover encryption keys, network packets, injected code, hidden processes and communications from volatile memory.

While there are many memory-acquisition tools and analysis programs for Windows operating systems, there are only a few for Macintosh systems. Ligh et al. (2014) provides a survey of information pertaining to Macintosh OS X memory forensics. A resource is the Rekall Memory Forensic Framework which began as a branch within the Volatility Project (Volatility, 2015) and became a stand-alone project in December 2013 (Rekall, 2015). Since main-memory capture is challenging, it is helpful to compare these tools to see what differences they have.

2 Methodology

This work tested three tools: BlackBag Technologies MacQuisition, Version 2014R1; OSXPMem, Version RC3; and Sumuri Forensics RECON, Version 1.0.11 (Leopard, 2015). The systems were first tested with OS X Mavericks (10.9.5), and then after

© ICST Institute for Computer Sciences, Social Informatics and Telecommunications Engineering 2018
P. Matoušek and M. Schmiedecker (Eds.): ICDF2C 2017, LNICST 216, pp. 175–180, 2018.
https://doi.org/10.1007/978-3-319-73697-6_13

upgrading to Yosemite 10.10.1 and 10.10.2. Each tool was directed to write a memory capture to an external USB 3 hard drive (7200RPM). In total 450 captures were performed (50 machines, 3 operating systems, and 3 forensic tools).

We evaluated the success rate with respect to (1) the ability of the tools to write a physical-memory capture without crashing the computer system; (2) how obtrusive the tool was (what its memory footprint was and how long it took to run); and (3) its ability to produce a capture from which standard forensic artifacts could be recovered using two memory-analysis tools, the Volatility Framework and the Rekall Memory Forensic Framework. The Rekall plugins used were arp, ifconfig, lsof, mount, netstat, psaux, and route, and the Volatility plugins used were mac_arp, mac_bash, mac-ifconfig, mac_lsof, mac-mount, mac_netstat, mac_psaux, and mac_route. We were particularly interested in differences between the memory snapshots obtained since they could indicate functional differences or coverage gaps of the tools.

The Passware Password Recovery Kit Forensic Version 13.1 was used to the confirm that encryption keys for FileVault2 were located within the OS X memory captures and could be used to decrypt the volume. To do this, FileVault2 was enabled on a MacBook Pro and a Mac Pro computer running Mavericks as well as on a MacBook Pro and a Mac Pro computer running Yosemite. Memory captures were done with MacQuisition, OSXPMem, and RECON on both the MacBook Pro and Mac Pro computers running Mavericks. RECON failed to capture physical memory from the Mac Pro computers. OSXPMem was used to capture memory from the Mac Pro and MacBook Pro running Yosemite. MacQuisition does not support Yosemite.

The rate at which memory changes affects the memory dumps acquired by tools. To analyze this we created a virtual machine using VMware Fusion Professional version 7.1.1, and used VMware to take a series of snapshots. The virtual machine ran Mavericks and was configured to use two processor cores and 8 GiB of memory. The host machine was a MacBook Pro (Retina, 15-inch, Mid 2014) with a 2.8 GHz Intel i7 processor and 16 GiB of 1600 MHz DDR3 memory. Our procedure was: (1) log into the VM and take a snapshot every fifteen minutes; (2) use the Volatility plugin to decompress the snapshots; (3) create MD5 hashes for every 4 KiB block using MD5Deep; (4) compare the MD5 hashes with the original hashes and note differences; (5) and repeat three times. We compared memory captured by each of our tools against the VM Snapshot that completed at a time closest to when each capture completed. We then compared the memory captures taken with the tools. To control for potential variations due to VMware's environment, we tested the tools on a physical Mac Mini (late 2014) with a 2.6 GHz Intel i7 processor, and 8 GiB of 1600 MHz DDR3 memory, running Mavericks. The memory captures were taken over a period of 30 min.

3   Results

Memory-acquisition speeds were within 7% for the three tools. Physical memory sizes were 67.45 MiB for MacQuisition, 0.944 MiB for OSXPmem, and 206.7 MiB for RECON, and shared memory and private memory sizes were proportional. OSXPmem had the advantage that it is a command-line tool without a graphical user interface.

We observed several crashes caused by tools. The machines that crashed were not the same nor did any one machine crash more than once. After a crash, a second acquisition attempt was often successful after the machines restarted. The exception was when RECON was used to acquire memory from the Mac Pros with 64 GiB of RAM; all the machines crashed and additional attempts also failed. Valuable forensic data is often permanently lost in a crash, so crash danger is important. Nonetheless, our experiments confirmed that if a memory capture was completed without a crash, then the capture contained every forensic artifact found by the other tools on any run.

The Passware Password Recovery Kit located the encryption keys in all of the memory captures and successfully decrypted the FileVault2 volumes. The OS X user's login password was located within all the memory captures using the hex editor iBored by searching for the term "longname" which we found frequently near a user's password. The password remained in the same block of memory during the thirty-minute period on all captures.

In another experiment, VM snapshots were taken over a period on a VM with Mac OS version Mavericks installed. A Python script counted the 4 KiB blocks whose hash values changed from the original snapshot. Results showed that on average only 5.33% of the blocks had changed after 30 min when running default processes.

Memory captures were considerably larger than the allocated physical memory due to the presence of reserved areas. The datasheet for 4th Generation Intel Core Processor Address Map describes reserved areas below 4 GiB that do not belong to the DRAM. A similar structure was observed in the virtual machines. The vmem files containing the memory in the VM snapshots were converted to raw images. Each vmem file as well as each tool memory capture was 9 GiB in size, though the VM configuration allocated 8 GiB to physical memory. (Stuttgen and Cohen, 2015) discuss how physical memory addresses are used for communication with devices (video cards, PCI cards, and flash memory) on the motherboard with memory-mapped I/O. The 1 GiB block ranges observed between 3 GiB and 4 GiB appear to be reserved for this. The chipset routes memory access around these reserved regions so that all RAM is used. This increases the size of memory captures.

All three tools captured the same range of null values observed in the first half of the memory graphs. The MacQuisition device log reported "bad addresses" were padded with zeroes beginning at block 786432 and ending at block 1048575. Each block contained 4096 bytes resulting in approximately 1 GiB of null characters. We inspected the block range in all three tool memory captures with a hex editor and confirmed that all the tools padded the same block range with zeroes.

Comparisons were done of the tool memory captures and the VM memory snapshots taken at 1 min after logging in to system, as well as the results of each tool memory capture compared to each other. Overall, we saw similar regions of non-null matches in all comparisons. However, the tool memory captures showed that most of the null characters observed in the VM snapshots were overwritten with data when the acquisition tools themselves acquired the memory. This would suggest as the memory-capture tools run, blocks of memory containing null characters get changed while other blocks remain mostly unchanged. Since these regions are large and outside the memory space used by the tools, it is unlikely that the tools themselves are changing the data directly. Rather, we conclude that some other mechanism of the operating system is writing to unused space in memory during the acquisition process.

Figure 1 shows example 4 KiB block matches between the tool-acquired memory captures and the VM snapshot SV1 (initiated at time = 1 min). The three plots show MacQuisition, OSXPmem, and RECON. Red blocks represent matches to the initial memory state which do not contain null (zero) characters; grey blocks represent blocks that match but contain null characters; and the white blocks represent blocks that have changed and do not match. The top of the diagram represents the beginning of memory, and each row represents 1024 blocks from left to right in 4 KiB block increments, so each horizontal slice represents 4 MiB of memory.

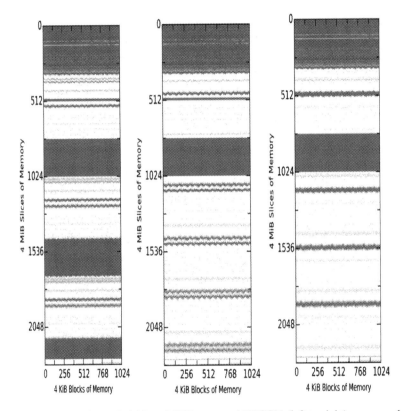

Fig. 1. Comparison of MacQuisition, OSXPmem, and RECON (left to right) on an analogous memory state. (Color figure online)

The OSXPmem data shows a reserved area that appears to agree with the output of the MacQuisition captures, again beginning at approximately the 2 GiB and continuing to 4 GiB. A range of blocks located just before the 6 GiB mark changed between OM2.5 and OM30. The edge of the red area in the figure on the right has shifted and the region of matching blocks is less. The RECON data agree with other tools about the location of reserved regions. The graphs also showed that a range of blocks, located just before the 6 GiB mark, changed between the memory capture at T2.5 and the capture at T30. The edge of the red areas between the figures was similar to before.

Data showed that the matching blocks without null characters (red) change over time by a relatively small percentage. These results were supported by the VM snapshots. It is clear that certain regions of memory are consistently captured while other regions are always in flux. Tests showed that slightly more than the first GiB of the memory capture always matches the VM snapshot. Many null values occur between the third and fourth GiB of memory which appears to be a reserved area. Two more significant blocks of null characters follow while the remaining memory appears to have changed during the acquisition.

Our tests showed that the tools represented the non-match regions (white areas) differently. This suggests not only that the tools are introducing considerable change to the memory space during the acquisition process, but also that each is changing the space in a unique way, so the changes from different tools do not match each other.

The memory-acquisition tools were also tested in non-virtual environment. The Mac Mini was configured with 8 GiB of physical memory, and each tool acquired a 9.74 GiB raw file. All three tools captured the same range of null values in the first half of the capture. This reserved area appears to be larger than in the VM memory images. Analysis with a hex editor determined that the reserved region began at 2.17 GiB and continued until 4 GiB. Data also showed that the block matches that contain non-null characters begin at approximately 30% of the total captured material, but remain relatively stable, declining by less than 10% over a 30 min period (Fig. 2). The match percent was less than what observed in the virtual environment.

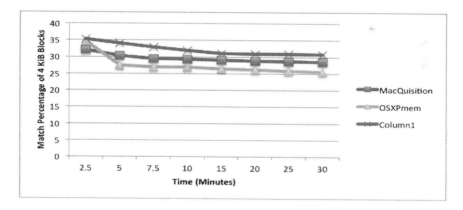

Fig. 2. Match Percentage Comparison over Time ("Column 1" = RECON).

4   Conclusions

MacQuisition, RECON, and OSXPmem were all successful in capturing memory from OS X Mavericks on Macintosh computers. They captured valuable artifacts such as FileVault2 encryption keys and volatile system data. Nonetheless, (Ligh et al., 2015) acknowledges the risk of memory-acquisition tools causing system crashes as we observed since these can be sensitive to the OS X version or the installed hardware on the system. The tool may access a reserved region or interfere with a system-critical function.

Our results showed that size of the memory capture was constant over the tools. Memory dumps were larger than the amount of physical memory (17.99 GiB versus 16 GiB for MacBook Pro was typical) due to regions reserved for firmware, ROM, and other PCI resources.

Comparison of the VM snapshots taken over thirty minutes showed that with only the default processes, memory changed only slightly. Volatility and Rekall revealed many valuable forensic artifacts remaining such as encryption keys and volatile system data. Our evidence further suggested that the tools are acquiring the blocks of memory that are not changing between captures. Though there were significant regions of memory that did not match between the tool-acquired dumps and the VM snapshots, these regions corresponded with memory blocks that contained nulls in the baseline. Our analysis of forensic artifacts using the Volatility and Rekall frameworks failed to detect any situations in which the non-matching regions corresponded to a loss of forensic evidence, since the regions or memory appear to have contained nulls before the memory acquisition.

The experiments with a non-virtual environment showed the tools successfully captured memory from a Mac Mini running Mavericks. We observed the memory captures from all three of the tools appeared similar as far as the blocks that matched and did not match as well for the blocks containing null characters. The results also agree with the results of our tests in the virtual environment in that the regions of memory that match between comparisons did not change much over time.

Future work will examine in more detail the exact changes in files over time and the discrepancies between different tools. Discrepancies suggest, without having to analyze the operating system, where volatile memory stores key operating-system parameters and links. Future work will also investigate the effects of simultaneously running various kinds of software on the operating-system memory images.

Acknowledgements. The views expressed are those of the authors and do not represent the U.S. Government.

References

Intel Corporation: Desktop 4th Generation Intel Core Processor Family, Desktop Intel Pentium Processor Family, and Desktop Intel Celeron Processor Family (2012). www.intel.com/content/dam/www/public/us/en/documents/datasheets/4th-gen-core-family-desktop-vol-2-datasheet.pdf. Accessed 25 May 2015

Leopard, C.: Memory forensics and the Macintosh OS X operating system. M.S. thesis, U.S. Naval Postgraduate School, June 2015

Ligh, M., Case, A., Levy, J., Walters, A.: Art of Memory Forensics. Wiley, Indianapolis (2014)

Rekall Team: Rekall Memory Forensic Framework: About the Rekall Memory Forensic Framework (2015). www.rekall-forensic.com/about.html. Accessed 13 March 2015

Stuttgen, J., Cohen, M.: Anti-forensic resilient memory acquisition. Digital Invest. **10**, S105–S115 (2013)

Volatility foundation: the volatility foundation – open source memory forensics (2015). www.volatilityfoundation.org/#!about/cmf3. Accessed 13 March 2015

Sketch-Based Modeling and Immersive Display Techniques for Indoor Crime Scene Presentation

Pu Ren[1,2], Mingquan Zhou[1,2], Jin Liu[3], Yachun Fan[1,2],
Wenshuo Zhao[4], and Wuyang Shui[1,2(✉)]

[1] College of Information Science and Technology,
Beijing Normal University, Beijing, China
sissun@126.com
[2] Engineering Research Center for Virtual Reality Applications,
MOE, Beijing, China
[3] Institute of Forensic Science, Ministry of Public Security, Beijing, China
[4] General Office, Ministry of Public Security, Beijing, China

Abstract. The reconstruction of crime scene plays an important role in digital forensic application. Although the 3D scanning technique is popular in general scene reconstruction, it has great limitation in the practice use of crime scene presentation. This article integrates computer graphics, sketch-based modeling and virtual reality (VR) techniques to develop a low-cost and rapid 3D crime scene presentation approach, which can be used by investigators to analyze and simulate the criminal process. First, we constructed a collection of 3D models for indoor crime scenes using various popular techniques, including laser scanning, image-based modeling and software-modeling. Second, to quickly obtain an object of interest from the 3D model database that is consistent with the geometric structure of the real object, a sketch-based retrieval method was proposed. Finally, a rapid modeling system that integrates our database and retrieval algorithm was developed to quickly build a digital crime scene. For practical use, an interactive real-time virtual roaming application was developed in Unity 3D and a low-cost VR head-mounted display (HMD). Practical cases have been implemented to demonstrate the feasibility and availability of our method.

Keywords: Forensic science · Indoor crime scene presentation
3D model database · Sketch-based retrieval · Rapid modeling
Immersive display

1 Introduction

In case of criminal incidents, the first phase of inspection and investigation is to rapidly record a complete, objective crime scene representation without erroneous information [1]. In comparison to traditional methods, i.e., verbal descriptions, hand-drawn sketches, photos, videos, etc., the use of 3D crime scene presentation is more intuitive and effective [2, 3]. Although 2D photos, videos and spherical photographs have been used in the courtroom, there are challenges in using these resources to describe and present the crime

© ICST Institute for Computer Sciences, Social Informatics and Telecommunications Engineering 2018
P. Matoušek and M. Schmiedecker (Eds.): ICDF2C 2017, LNICST 216, pp. 181–194, 2018.
https://doi.org/10.1007/978-3-319-73697-6_14

scene because these resources only provide information from a given view [4, 5]. 3D presentation enables investigators to virtually experience the crime scene, measure the distances between different objects and simulate the criminal activity. A powerful and effective way of presenting a 3D crime scene was proposed in this context.

In recent studies of forensic investigation, the use of a terrestrial laser scanner (TLS) or RGB-D camera has become a popular technique for the acquisition of 3D models of indoor crime scenes and evidence. The time-of-flight laser scanner, structure-light scanner and triangulation-based scanner have been used to acquire both the large-scale geometric information of crime scenes and the small-scale geometric information of evidence and victims [1, 3, 4, 6, 7]. These noninvasive scanners can be used to accurately generate a digital model after registration of range images and mesh processing. However, these devices are always expensive and the generation of digital models from unorganized point clouds is always based on manual and expert procedures. It is difficult to widely promote the application of this technique in local police stations. To address this problem, another type of modeling method is to produce a realistic 3D digital model from a series of images, the procedures for which comprise camera calibration, dense point-cloud computation, surface reconstruction and post-processing [8–11]. The quality of a reconstructed model depends largely upon the algorithm used to calculate feature correspondence and camera calibration. Furthermore, it is time consuming and expensive to use these optical device based methods.

Considering investigators would like to quickly represent the spatial information of crime scenes, the use of professional software, for example AutoCAD, 3Ds Max, SketchUp, etc., is the most common, intensive and powerful technique for 3D crime scene representation [12–15]. However, one potential problem of this technique is that investigators have no professional training or experience in producing 3D models using software. In addition, this work is tedious and time consuming, because hundreds of 3D models should be generated for a crime scene.

We have observed that in traditional practical crime investigations, policemen are often tasked with recording the indoor layout in hand-drawn sketches. Inspired by this observation and existing literature, this article presents an effective way to build a digital indoor crime scene to record the spatial relationships of objects for crime analysis and presentation. Additionally, rather than relying on sketches of the layout and objects, investigators can directly obtain a 3D scene using our system and explore this virtual scene anywhere and at any time.

2 Materials and Methods

2.1 A Specialized 3D Model Collection

The high quality and large number of 3D models in the collection improved the presentation of the 3D crime scene. By collecting more categories and a larger number of models in each category, one can retrieve a larger number of appropriate objects. In this study, we used existing laser-scanning, image-based modeling and software-modeling techniques to generate 3D models. We have constructed a 3D model database including crime-related models and common models in indoor scenes.

Some objects that appear in a crime scene are unique and cannot be replaced by the existing models in the database. Thus, we used laser-scanning and image-based modeling techniques to capture real data of critical evidence. We used a high-precision hand-held laser scanner HandySCAN 700 (Creaform Company, Canada) to reconstruct 3D models of objects. The benefit of this laser scanner is that it automatically produces complete single mesh models, without the procedure of manual range-image registration in other scanners (e.g., Vivid 910 laser scanner). Figure 1 shows some examples of 3D models captured by laser scanner. In addition to some crime tools there are two shoes and soles (usually very important evidence) in this figure. The main benefit of this technique is that it acquires high-quality 3D models with more details. However, the high cost of the device prohibits its widespread use.

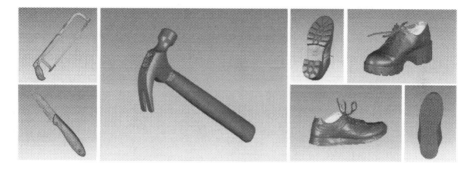

Fig. 1. 3D models capture by laser scanner. (Crime-fighting tools and shoe soles.)

The structure-from-motion (SFM) technique is used as a substitute in cases in which the laser scanner cannot be used. Inputting a set of photos of the object, a powerful and free tool called VisualSFM [16, 17] was used to generate a dense 3D point cloud with color. Figure 2 shows some examples of 3D models acquired by the SFM technique.

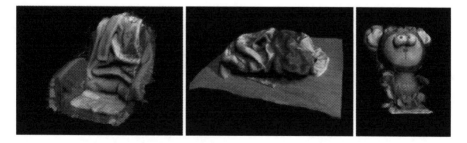

Fig. 2. 3D models reconstructed by SFM technique. Left: a chair with clothes on it. Middle: a mass of clothes. Right: a plush toy. (Color figure online)

To construct a mesh model from point clouds, the open-source software Meshlab was used to realize surface reconstruction and post-processing [18]. In Meshlab, the normal vector at every point was estimated and the Poisson surface reconstruction algorithm was used to generate a mesh model. This technique is easier to use than 3D scanning since it is convenient to acquire multiple photos for evidence.

To extend the number and categories of 3D models, we collected 3D models from online public-domain galleries, such as the Google 3D Warehouse, which offers thousands of models online [12], and the public database from literature [19]. As a supplement, some models were created by professional designers using geometric modeling software. Figure 3 shows some examples of 3D models created using commercial software (SketchUp, 3Ds Max). Figure 3(a) shows 3D models of furniture. Moreover, the victim's posture plays a significant role in crime investigation. Thus, multiple types of human models with various postures are available in our database to ensure that the most similar one to the real situation would be found (Fig. 3(b)). In summary, we offered a total of 2,564 models and 18 categories in our collection, including windows, doors, home appliances, furniture, human bodies, and criminal tools. Table 1 lists the main types of models from different sources in our database. The decisive evidence refers to some material evidence which play a decisive role in the real investigation.

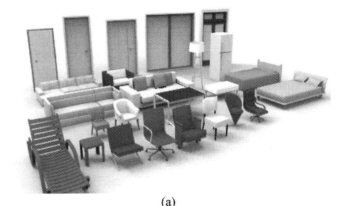

(a)

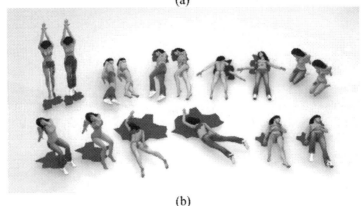

(b)

Fig. 3. A collection of 3D models in the crime scene. (a) Furniture models with various shapes. (b) Human models with various postures.

Table 1. 3D model database.

Source	Online libraries	Open literature	Software modeling	Laser scanning	Image-based modeling	Total
Indoor models	1,123	659	361	0	18	2,161
Murder related	240	0	135	12	6	393
Decisive evidence	0	0	2	3	5	10
Total						2,564

2.2   Method

I. Sketch-based indoor scene modeling

It is a challenge to rapidly obtain the appropriate model from large collections of 3D models since public collections are often insufficiently annotated [20]. To address this problem, the content-based retrieval technique is a powerful and effective tool. The general idea of the sketch-based method is that the user retrieves the desired model through the input of a hand drawing. In this study, our sketch-based retrieval was divided into two stages: offline index and online query. To save time in a real-time query, we perform the computation offline as much as possible. Figure 4 shows the framework of our algorithm and Fig. 5 shows one of the retrieval results. The input sketch is shown on the upper left, and the first couch model is the most similar model in the database. The key steps of our algorithm are described below.

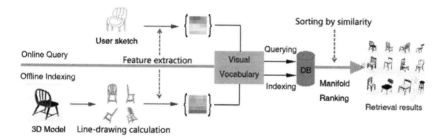

Fig. 4. The framework of our sketch-based retrieval algorithm.

Fig. 5. Retrieval results using sketch-based technique. The left figure shows an input of hand drawing by user. Right figure shows the first nine most similar models.

Step 1: Line-drawing calculation. The essence of 3D model retrieval is to evaluate the similarity between hand-drawn sketches and models. Towards this end, 3D information should be first projected into 2D images. 2D line drawings are extracted from 102 viewpoints of geodesic geometry for each model in the database, reflecting the visual information as much as possible. Different from most of the previous line-drawing extraction algorithms, which were only available for homogeneously distributed dense meshes, we proposed a depth map-based difference-of-Gaussian (DoG) method to extract lines, including the boundaries and creases formed by differences in depth. The information in the depth buffer is used to generate depth images with different Gaussian parameters, called D1 and D2, and the line drawing is generated by calculating the inverse of binary image, i.e., the Gaussian difference of D1 and D2. To overcome the saw tooth noise problem, the Bezier curve approximation is used to perform the line stylization and obtain a smooth contour line [22].

Step 2: Feature extraction. We used a spatial, high-dimensional local feature-description algorithm to extract features. As a type of short-time Fourier transform, Gabor transform is sensitive to the edges of an image. It can provide good selection for frequency and orientation. In addition, the Gabor filter is similar to the mammalian visual system in the expression of frequency and orientation. It is suitable for sketch retrieval requests. Thus, we use an algorithm called the Space Pyramid of Gabor Local Feature Extraction and obtain better results [20]. Next, we define a set of Gabor filters $g_i(i = 1, 2, \ldots, k)$ to calculate the basic transform of the feature region, and the information on the spatial distribution is obtained in the space pyramid of the image. For each g_i and image I, a convolution computation is employed to obtain a response image R_i:

$$R_i = \|\text{idft}(g_i * \text{dft}(I))\| \tag{1}$$

where $*$ denotes point-wise multiplication, and the function dft() and idft() respectively denote the discrete Fourier transform and the inverse discrete Fourier transform. A grid-sampling method is used for feature-point sampling. For a local shape feature, we divide the region into $n \times n$ cells C_{rc}, in which r and c respectively denote the row and column coordinates. The descriptor in the i direction is a feature vector of size $n \times n$.

$$F(r, c, i) = \frac{1}{N} \sum_{(x,y) \in C_{rc}} R_i(x, y) \tag{2}$$

where N denotes the sample number for which $R_i(x, y) \neq 0$ in the i direction. The local feature is a $k \times n \times n$ dimensional vector.

Step 3: Sorting by similarity. We employed TF-IDF [21] to calculate the similarities of feature vectors among various models. In an ideal situation, the first-place model is the desired model, and then we import it into the crime scene. As the retrieval algorithm is not the focus of this work, readers can find more complete algorithm details in our other work [22].

II. System interface

Our system was developed on the basis of open-source software SweetHome3D licensed under the GNU General Public License [23]. We developed the sketch-based algorithm in Microsoft Visual Studio in C++ and exported to a Dynamic-link library (dll) file. This dll file was imported as a plugin on a new user interface implementing sketch-based function. Our proposed 3D crime scene representation system contains five modules (see Fig. 6): (a) the user draw a sketch of the desired from any viewpoint at the left-top area, and the retrieval results are displayed on the bottom, sorted according to similarity; (b) a 2D plan view that referring to the ichnography, can be loaded into this module as a base map where the layout of the indoor scene and the selected model can be transformed to the designated location (translation, rotation and scale); (c) a 3D display view where the 3D model scene corresponding to the 2D plan view is displayed and the user can observe the scene from any view and roam the scene as a virtual character; (d) a model classification and viewing tree in which a collection of 3D models is classified according to the given classification scheme and every model can be selected and viewed; and (e) a scene management interface where the parameters and statues of every model can be edited.

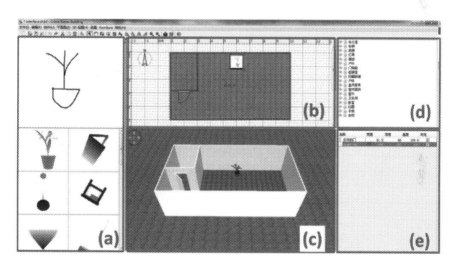

Fig. 6. Interface of our system. (a) Sketch retrieval interface. (b) 2D plan view. (c) 3D display view. (d) Model classification and viewing tree. (e) Scene management interface.

The major advantage of our system is that simple 2D sketches can be rapidly transformed into a complex 3D crime scene. In the first stage, users need to draw a sketch on the sketch-retrieval interface to obtain the desired objects from the database directly. Second, the retrieved models are placed on the 2D plane view and the corresponding 3D scene is simultaneously rendered on the 3D display view. The user can either view the 3D scene from any directions or roam in it anywhere and at any time. In the scene-management module, users can adjust the parameters and status of the chosen model, including visibility, texture, object position and size. Another notable feature of our system is that it is easy to measure the distance between two objects (Fig. 7). In the 3D scene shown in (a), the distance between the body and the murder weapon can be easily measured by connecting them with a line as shown in (b). Finally, the 3D crime-scene representation can be exported as a standard .obj files.

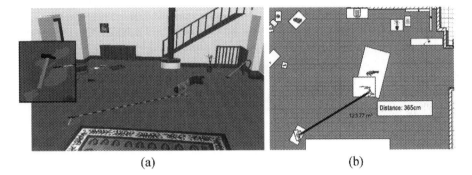

(a)   (b)

Fig. 7. The distance measuring function of the system.

III. Immersive display

As a supplement to the virtual roaming function provided by our system, a helmet-mounted display (HMD) device, such as HTC Vive, can be used to increase the immersive VR effect. This device has a high resolution of pixels, resulting in a resolution of pixels for each eye. HTC Vive provides a pair of handheld controllers and positioning-system tracking display, which allow the user to move within a certain scope and interact with the virtual scene using the handle [4]. These advantages are very suitable for the virtual representation of crime scenes.

Utilizing the encapsulated SDK in the cross-platform game engine Unity3D (Unity Technologies, San Francisco, USA), we developed a VR roaming system for crime scenes. The 3D model scene built with our proposed sketch-based indoor-scene system can be imported into Unity3D and real-time interactive virtual-experience systems are developed using Microsoft Visual Studio C#. In comparison to the traditional PC screen, the immersive display offers a larger viewing volume and more realistic experience. With the headset and handle, the investigator can enter the crime scene in digital space, observe 3D models of physical evidence, and analyze the case from a more intuitive angle.

3   Illustrative Example

To demonstrate the availability and effectiveness of our system, we quickly present an example of how to create an acceptable 3D crime scene for presentation from series of 2D sketches. We took a criminal case happened fifteen years ago as an example;

specifically, three adults and one child were killed in an apartment (Fig. 8). The only remaining visual documents for this case are several low-resolution photos and a hand-drawn floor plan of the crime scene. Using our system, we can rapidly reconstruct this indoor scene and develop a roaming system in VR space.

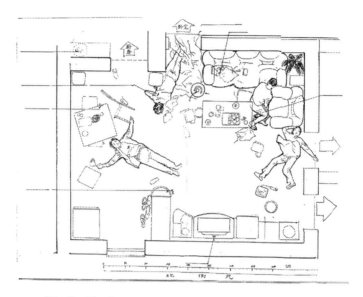

Fig. 8. The floor plan of the crime scene in our example.

Although very few visual records of this case are available, the floor plan is a crucial piece of physical evidence for crime-scene reconstruction. By importing the hand-drawn floor plan into our system as a base map, we obtained the measurements and layout information of 3D models (Fig. 9a). Then, the user dragged the mouse to draw 2D shapes of walls on the 2D plan view according to the tracing lines of the imported base map, and the 3D scene was rendered in the 3D display view in real time (Fig. 9b). To enable the accurate representation of the 3D crime scene, the user scaled each shape according to the real measurement values, i.e., user defined the length, height and width of the indoor scene. The main contribution of our approach is the sketch retrieval function in this system. Figure 9c shows an example of retrieving the sofa. The retrieved model was imported into the 2D plan view and placed at the designated location, according to the base map. All the textures of imported models can be exchanged according to the real scenario (Fig. 9d). These steps were repeated until all objects were imported and transformed to the correct locations.

Figure 10 shows the 3D scene of this crime that was constructed using our system, which consisted of a total of 58 digital models and was rebuilt in a total of 13 min. The top two screenshots are bird's eye view and the bottom two are roaming perspective.

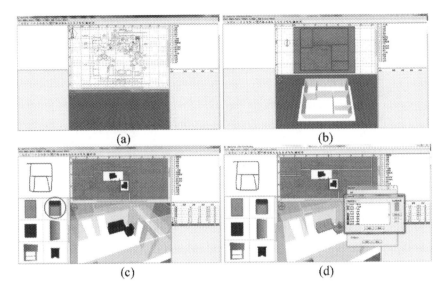

Fig. 9. Sketch-based modeling for the indoor crime scene. (a) Importing the hand-drawn floor plan as a base map. (b) Reconstruct the walls. (c) Retrieving 3D models by sketches. (d) Changing the textures.

Fig. 10. The creation of 3D indoor crime scene using our system.

To virtually experience this crime scene in an immersive display, the created crime scene can be exported as a standard .obj file, and an interactive virtual roaming system was developed in Unity3D, enabling investigators to experience the crime scene from a fixed viewpoint or different views to examine more details of the evidence of interest. Figure 11 shows the immersive roaming effect using HTC Vive. In this application, the user can intuitively simulate and analysis the shooting and walking routes of the criminal in the virtual space.

Fig. 11. Interactive crime scene experience in the immersive display using HTC Vive. Left: photo of the experiencer. Right: real-time screenshot.

4 Discussion

In comparison to traditional recording approaches, e.g., 2D hand-drawn sketches, photos, videos, 3D digital scenes and animations have been used to enhance clarity and understanding in crime-scene investigation [2, 3, 7, 12, 14]. Although the laser-scanning technique provides life-like and accurate 3D models of crime scenes, it has limitations for widely promotion. For one hand, the devices are expensive. For another hand, it is still a great challenge to convert dense triangle meshes (more than hundreds of thousands of triangle meshes) into a simplified model to meet the requirement of real-time virtual experience. Another limitation is that many crime scenes cannot be entered after the criminal incident. In this situation, investigators need to model the scene manually. Clair et al. introduced the application of the easy-to-use modeling software SketchUp (version 8) to generate 3D indoor crime-scene models [12]. It was an extremely time-consuming process to generate every model. To solve this problem, Howard et al. constructed a collection of 3D models and generated the non-critical areas of digital crime scenes using the existing models [14].

One of the contributions of our work is utilizing multiple techniques to construct a large collection of 3D models for indoor scene. The 3D models with complex structures and more details, e.g., guns, knives, shoe soles, etc., were generated by laser-scanning or image-based modeling techniques. To enable real-time rendering of this model in Unity 3D, the open-source Meshlab software was used to convert this 3D model to a simplified model and texture.

Another contribution of our work is the sketch-based model retrieval. Because of the large number of models in the collection, investigators have become more comfortable and it has become easier to generate a crime scene by our method. However, it is also a challenge for investigator to rapidly obtain the desired model from datasets. Compared with the traditional text-based retrieval methods, the 2D hand-drawn sketch-based approach has much more potential in our application since few annotations are available for each 3D model. In this paper, we propose a sketch-based approach to obtain a suitable model with geometric structure similar to that of the real object from the database. To achieve real-time retrieval, we have extracted and archived the feature lines of every model in advance. Because of this main part of our work, crime scenes can be rebuilt quickly using policemen's hand-drawn sketches rather than those of professional designers.

To better provide a crime-scene model, a multi-participant, large-screen stereoscopic projector system [14], an immersive display VR headset [4], and the augmented-reality technique have been used in previous studies [24]. In our article, we provided a general system covering the functions of rebuilding an indoor crime scene and rendering it in 3D space. To realize immersive display, the rebuilt scene model was imported into Unity 3D to develop a VR roaming system in HTC Vive.

There are still some limitations of our approach. We have successfully extended the crime scene model database, but both the number of category in the database and the number of models in each category are insufficient for crime-scene presentation. We will continue to generate multiple kinds of models to build an extensive crime-scene model database. A system allowing the user to retrieve multiple 3D models at the same time is also helpful in practice.

5   Conclusion

Based on the 3D model collection, a sketch-retrieval based modeling system was developed. Because of the TF-IDF algorithm, our method achieves high retrieval accuracy and time efficiency. Using our approach, police investigators can rapidly record the spatial relationships of objects while constructing a digital model of the indoor crime scene. In comparison to laser-scanning and software-modeling techniques, the main advantage of our method is that it is low cost and rapid, making it very suitable for criminal investigation. In terms of digital forensics and educational training applications, the immersive-display we developed has broad prospects because of the VR interactive experience in the crime scene.

Acknowledgement. The authors would like to thank the anonymous reviewers. Special thanks to all the members of SweetHome3D project. This work is supported by the National Natural Science Foundation of China (No. 61402042), the open subject of the key laboratory of traces of science and technology of Ministry of Public Security (No. 2014FMKFKT04) and the National Key Technology Research and Development Program of China (No. 2012BAH33F04).

References

1. Sansoni, G., Cattaneo, C., Trebeschi, M., Gibelli, D., Poppa, P., Porta, D., et al.: Scene-of-crime analysis by a 3-dimensional optical digitizer: a useful perspective for forensic science. Am. J. Forensic Med. Pathol. **32**, 280–286 (2011)
2. Ma, M., Zheng, H., Lallie, H.: Virtual reality and 3D animation in forensic visualization. J. Forensic Sci. **55**, 1227–1231 (2010)
3. Hołowko, E., Januszkiewicz, K., Bolewicki, P., Sitnik, R., Michoński, J.: Application of multi-resolution 3D techniques in crime scene documentation with bloodstain pattern analysis. Forensic Sci. Int. **267**, 218–227 (2016)
4. Ebert, L.C., Nguyen, T.T., Breitbeck, R., Braun, M., Thali, M.J., Ross, S.: The forensic holodeck: an immersive display for forensic crime scene reconstructions. Forensic Sci. Med. Pathol. **10**, 623–626 (2014)
5. Tung, N.D., Barr, J., Sheppard, D.J., Elliot, D.A., Tottey, L.S., Walsh, K.A.: Spherical photography and virtual tours for presenting crime scenes and forensic evidence in New Zealand courtrooms. J. Forensic Sci. **60**, 753–758 (2015)
6. González-Jorge, H., Zancajo, S., González-Aguilera, D., Arias, P.: Application of Kinect gaming sensor in forensic science. J. Forensic Sci. **60**, 206–211 (2015)
7. Buck, U., Naether, S., Räss, B., Jackowski, C., Thali, M.J.: Accident or homicide–virtual crime scene reconstruction using 3D methods. Forensic Sci. Int. **225**, 75–84 (2013)
8. Gibson, S., Howard, T.: Interactive reconstruction of virtual environments from photographs, with application to scene-of-crime analysis. In: ACM Symposium on Virtual Reality Software and Technology, pp. 41–48 (2000)
9. Se, S., Jasiobedzki, P.: Instant scene modeler for crime scene reconstruction. In: 2005 IEEE Computer Society Conference on Computer Vision and Pattern Recognition Workshops, CVPR 2005, pp. 123–128. IEEE (2005)
10. Leipner, A., Baumeister, R., Thali, M.J., Braun, M., Dobler, E., Ebert, L.C.: Multi-camera system for 3D forensic documentation. Forensic Sci. Int. **261**, 123–128 (2016)
11. Bostanci, E.: 3D reconstruction of crime scenes and design considerations for an interactive investigation tool. Computer Science, pp. 896–900 (2015)
12. Clair, E.S., Maloney, A., Schade, A.: An introduction to building 3D crime scene models using SketchUp. J. Assoc. Crime Scene Reconstr. **18**, 29–47 (2012)
13. Maksymowicz, K., Tunikowski, W., Kościuk, J.: Crime event 3D reconstruction based on incomplete or fragmentary evidence material–case report. Forensic Sci. Int. **242**, e6–e11 (2014)
14. Howard, T.L., Murta, A.D., Gibson, S.: Virtual environments for scene of crime reconstruction and analysis. In: Electronic Imaging: International Society for Optics and Photonics, pp. 41–48 (2000)
15. Bevel, T., Gardner, R.M.: Bloodstain Pattern Analysis with an Introduction to Crime Scene Reconstruction. CRC Press, Boca Raton (2008)
16. Wu, C.: Towards linear-time incremental structure from motion. In: 2013 International Conference on 3D Vision-3DV 2013, pp. 127–134. IEEE (2013)
17. Jancosek, M., Pajdla, T.: Multi-view reconstruction preserving weakly-supported surfaces. In: 2011 IEEE Conference on Computer Vision and Pattern Recognition (CVPR), pp. 3121–3128. IEEE (2011)
18. Cignoni, P., Callieri, M., Corsini, M., Dellepiane, M., Ganovelli, F., Ranzuglia, G.: MeshLab: an open-source mesh processing tool, pp. 129–136. Eurographics Association (2008)

19. Fisher, M., Ritchie, D., Savva, M., Funkhouser, T., Hanrahan, P.: Example-based synthesis of 3D object arrangements. ACM Trans. Graph. **31**, 135 (2012)
20. Eitz, M., Richter, R., Boubekeur, T., Hildebrand, K., Alexa, M.: Sketch-based shape retrieval. ACM Trans. Graph. **31**, 31:1–31:10 (2012)
21. Zobel, J., Moffat, A.: Inverted files for text search engines. ACM Comput. Surv. **38**, 1–56 (2006). Article no. 6
22. Qian, L., Fan, Y., Zhou, M., Luan, H., Ren, P.: Manifold ranking for sketch-based 3D model retrieval. In: Pan, Z., Cheok, A.D., Müller, W., Zhang, M. (eds.) Transactions on Edutainment XIII. LNCS, vol. 10092, pp. 149–164. Springer, Heidelberg (2017). https://doi.org/10.1007/978-3-662-54395-5_14
23. http://www.sweethome3d.com/
24. Gee, A.P., Escamilla-Ambrosio, P.J., Webb, M., Mayol-Cuevas, W., Calway, A.: Augmented crime scenes: virtual annotation of physical environments for forensic investigation. In: Proceedings of the 2nd ACM Workshop on Multimedia in Forensics, Security and Intelligence, pp. 105–110. ACM (2010)

An Overview of the Usage of Default Passwords

Brandon Knieriem, Xiaolu Zhang, Philip Levine, Frank Breitinger[✉],
and Ibrahim Baggili

Cyber Forensics Research and Education Group (UNHcFREG),
Tagliatela College of Engineering, University of New Haven,
West Haven, CT 06516, USA
{bknie1,plevi1}@unh.newhaven.edu,
{XZhang,FBreitinger,IBaggili}@newhaven.edu

Abstract. The recent Mirai botnet attack demonstrated the danger of
using default passwords and showed it is still a major problem. In this
study we investigated several common applications and their password
policies. Specifically, we analyzed if these applications: (1) have default
passwords or (2) allow the user to set a weak password (i.e., they do not
properly enforce a password policy). Our study shows that default passwords are still a significant problem: 61% of applications inspected initially used a default or blank password. When changing the password, 58%
allowed a blank password, 35% allowed a weak password of 1 character.

Keywords: Default passwords · Applications · Usage · Security

1 Introduction

In October 2016, a large section of the Internet came under attack. This attack
was perpetuated by approximately 100,000 Internet of Things (IoT) appliances,
refrigerators, and microwaves which were compromised and formed the Mirai
botnet. Targets of this attack included *Twitter*, *reddit* and *The New York Times*
all of which shut down for hours. The Mirai botnet was created by abusing
default credentials in IoT devices [7,14]. Besides devices, there are also applications permitting users access to critical central resources such as Database Management Systems (DBMS), Web Server Applications, and Content Management
Systems (CMS). For instance, in July 2014 hackers attacked HealthCare.gov [18].
Fifteen days later HealthCare.gov released a statement that only the test servers
were hacked and no personal information was compromised. The attack occurred
because the manufacturer's default password on the server had not been changed.
Days later, despite reporting on this vulnerability, the default password had still
not been updated [2].

These findings motivated us to perform two short surveys with the goal to
start a discussion in the field about the usage of develop passwords: The first was
to examine applications such as DBMS, Web Server Applications, and CMSs
that enable a default password during initial configuration. Results show the

ⓒ ICST Institute for Computer Sciences, Social Informatics and Telecommunications Engineering 2018
P. Matoušek and M. Schmiedecker (Eds.): ICDF2C 2017, LNICST 216, pp. 195–203, 2018.
https://doi.org/10.1007/978-3-319-73697-6_15

most applications have default credentials. The second survey was conducted on developers to understand the use of default passwords. The results indicate that many services are designed with default passwords to bypass authentication to provide immediate, temporary access for quick, convenient initial set up of infrastructure and should only be used during this installation phase.

Remark: The extended version of this article named 'An Overview of the Usage of Default Passwords (extended version)' can be accessed through digital commons[1].

2   Literature Review

"Passwords are an ubiquitous and critical component of many security systems" [19]. Therefore, it is important to create secure passwords that are difficult to compromise. For instance, according to [9], a strong password policy requires a minimum number of characters, different types of characters, and specify how frequently users should change their passwords. More recently, National Institutes of Standards and Technology (NIST) Digital Authentication Guidelines have suggestions for improving security and reduce common issues [6]. These suggestions can be broken down into several main categories: hashing passwords, increasing user friendliness, enforcing an 8-character minimum, and banning common passwords. It suggests avoiding password rules, password hints, security questions, and never forcing arbitrary password changes [22]. These suggestions are a step in the right direction for new password policy, though despite being nearly a year old, have yet to be implemented by many application developers.

2.1   Breaches Exploiting Default User Credentials

Although guidelines and warnings regarding default passwords exist, there are still many incidents involving default credentials. According to [4], "very few open source vendor advisories have mentioned default passwords, whereas they appear with some regularity in closed source advisories, even in the top 10 [vulnerabilities] as recently as 2005".

A newer study named the Verizon Data Breach Report examined 621 corporate breaches. "The analysis found that 78% of initial intrusions into corporate networks were elementary. Many attackers use a phishing attack, convincing employees to give up credentials, or brute force attack, taking advantage of weak or default passwords on remote services to gain initial access to the network" [20]. Unfortunately, the report did not mention, out of 78% how many constituted weak passwords or default passwords. Notwithstanding, some of the recent breaches that were attributed to the misuse of default passwords. Utah Department of Health] suffered a breach of 780 k Medicaid patient health records [12] in addition to compromising more than 255,000 social security numbers [17]. Attackers achieved complete access to the system using a default password.

---

[1] http://digitalcommons.newhaven.edu.

A Bank of Montreal's ATM was hacked by two 14 year old children; they used the machine's default password [11]. Emergency Alert System (EAS)] equipment used to broadcast warnings was hacked by exploiting default passwords. After the breach, the hackers sent out an alert warning the public of a 'zombie attack.' [11]. Electronic Highway Billboards were attacked in June 2014. The hacker changed the signs to display their Twitter/hacker handle for all the highway drivers to see. This was an act of mischief reported by [8].

A recent WordPress incident demonstrated that the usage of a default username can result in a tremendous security risk. In case of WordPress, the default username is always 'admin'. Hackers used that knowledge and used a botnet to brute force 90,000 IP addresses hosting different software [1]. Unfortunately, the report did not release how successful this attack was.

2.2 Taking Advantage of Default Passwords - Tools, Scripts and Malware

Attackers, often taking an opportunistic approach, realized the potential in abusing default passwords to access a system. Thus, there are several tools, scripts, and malware that can be used for this purpose. Work [16] states "the most common password lists found using Internet search engines were default password lists. These lists contain passwords used by hardware manufacturers as the default security setting". In a recent article, [3] mentioned several tools that focus on exploiting default passwords. For instance, Cisco OCS Perl Script scans Cisco devices on a network by inputting 'cisco' into the password form. Metasploit includes multiple modules used for network default password scanning.

On the other hand, several worms exist that use default passwords to propagate. According to [13], the 'Voyager Alpha Force' worm was used to demonstrate a vulnerability on Microsoft's SQL Server with an administrator blank password using the default port: 1433. Similarly, MySQL required no password at the time of installation. A worm named "MySpooler" infected 8000 hosts at a rate of 100 hosts per hour [10]. In 2005, an anonymous developer disclosed a proof-of-concept worm that targeted Oracle databases using default usernames and passwords [23]. A particularly malicious worm implementation uses blending viruses; which are viruses that run a daily Internet scan for vulnerabilities. One of the main functions of them are to find well known default passwords [5].

Work [15] triggered malnets; a combination of malware and bots initiated malware attacks on routers. A similar experiment was also performed by [24]. Regarding wireless malware propagation: 16.7% of routers were set to be configured with default settings. Only 10% of these routers used default passwords or did not have passwords set.

3 Applications Analysis

To analyze the impact of default passwords we examined database management systems, Web server applications, and content management systems. We decided to focus on web applications as they are easily accessible and cater to a broad audience. More precisely, we investigated Relational Database Management Systems (RDBMS), Web Server Applications (WSA), and Content Management Systems (CMS). After locating a comprehensive list containing the major applications in all three categories, our methodology is as (1) For each identified application, search for documentation and identify the default credentials/settings. (2) Download and install a free or evaluation version of each application. Prioritize installation on Windows 10 (64-bit), then Ubuntu Linux 16.04.2, and finally Mac OS Sierra 10.12.5. Use default configurations and procedure; do not use advanced or customized installation options. (3) If a default database is not created during installation, create one immediately after installation. (4) Note any prompts, or lack thereof, regarding security policy enforcement. (5) Assign each conclusive application a password policy quality value on a scale of 0 to 4. This was loosely based on an IBM's classification [21].

3.1   Results

In total, $n = 90$ applications were analyzed where 62 applications yielded conclusive results and 28^2 had inconclusive results due to licensing restrictions. An overview of the results is given in Table 1. Of the 62 conclusive applications, 41 applications had commercial licenses and 21 were open source. To analyze the applications, 51 applications were installed on Windows 10 (64-bit), 8 were installed on Linux-x86, four were web services, and one was installed on Mac OS. Note, two applications were a pre-release version (0.1–0.9/Alpha/Beta), the remaining 60 applications were a release version (1.0+) (97%).

In total, 30 applications featured a default user name, the most frequent were "Admin" or "root". 6 (10%) applications featured a default password. 32 (52%) applications featured a default blank password for the default user account. All applications featuring a default password also featured a default user name.

Lastly, we analyzed the quality of the passwords according the IBM classification [21]. Overall, 36 (58%) applications were categorized as having a level 0 policy, 22 (35%) applications were categorized as having a level 1 policy. Two applications were categorized as having a level 2 policy. One application was categorized as having a level 3 policy. Finally, only one application that met the requirements for a level 4 policy, which is interesting as this is what most modern online portals require.

4   Qualitative Survey of Default Credential Use

This section tries to understand why default user credentials/passwords are still so widely used. Therefore, we created a question for software developers, computer engineers, and security experts: why many applications still come with a

---

[2] Actian Ingres, Actian Vector, CA Datacom, CA IDMS, Clarion, Clustrix, Empress Embedded Database, EXASolution, eXtremeDB, GroveSite, IBM PureSystems, Infobright, Linter, Microsoft Visual FoxPro, NexusDB V4 Windows, NonStop SQL, Openbase, Postgres Plus Advanced Server, R:Base, SAP ADS, SAP Anywhere, SAP HANA, SAP Sybase ASE, SAP Sybase IQ, SQL Azure, SQream DB, UniData, Vertica.

default user name password and do not require the user to set new credentials according to a reliable password policy? The question was distributed online in 20 software developer forums, advertised to 30 groups on Quora, and other forums.

Table 1. Surveyed applications

Name	Version/ release	Platform	Commercial/ open-source	License	Default username	Default password	Password policy quality
4th Dimension	16.1	Windows	Commercial	30-Day evaluation	"Administrator"	None	0
Adabas	2016 April	Windows	Commercial	Community edition	Inherits user account	Inherits user password	0
Alpha five	V12	Windows	Commercial	30-Day evaluation	"Admin"	None	0
Altibase	6.5	Linux-x86	Commercial	Community edition	None	None	0
Amazon aurora	N/A	Web-service	Commercial	N/A	None	None	2
Apache derby	10.13.1.1	Windows	Open-source	N/A	None	None	0
Apache OpenOffice.org base	4.1.3	Windows	Open-source	N/A	N/A	N/A	0
Apache trafodion	2.1.0	Windows	Open-source	N/A	None	None	1[b]
Base X	8.6	Windows	Open-source	Free version	"admin"	"admin"	0
ClickHouse	1.1.54189	Linux-x86	Open-source	N/A	None	None	0
CSQL	3.3	Linux-x86	Open-source	N/A	None	None	0
CUBRID	10.0.0.1376	Windows	Open-source	N/A	"admin"	"admin"	2[c]
Database management library (C++)	1.0	Windows	Open-source	N/A	None	None	0
DataEase	6.5 Demo	Windows	Commercial	N/A	"labadmin"	None	0
Dataphor	3.1.6143	Windows	Open-source	N/A	"admin"	None	0
dBase PLUS	11.2	Windows	Commercial	30-Day evaluation	None	None	0
Drupal	8.3.2	Windows	Commercial	Free version	None	None	1
EnterpriseDB	9.6	Windows	Commercial	Standard version	"postgresql"	None	1
FileMaker pro	15	Windows	Commercial	Trial version	"Admin"	None	0
Firebird	3.0.2	Windows	Open-source	N/A	N/A	N/A	1
FrontBase	8.28	Windows	Commercial	Free version	None	None	0
Google fusion tables	N/A	Web service	Commercial	Free version	Google account	Google account	3[d]
Greenplum	5.0.0-alpha.3	Linux-x86	Open-source	N/A	None	None	0
H2	1.4.195	Windows	Open-source	N/A	"sa"	None	0
Helix	7.0.2	Mac OS	Commercial	Demo version	None	None	0
HSQL	2.4.0	Windows	Open-source	N/A	"SA"	None	0
IBM DB2	11.1	Windows	Commercial	Trial version	"db2admin"	None	1

(continued)

Table 1. (*continued*)

Name	Version/ release	Platform	Commercial/ open-source	License	Default username	Default password	Password policy quality
IBM DB2 Express-C	11.1	Windows	Commercial	Trial version	"db2admin"	None	1
Informix enterprise	12.10	Windows	Commercial	Time-limited	"informix", "ifxjson"	None	0
InterBase	2017	Windows	Commercial	Trial version	"SYSDBA"	N/A	1
InterSystems CachÃ©	2017.1	Windows	Commercial	Evaluation Version	"_SYSTEM", "Admin", "SuperUser", "forensics", "CSPSystem"	N/A	1[b]
JBoss Web Console	6	Windows	Commercial	Free version	"Admin"	"Admin"	0
Joomla	3.7	Windows	Commercial	Free version	"admin"	None	1
LibreOffice base	5.3.3	Windows	Open-source	N/A	None	None	0
MariaDB	10.3	Windows	Open-source	Free version	"root"	N/A	1
Microsoft access	16.0	Windows	Commercial	Office 2016	None	None	0
Microsoft SQL server	2016 SP1	Windows	Commercial	Express edition	"sa"	None	0
Mimer SQL	10.1	Windows	Commercial	Trial version	"SYSADM"	N/A	1
MonetDB	11.25.21	Windows	Open-source	Free version	None	None	0
mSQL		Linux-x86	Commercial	Free version	"root"	None	0
MySQL	5.7.18.1	Windows	Commercial	Community edition	"root"	None	0
neo4j	3.2	Windows	Commercial	Evaluation	"neo4j"	None	1[a]
NexusDB	V4	Windows	Commercial	Server trial version	N/A	N/A	1
NuoDB database	2.6.1	Windows	Commercial	Community edition	"dba"	"goalie"	1[a]
NuoDB Domain		Web service	Commercial	Community edition	None	None	1
OpenLink virtuoso	6.0	Windows	Commerical	Trial version	N/A	N/A	1
Oracle RDBMS	7.3	Windows	Commerical	Free version	N/A	N/A	0
Oracle TimesTen		Windows	Commercial	Free version	N/A	N/A	1[b]
Orange HRM	3.3.1	Windows	Open-source	N/A	None	None	1[b]
Polyhedra	8.6.1	Windows	Commercial	Lite version	None	None	0
PostgreSQL	9.6	Windows	Open-source	N/A	"postgres"	None	0
RDM Server	8.4	Windows	Commercial	Trial version	N/A	N/A	1[b]
SAND CDBMS	8.1	Windows	Commercial	Free version	"DBA"	None	0
SAP MaxDB	7.8.02.39	Windows	Commercial	Free	"DBADMIN"	N/A	1
ScimoreDB	4.0	Windows	Commercial	Freeware	None	None	0
SQLBase	12.0	Windows	Commercial	Trial version	"SERVER1"	"SECRET"	0
SQLite	3.18	Windows	Open-source	N/A	None	None	0
Tableau (local)	10.2.2 64-bit	Windows	Commercial	14-Day evaluation	N/A	N/A	0
Tableau (online)	10.2.2 64-bit	Windows	Commercial	14-Day evaluation	N/A	N/A	4

(*continued*)

Table 1. (*continued*)

Name	Version/ release	Platform	Commercial/ open-source	License	Default username	Default password	Password policy quality
Tibero	6.0	Windows	Commercial	30-Day evaluation	"root", "sys", "syscat", "sysgis", "outln", "tibero", "tibero1"	"tibero", "tibero", "syscat", "sysgis", "outln", "tmax", "tmax"	1
txtSQL	3.0.0b	Windows	Open-source	N/A	"root"	None	0
Wordpress	4.7.4	Web service	Open-source	N/A	None	None	1

0: No password policy.
1: Password policy only requires a single character.
2: Requires a minimum number of characters but can be compromised without a computer.
3: Requires a minimum number of characters but can still likely be compromised with a computer.
4: Requires a minimum number of characters, numbers, and special characters, and would be difficult to compromise.
[a]: Fully custom credentials required.
[b]: Forces custom credentials following login with defaults.
[c]: Two-factor authentication required.

The question was also sent directly to 35 users on Quora who are known developers and 10 professors from the University of New Haven and the University of Bridgeport (IRB approval was obtained prior to the start). The question received high exposure; in one instance over 2,800 individuals accessed or viewed the question on Quora. However, the response rate was low. In total, we only received 20 responses. 6 users blamed the developers for writing a sloppy code. A Web Development project manager on Quora described a situation: "I ran across a custom WordPress/Yii app that used the same password by default. As the dev manager, I pointed out that this was a major flaw. Got told that it was but wasn't urgent. Until a hack happened..." The CEO of mid-size online company on LinkedIn explained a situation where a default password is used: "I need to install my Lazarus application on 20 clients. Can you imaging running through the setup process with password policies right from the start? Do you see how much more time you'll need to spend? ... I imagine you know the hassle of dealing with OS permissions, DB permissions (different user), application permissions, and then user roles. Yes, it is possible to have a security policy in place from the start, but do you see how much more difficult it gets?"

5   Discussion and Conclusion

Applications are designed to provide the best user experience to their customers and reduce setup time. Especially when the administrator needs to install the application on multiple devices in succession. The default passwords in this study demonstrate this by being easy to remember and utilize for multiple devices. For instance, most of applications used 'password', 'admin', 'dba' etc. as default passwords.

Many of these applications accepted a single character as a valid user name or password. A user may choose a more complex password, but because there is often no requirement for special characters or total character count, the user may choose the easiest, most convenient credential solution.

In summary, this article surveyed a well-known default password issue on 21 open-sourced applications and 41 commercial applications. Out of the 62 applications, we found that 32 applications featured a default user name, 6 applications featured a default password and 32 applications accepted empty passwords. In total, 38 applications surveyed can lead an administrator using default user credentials. Meanwhile, in order to evaluate the password policy we also scored the applications with IBM password quality scale. 36 of applications scored with '0', having no password policy. 22 of applications scored a '1', meaning that a single character password is acceptable, the weakest possible password policy. Only 4 applications had an acceptable password policy. To explain why practitioners may keep default user credentials of the DBMS on their own database system, we distributed a survey on Quora and responded by variety roles such as web developer, system manager, CEO etc. (Sect. 4).

Acknowledgements. Special thanks go to Mohammed Nasir who initially started this research project and Matthew Vastarelli for supporting us.

References

1. Booker, L.: Brute force attack targets WordPress sites with default admin username (2013)
2. Carroll, R.: Breached healthcare.gov server still had default password (2014)
3. Casey, B.: Network security risks: the trouble with default passwords (2014)
4. Christey, S., Martin, R.A.: Vulnerability type distributions in cve. Mitre report, May 2007
5. Gordineer, J.: Blended threats: a new era in anti-virus protection. Inf. Syst. Secur. **12**(3), 45–47 (2003)
6. Grassi, G.: Digital identity guidelines. National Institute of Standards and Technology (2016)
7. Hypponen, M., Nyman, L.: The internet of (vulnerable) things: on hypponen's law, security engineering, and IoT legislation. Technol. Innov. Manag. Rev. **7**(4), 5–11 (2017)
8. http://KrebsonSecurity.com. They hack because they can (2014)
9. Martins, F.: Creating strong password policy best practices (2014)
10. Northcutt, S.: The risk of default passwords (2007)
11. Pham, T.: Default passwords: breaching ATMs, highway signs and POS devices (2014)
12. Duo Security: Utah department of health (UDOH) breach (2012)
13. Microsoft Customer Support: An unsecured SQL server server that has a blank (NULL) system administrator password allows vulnerability to a worm (2005)
14. Symantec Security Response. Mirai: what you need to know about the botnet behind recent major DDoS attacks, Oct 2016

15. Traynor, P., Butler, K., Enck, W., McDaniel, P., Borders, K.: Malnets: large-scale malicious networks via compromised wireless access points. Secur. Commun. Netw. **3**(2–3), 102–113 (2010)
16. Van Heerden, R.P., Vorster, J.S.: Statistical analysis of large passwords lists, used to optimize brute force attacks (2009)
17. Vijayan, J.: Weak passwords still the downfall of enterprise security (2012)
18. Vinton, K.: Data breach bulletin: home depot, healthcare.gov, JP morgan (2014)
19. Vu, K.P.L., Proctor, R.W., Bhargav-Spantzel, A., Tai, B.L.B., Cook, J., Schultz, E.E.: Improving password security and memorability to protect personal and organizational information. Int. J. Hum. Comput. Stud. **65**(8), 744–757 (2007)
20. Westervelt, R.: Verizon data breach report finds employees at core of most attacks (2013)
21. Williams, C., Spanbauer, K.: Understanding password quality (2001)
22. Wisniewski: Naked security (2016)
23. Wright, J.: Oracle worm proof-of-concept (2005)
24. Zanero, S.: Wireless malware propagation: a reality check. IEEE Secur. Priv. **7**(5), 70–74 (2009)

Hacking

Automation of MitM Attack on Wi-Fi Networks

Martin Vondráček[(✉)], Jan Pluskal, and Ondřej Ryšavý

Brno University of Technology, Božetěchova 2, Brno, Czech Republic
xvondr20@stud.fit.vutbr.cz, {ipluskal,rysavy}@fit.vutbr.cz
http://www.fit.vutbr.cz/
https://mvondracek.github.io/wifimitm/

Abstract. Security mechanisms of wireless technologies often suffer weaknesses that can be exploited to perform Man-in-the-Middle attacks, allowing to eavesdrop or to spoof network communication. This paper focuses on possibilities of automation of these types of attacks using already available tools for specific tasks. Outputs of this research are the *wifimitm* Python package and the *wifimitmcli CLI* tool, both implemented in Python. The package provides functionality for automation of *MitM* attacks and can be used by other software. The *wifimitmcli* tool is an example of such software that can automatically perform multiple *MitM* attack scenarios without any intervention from an investigator.

The results of this research are intended to be used for automated penetration testing and to help with forensic investigation. Finally, a popularization of the fact that such severe attacks can be easily automated can be used to raise public awareness about information security.

Keywords: Man-in-the-Middle attack
Accessing secured wireless networks · Password cracking
Dictionary personalization · Tampering network topology
Impersonation · Phishing

1   Introduction

The main focus of this paper is security of wireless networks. It provides a study of widely used network technologies and mechanisms of wireless security. Analyzed technologies and security algorithms suffer weaknesses that can be exploited to perform Man-in-the-Middle attacks. A successful realization of this kind of attack allows not only to eavesdrop on all the victim's network traffic but also to spoof his communication [1], [16, pp. 101–120].

In an example scenario, the victim is a suspect conducting illegal activity on a target network. The attacker is a law-enforcement agency investigator with appropriate legal authorization to intercept the suspect's communication and to perform a direct attack on the network. In some cases, the suspect may be aware that his communication can be intercepted by the ISP[1] and harden his network.

---

[1] Internet Service Provider

© ICST Institute for Computer Sciences, Social Informatics and Telecommunications Engineering 2018
P. Matoušek and M. Schmiedecker (Eds.): ICDF2C 2017, LNICST 216, pp. 207–220, 2018.
https://doi.org/10.1007/978-3-319-73697-6_16

For example, he could use an overlay network technology, e.g., *VPN* (implemented by *L2TP*, *IPsec* [9, pp. 09–10], *PPTP*) or anonymization networks (Tor, I2P, etc.) to create an encrypted tunnel configured on his gateway, for all his external communication. This concept is easy to implement and does not require any additional configuration on endpoint devices. Generally, this would not be considered a properly secured network [5, pp. 425–431], but this scheme, or similar, is often used by large vendors like Cisco [2] or Microsoft [19] for branch office deployment and can also be seen in home routers[2]. In such cases, intercepting traffic on the ISP level would not yield meaningful results, because all the communication is encrypted by the hardening. On the other hand, direct attack on the suspect's LAN will intercept plain communication. But, even when an investigator is legally permitted to carry out such an attack to acquire evidence, it is scarcely used, because it requires expert domain knowledge. Thus, this process of evidence collection is very expensive and human resource demanding.

The aim of this research is to design, implement and test a tool able to automate the process of accessing a secured *WLAN* and to perform data interception. Furthermore, this tool should be able to tamper with the network to collect more evidence by redirecting traffic to place itself in the middle of the communication and tamper with it, to access otherwise encrypted data in plain form. Using the automated tool should not require any expert knowledge from the investigator.

We designed a generic framework, see Fig. 1, capable of accessing and acquiring evidence from a wireless network regardless of used security mechanisms. This framework can be split into several steps. First, it is necessary for an investigator to obtain access to the *WLAN* used by the suspect. Therefore, this research focuses on exploitable weaknesses of particular security mechanisms. Upon successful connection to the network, the investigator needs to tamper with the network topology. For this purpose, weaknesses of several network technologies can be exploited. From this point on, the investigator can start to capture and break the encryption on the suspect's communication.

Specialized tools focused on exploiting individual weaknesses in security mechanisms currently used by *WLAN*s are already available. There are also specialized tools focused on individual steps of *MitM* attacks. Tools that were analyzed and used in implementation of the *wifimitm* package are outlined in Sect. 2.

Based on the acquired knowledge, referenced studies and practical experience from manual experiments, authors were able to create an attack strategy which is composed of a suitable set of available tools. The strategy is then able to select and manage individual steps for a successful *MitM* attack tailored to a specific *WLAN*. This strategy also includes options for impersonation and phishing for situations, when the network is properly secured, and the weakest part of the overall security is the suspect.

The created software can perform a fully automated attack and requires zero knowledge. We tested the final implementation on carefully devised experiments,

---

[2] Asus RT-AC5300 – Merlin WRT has an option to tunnel all traffic thought Tor.

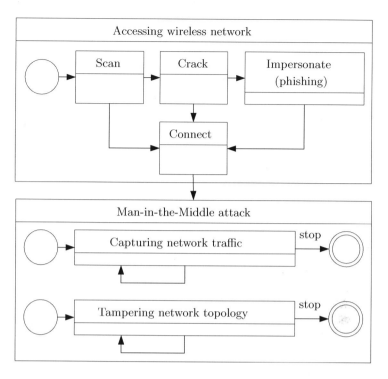

Fig. 1. During the first phase – *Accessing wireless network*, the tool is capable of an attack on *WEP OSA*, *WEP SKA*, *WPA PSK* and *WPA2 PSK* secured *WLAN*s. In a case of the dictionary attack on the device deployed by the UPC company, used dictionaries are personalized by the implicit passwords. In the case of properly secured *WLAN*, impersonation (phishing) can be employed. Using this method, an investigator impersonates the legitimate network to obtain the *WLAN* credentials from the user. During the second phase – *Tampering network topology*, the tool needs to continuously work on keeping the network *stations* (*STA*s) persuaded that the spoofed topology is the correct one. An investigator is now able to capture or modify the traffic. The successful *MitM* attack is established.

with available equipment. The tool is open source and can be easily incorporated into other software. The main use cases of this tool are found in automated penetration testing, forensic investigation, and education.

2   Security Weaknesses in WLAN Technologies

Following network technologies (Sects. 2.1 and 2.2), which find a significant utilization, unfortunately, suffer from security weaknesses in their protocols. These flaws can be used in the process of the *MitM* attack.

2.1   Wireless Security

Wired Equivalent Privacy (*WEP*) is a security algorithm introduced as a part of the IEEE 802.11 standard [6, p. 665], [8, pp. 1167–1169]. At this point, *WEP* is deprecated and superseded by subsequent algorithms, but is still sometimes used, as can be seen from Table 1 available from *Wifileaks.cz*[3]. *WEP* suffers from weaknesses and, therefore, it has been broken [4]. There are already implemented tools to provide access to wireless networks secured by *WEP* available [18]. Regarding *WEP* secured *WLANs*, authentication can be either *Open System Authentication (OSA)* or *Shared Key Authentication (SKA)* [8, pp. 1170–1174]. In the case of *WEP OSA*, any *station (STA)* can successfully authenticate to the *Access Point (AP)* [17, pp. 4–10]. *WEP SKA* provides authentication and security of transferred communication using a shared key. Confidentiality of transferred data is ensured by encryption using the *RC4* stream cipher. Methods used for cracking access to *WEP* secured networks are based on analysis of transferred data with corresponding *Initialization Vectors (IVs)*.

Table 1. Following table summarizes *WLAN* statistics provided by *Wifileaks.cz*. Users of this service voluntarily scan and publish details about *WLANs* in the Czech Republic. Information in the table show that a significant number of *WLANs* still use deprecated security algorithms. The statistics consisting of 97 192 922 measurements of 2 548 054 *WLANs* were published on May 26, 2017.

Security	Count	Ratio
WPA2	1 429 518	56%
WEP	393 579	15%
WPA	375 984	15%
open	67 388	3%
other	281 585	11%

Wi-Fi Protected Access® *(WPA)* was developed by the Wi-Fi Alliance® as a reaction to increasing number of security flaws in *WEP*. The main flaw of *WPA* security algorithm can be identified at the beginning of client device's communication, where an unsecured exchange of confidential information is performed during the four-way handshake. An investigator can obtain this unsecured communication and use it for consecutive cracking of the *Pre-Shared Key (PSK)*.

Wi-Fi Protected Access® *2 (WPA2^{TM})* is a successor of *WPA*, but security flaws of the *WPA PSK* algorithm remain significant also for the *WPA2 PSK*. Information exposed during the handshake can be used for the dictionary attack, which can be further improved by precomputing the *Pairwise Master Keys (PMKs)* [12, pp. 37–38], [13, p. 3]. Precomputed lookup tables are already available online[4].

A critical security flaw in wireless networks secured by *WPA* or *WPA2* is the functionality called *Wi-Fi Protected Setup^{TM} (WPS)*. This technology was introduced with an aim to provide a comfortable and secure way of connecting

---

[3] http://www.wifileaks.cz/statistika/
[4] https://www.renderlab.net/projects/WPA-tables/

to the network. For a connection to the *WLAN* with *WPS* enabled, it is possible to use an individual *PIN*. However, the process of connecting to the properly secured network by providing *PIN* is very prone to brute-force attacks [7]. Because *WPS* is a usual feature in today's access points and that *WPS* is usually turned on by default, *WPS* can be a very common security flaw even in networks secured by *WPA2* with a strong password. Currently, there are already available automated tools for exploiting *WPS* weaknesses, e.g., *Reaver Open Source*[5].

Newly purchased access points usually use *WPA2* security by default. Currently, many access points can be found using default passwords not only for wireless network access, but even for *AP*'s web administration. In a case of possible access to the *AP*'s administration, the investigator could focus on changing the network topology by tampering the network configuration. Access to the network management further allows the investigator to lower security levels, disable attack detections, reconfigure *DHCP* together with *DNS* and also clear *AP*'s logs. There are already implemented tools, which exploit relations between *SSID*s and default network passwords, e.g., *upc_keys*[6] by Peter Geissler.[7] These tools could be used in an attack on the network with default *SSID* to improve dictionary attack using possible passwords. High severity of these security flaws is also proven by the fact that a significant amount of *WLAN*s was found using unchanged passwords, as it is shown in Table 2.

Table 2. Results of wardriving in Bratislava and Brno focused on UPC vulnerabilities concerning default *WPA2 PSK* passwords [11]. Detailed article about these security flaws is available online [10].

Bratislava (capital of Slovakia) 2016-10-01	Count	Ratio
Total networks	22 172	
UPC networks	3 092	13.95%
UPC networks, vulnerable	1 327	42.92% UPC
Brno (city in the Czech Republic) 2016-02-10	Count	Ratio
Total networks	17 516	
UPC networks	2 868	16.37%
UPC networks, vulnerable	1 835	63.98% UPC

2.2 Network Technologies Used in WLANs

In the context of a MitM attack on a *WLAN*, we are targeting some common network protocols:

- *DHCP* automates network device configuration without a user's intervention [3].

---

[5] https://code.google.com/archive/p/reaver-wps/
[6] https://haxx.in/upc-wifi/
[7] UPC company is a major ISP in the Czech Republic, URL: https://www.upc.cz

– *ARP* translates an *IPv4* address to a destination *MAC* address of the next-hop device in the local area network [14].
– *IPv6* networks utilize *ICMPv6 Neighbor Discovery* functionality to achieve similar functionality to *ARP* in *IPv4* networks.

These network protocols are vulnerable and a *MitM* attack is a coordinated attack on each of these protocols, effectively changing the network topology.

– *DHCP Spoofing* generates fake *DHCP* communication. This attack can also be referred to as *Rogue DHCP*. An investigator can perform this kind of attack to provide devices in the network with malicious configuration, most often a fake default gateway address or *DNS* address
– *ARP Spoofing* provides the network devices with fake *ARP* messages. This persuades the suspect's device to believe that the attacking device's *MAC* address is the default gateway's *MAC* address.
– *IPv6 Neighbor Spoofing* is a similar concept to *ARP Spoofing*.

ARP Spoofing technique was selected from the researched methods. This method proved itself with reasonable performance during experiments. Possible counter-measures to these attacks are further described in the thesis [20].

2.3 Available Tools for Specific Phases of the MitM Attack on Wireless Networks

From perspective of the intended functionality of the implemented tool, the whole process of *MitM* attack on wireless networks can be divided into three main phases: *Accessing wireless network*, *Tampering network topology* and *Capturing network traffic*, as explained in Fig. 1.

To access secured wireless networks, *Aircrack-ng suite*[8] is considered a reliable software solution. Considering the phase *Accessing wireless network* (Fig. 1), following tools were utilized. *Airmon-ng* can manage modes of a wireless interface. *Airodump-ng* can be used to scan and detect attacked *AP*. *Aircrack-ng* together with *aireplay-ng*, *airodump-ng* and *upc_keys* can be utilized for cracking *WEP OSA*, *WEP SKA*, *WPA PSK* and *WPA2 PSK*. The tool *wifiphisher*[9] can be used to perform impersonation and phishing. Connection to the wireless network can be established by *netctl*[10]. *MITMf*[11] with its *Spoof* plugin can be used during the *Tampering network topology* phase. *Capturing traffic* can be done by the tool *dumpcap*[12], which is part of the *Wireshark*[13] distribution. Behaviour, usage and success rate of individual tools, as well as possibilities of controlling them by the implemented tool, were analyzed. The software selected for individual tasks of the automated *MitM* attack were chosen from the researched variety

---

[8] http://www.aircrack-ng.org/
[9] https://github.com/sophron/wifiphisher
[10] https://www.archlinux.org/packages/core/any/netctl/
[11] https://github.com/byt3bl33d3r/MITMf
[12] https://www.wireshark.org/docs/man-pages/dumpcap.html
[13] https://www.wireshark.org/

of available tools based on performed manual experiments, further described in the thesis [20].

3 Attack Automation Using Developed wifimitm Package and wifimitmcli Tool

The implemented tool is currently intended to run on *Arch Linux*[14], but it could be used on other platforms which would satisfy specified dependencies. This distribution was selected because it is very flexible and lightweight. Python 3.5 was selected as a primary implementation language for the automated tool and Bash was chosen for supporting tasks, e.g., installation of dependencies on *Arch Linux* and software wrappers.

The functionality implemented in the *wifimitm* package could be directly incorporated into other software products based on Python language. This way the package would work as a software library. Schema of the *wifimitm* package is in Fig. 2.

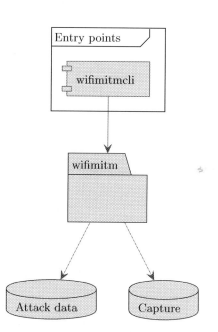

Fig. 2. This figure shows the basic structure of the developed application. The tool *wifimitmcli* uses a functionality offered by the package *wifimitm*. The package is also able to manipulate attack data useful for repeated attacks and capture files with intercepted traffic. Detailed structure of the package is described in Sect. 3.

The *wifimitm* package consists of following modules. The `access` module offers an automated process of cracking selected *WLAN*. It uses modules `wep`

---

[14] https://www.archlinux.org/

and `wpa2`, which implement attacks and cracking based on the used security algorithm. The `wep` module is capable of fake authentication with the *AP*, *ARP replay* attack (to speed up gathering of *IV*s) and cracking the key based on *IV*s. In the case of *WPA2* secured network, the `wpa2` module can perform a dictionary attack, personalize used dictionary and verify a password obtained by phishing. Verification of the password and dictionary attacks are done with a previously captured handshake. The `common` module contains functionality which could be used in various parts of the process for scanning and capturing wireless communication in monitor mode. The `common` module also offers a way to deauthenticate *STA*s from selected *AP*.

If a dictionary attack against a correctly secured network fails, a phishing attack can be managed by the `impersonation`[15] module. The `topology` module can be used to change network topology. It provides functionality for *ARP Spoofing*. The `capture` module focuses on capturing network traffic. It is intended to be used after the tool is successfully connected to the attacked network and network topology was successfully changed into the one suitable for *MitM* attack.

3.1   Attack Data

Various attacks executed against the selected *AP* require some information to be captured first. ARP request replay attack on *WEP* secured networks requires an ARP request to be obtained in order to start an attacking procedure. Fake authentication in *WEP SKA* secured network needs *PRGA XOR*[16] obtained from a detected authentication. Dictionary attack against *WPA PSK* and *WPA2 PSK* secured networks requires a captured handshake. Finally, for the successful connection to a network, a correct key is required. When the required information is obtained, it can be saved for a later usage to speed up following or repetitive attacks. Data from successful attacks could be even shared between users of the implemented tool.

3.2   Dictionary Personalization

Weaknesses in default network passwords could be exploited to improve dictionary attacks against *WPA PSK* and *WPA2 PSK* security algorithms. The implemented tool incorporates *upc_keys* for generation of possible default passwords if the selected network matches the criteria. The *upc_keys* tool generates passwords, which are transferred to the cracking tool using pipes. With this approach, the implemented tool could be further improved for example to support localized dictionaries.

---

[15] For details concerning individual phishing scenarios, please see *wifiphisher*'s website. https://github.com/sophron/wifiphisher

[16] Stream of *Pseudo Random Generation Algorithm* generated bits.

3.3   Requirements

The implemented automated tool depends on several other tools, which are being controlled. The Python package can be automatically installed by its setup including Python dependencies. Non-Python dependencies can be satisfied by installation scripts and wrappers, which are currently developed for *Arch Linux*.

MITMf has a number of dependencies. Therefore, the installation script also creates a virtual environment dedicated to *MITMf*. After installation, *MITMf* can be easily run encapsulated in its environment. *Wifiphisher* is also installed in a virtualized environment and run using a wrapper. Tool *upc_keys* is compiled during installation. Some changes in *wifiphisher*'s source code were implemented, the installation script therefore applies a software patch. Other software dependencies are installed using a package manager.

Due to the nature of concrete steps of the attack, a special hardware equipment is required. During the scanning and capturing of network traffic without being connected to the network, an attacking device needs a wireless network interface in monitor mode. For sending forged packets, the wireless network interface also needs to be capable of packet injection. To be able to perform a phishing attack, a second wireless interface capable of master (*AP*) mode has to be available. The user can check whether his hardware is capable of packet injection

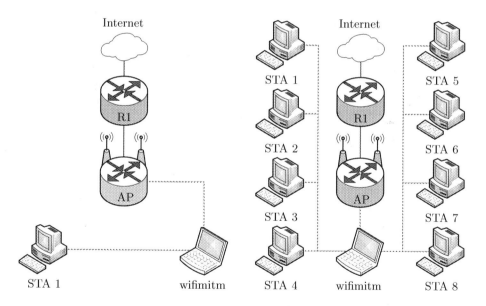

Fig. 3. This figure shows the network topology used for the first performance testing (Sect. 4) and success rate measurements (Sect. 5). Results of this performance testing are in Fig. 5.

Fig. 4. This figure shows the network topology consisting of 8 *STA*s and 1 *AP* which was used for the second performance testing (Sect. 4). Results of this performance testing are in Fig. 6.

using the *aireplay-ng* tool. Managing monitor mode of interface is possible with the *airmon-ng* tool.

4   Attack's Performance Impact

A scheme of the networks used for the experiments is shown in Figs. 3 and 4. The *STAs* were correctly connected to the *AP* and they were successfully communicating with the Internet. The implemented *wifimitmcli* tool was then started and automatically attacked the network.

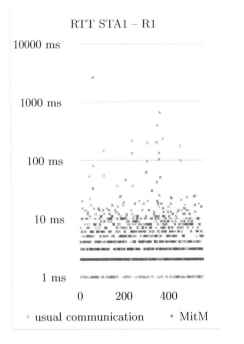

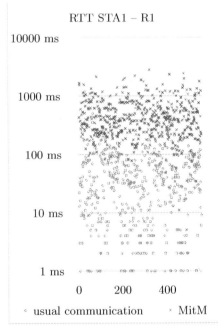

Fig. 5. The first *WLAN* for performance testing was the same as for the success rate measurements described in Sect. 5. Figure shows comparison of the measured *RTT* between *STA1* and *R1* during usual communication and during successful *MitM* attack. The results show the performance impact is not critical. Discussion with the users of the attacked network proved this attack unrecognizable.

Fig. 6. The second performance testing consisted of 8 *STAs* and 1 *AP* connected to the Internet – streaming videos, downloading large files, etc. The figure compares the *RTT* between *STA1* and *R1* similarly. The performance impact is more severe than in Fig. 5. Despite the performance impact, the users had no suspicion that they were under *MitM* attack. Instead, they blamed the amount of devices for network congestion.

The performance impact of the *wifimitm* was compared using setups based on SOHO[17] environment. Both experiments were also evaluated based on the fact, whether the attack being performed was revealed or whether the users had any suspicion about the malicious transformation of their *WLAN*. Results of the testing are presented in Figs. 5 and 6.

Table 3. This table presents results of the success rate measurements. A successful attack is marked using a *checkmark* symbol (✓) and unsuccessful attack is marked using a *times* symbol (×). In the case when the attack was not fully successful, the question mark (?) is used. Such partially successful test (? symbol) can for example happen in situation where the suspect is sending only a portion of his traffic through the investigator. Some of the used *STAs* lack *WEP SKA* settings (□ symbol). Testing *WPA PSK* and *WPA2 PSK* networks were configured with password "12345678" and *WEP* secured networks used password "A_b#1".

		Lenovo G580, Windows 10	Lenovo G505s, Windows 8.1	Dell Latitude E6500, Ubuntu 17.04	HTC Desire 500, Android 4.1.2	Apple iPhone 4, iOS 7.1.2
Linksys WRT610N	open	✓	✓	✓	✓	✓
	WEP OSA	✓	✓	✓	✓	✓
	WEP SKA	□	□	✓	✓	✓
	WPA PSK	✓	✓	✓	✓	✓
	WPA2 PSK	✓	✓	✓	✓	✓
Linksys WRT54G	open	✓	✓	✓	✓	✓
	WEP OSA	✓	✓	✓	✓	✓
	WEP SKA	□	□	✓	✓	✓
	WPA PSK	✓	✓	✓	✓	✓
	WPA2 PSK	✓	✓	✓	✓	✓
Linksys WRP400	open	✓	✓	✓	✓	✓
	WEP OSA	✓	✓	✓	✓	✓
	WEP SKA	□	□	✓	✓	✓
	WPA PSK	✓	✓	✓	✓	✓
	WPA2 PSK	✓	✓	✓	✓	✓
TP-LINK TL-WR841N	open	?	×	✓	✓	✓
	WEP OSA	?	×	✓	✓	×
	WEP SKA	□	□	✓	✓	×
	WPA PSK	?	×	✓	✓	×
	WPA2 PSK	?	×	✓	✓	×
D-Link DVA-G3671B	open	✓	✓	✓	✓	✓
	WEP OSA	✓	✓	✓	✓	✓
	WEP SKA	□	□	✓	✓	✓
	WPA PSK	✓	✓	✓	✓	✓
	WPA2 PSK	✓	✓	✓	✓	✓

---

[17] Small office/home office.

5   Experiments Concerning Various Network Configurations and Devices

The test was considered successful if the *wifimitmcli* was able to capture network traffic according to the concept of *MitM*. For the test to be correct, no intervention (help) from the investigator was allowed during the attack performed by *wifimitmcli*. Results of the success rate measurements are shown in Tables 3 and 4.

Table 4. The following table shows the results of public experiments. Visitors of the Brno University of Technology, Faculty of Information Technology were invited to let their devices be attacked. Testing network utilized *Linksys WRP400* device as an AP. A successful attack is marked using a *checkmark* symbol (✓).

Model	OS	Attack
HTC Desire 500	Android 4.1.2	✓
HTC Desire 820	Android 6.0.1	✓
Apple iPhone 6	iOS 10.3.1	✓
Apple iPhone 5s	iOS 10.2.1	✓
Apple iPhone 5	iOS 10.3.1	✓
Apple iPhone 5c	iOS 9.2.1	✓
Apple iPhone 4	iOS 7.1.2	✓

Results of experiments (Tables 3 and 4 and the thesis [20, pp. 42–43]) show, that open networks can be very easily attacked. *WEP OSA* and *WEP SKA* secured networks can be successfully attacked even if they use a random password. *WPA PSK* and *WPA2 PSK* secured networks suffer from weak passwords (dictionary attack), default passwords and mistakes of users (impersonation and phishing). As Figs. 5, 6 and Tables 3, 4 show, *MitM* attack using the *wifimitm* is successfully feasible in the target environments.

6   Conclusions

The goal of this research was to implement a tool that would be able to automate all the necessary steps to perform *MitM* attacks on *WLAN*s. The authors searched for and analyzed a range of software and methods focused on penetration testing, communication sniffing and spoofing, password cracking and hacking in general. To be able to design, implement and test the tool capable of such attacks, knowledge of different widespread security approaches was essential. The authors further focused on possibilities of *MitM* attacks even in cases where the target *WLAN* is secured correctly. Therefore, methods and tools for impersonation and phishing were also analyzed.

The authors' work and research resulted in creation of the *wifimitm* Python package. This package serves as a library which provides functionality for automation of *MitM* attacks on target *WLAN*s. The developed package can also be easily incorporated into other tools. Another product of this research is the *wifimitmcli* tool which incorporates the functionality of the *wifimitm* package. This tool automates the individual steps of a *MitM* attack and can be used from a *CLI*. The implemented software comes with a range of additions for convenient usage, e.g., a script that checks and installs dependencies on *Arch Linux*, a Python setuptools setup script and of course a manual page.

The *wifimitmcli* tool, and therefore *wifimitm* as well, was tested during experiments with an available set of equipment. As the results show, the implemented software product is able to perform an automated *MitM* attack on *WLAN*s successfully.

Upon successful deployment and execution of the implemented tool, an investigator can eavesdrop or spoof the passing communication. The goal of the tool was to automate *MitM* attacks on *WLAN*s. It does not focus on dissecting further traffic protections. This means that it does not interfere with *SSL/TLS*, *VPN*, or other encapsulations. Thanks to the tool's design, it can be easily used together with other software specialized on interception of encapsulated traffic. Traffic encapsulation is a sufficient protection against this tool. From the *WLAN* administrators point of view, available defense mechanisms are outlined in Sect. 2.2.

As explained earlier, all the suspect's network traffic is passing through the attacking device during a successful *MitM* attack. Unfortunately, there could be users on the network other than the ones that are subject to a court order. Making sure that only appropriate traffic is being captured may be important depending on the nature of the court order or the legislation. This challenge may be solved by setting corresponding filter rules for traffic capture software.

This research and its products can be utilized in combination with other security research carried out at the Brno University of Technology, Faculty of Information Technology. It can serve in investigations done by forensic researchers [15]. It can also be used in automated penetration testing of *WLAN*s.

In the future iterations of the development, the product could focus on exploiting the weaknesses of the widely used *WPS* technology. Concerning the current state of the product, it does not focus on enterprise *WLAN*s, which also suffer from their own weaknesses.

The authors disclaim any use of this research for any unlawful activities.

References

1. Callegati, F., Cerroni, W., Ramilli, M.: Man-in-the-middle attack to the HTTPS protocol. IEEE Security Privacy **7**, 78–81 (2009)
2. Deal, R., Cisco Systems Inc.: The Complete Cisco VPN Configuration Guide. Cisco Press Networking Technology Series. Cisco Press, Indianapolis (2006)
3. Droms, R.: Dynamic host configuration protocol. RFC 2131, IETF, March 1997

4. Fluhrer, S., Mantin, I., Shamir, A.: Weaknesses in the key scheduling algorithm of RC4. In: Vaudenay, S., Youssef, A. (eds.) Selected Areas in Cryptography. LNCS, pp. 1–24. Springer, Heidelberg (2001). https://doi.org/10.1007/3-540-45537-X_1

5. Godber, A., Dasgupta, P.: Countering rogues in wireless networks, vol. 2003-January, pp. 425–431. Institute of Electrical and Electronics Engineers Inc. (2003)

6. Halsall, F.: Computer Networking and the Internet. Addison-Wesley, Boston (2005)

7. Heffner, C.: Cracking WPA in 10 hours or less –/dev/ttys0 (2011). http://www.devttys0.com/2011/12/cracking-wpa-in-10-hours-or-less/

8. IEEE-SA. IEEE standard for information technology-telecommunications and information exchange between systems local and metropolitan area networks-specific requirements part 11: Wireless LAN medium access control (MAC) and physical layer (PHY) specifications. IEEE Std 802.11-2012 (Revision of IEEE Std 802.11-2007), pp. 1–2793, March 2012

9. Kent, S., Seo, K.: Security Architecture for the Internet Protocol. RFC 4301, IETF, December 2005

10. Klinec, D., Svítok, M.: UPC UBEE EVW3226 WPA2 password reverse engineering, rev 3. https://deadcode.me/blog/2016/07/01/UPC-UBEE-EVW3226-WPA2-Reversing.html. Accessed 5 Nov 2016

11. Klinec, D., Svítok, M.: Wardriving Bratislava 10/2016, 5 November 2016. https://deadcode.me/blog/2016/11/05/Wardriving-Bratislava-10-2016.html

12. Kumkar, V., Tiwari, A., Tiwari, P., Gupta, A., Shrawne, S.: Vulnerabilities of wireless security protocols (WEP and WPA2). Int. J. Adv. Res. Comput. Eng. Technol. (IJARCET) 1(2), 34–38 (2012)

13. Liu, Y., Jin, Z., Wang, Y.: Survey on security scheme and attacking methods of WPA/WPA2. In: 2010 6th International Conference on Wireless Communications Networking and Mobile Computing (WiCOM), pp. 1–4, September 2010

14. Plummer, D.: Ethernet address resolution protocol: or converting network protocol addresses to 48.bit ethernet address for transmission on ethernet hardware. RFC 826, IETF, November 1982

15. Pluskal, J., Matoušek, P., Ryšavý, O., Kmeť, M., Veselý, V., Karpíšek, F., Vymlátil, M.: Netfox detective: a tool for advanced network forensics analysis. In: Proceedings of Security and Protection of Information (SPI) 2015, pp. 147–163. Brno University of Defence (2015)

16. Prowell, S., Kraus, R., Borkin, M.: Man-in-the-middle. In: Prowell, S., Kraus, R., Borkin, M. (eds.) Seven Deadliest Network Attacks, pp. 101–120. Syngress, Boston (2010)

17. Robyns, P.: Wireless network privacy. Master's thesis. Hasselt University, Hasselt (2014)

18. Tews, E., Weinmann, R.-P., Pyshkin, A.: Breaking 104 bit WEP in less than 60 seconds. In: Kim, S., Yung, M., Lee, H.-W. (eds.) Information Security Applications. LNCS, pp. 188–202. Springer, Heidelberg (2007). https://doi.org/10.1007/978-3-540-77535-5_14

19. Thomas, O.: Windows Server 2016 Inside Out. Inside Out. Pearson Education, London (2017)

20. Vondráček, M.: Automation of MitM attack on WiFi networks. Bachelor's thesis. Brno University of Technology, Faculty of Information Technology (2016)

SeEagle: Semantic-Enhanced Anomaly Detection for Securing Eagle

Wu Xin[1,3], Qingni Shen[2,3], Yahui Yang[2,3], and Zhonghai Wu[2,3(✉)]

[1] School of Electronics and Computer Engineering,
Peking University, Shenzhen, China
xinwu@pku.edu.cn
[2] School of Software and Microelectronics, Peking University, Beijing, China
{qingnishen,yhyang,wuzh}@ss.pku.edu.cn
[3] Lab for Big Data Technology, Peking University, Beijing, China

Abstract. In order to ensure data security and monitor data behavior, eBay has developed Eagle, which can detect anomalous user behavior based on user profiles and can intelligently protect data security of Hadoop ecosystem in real-time. By analyzing the kernel density estimation (KDE) algorithm and source code implemented in Eagle, we recognize that there are two security risks: One is that user profiles are models of operations, but the objects of operations are not analyzed; The other is that the owner of HDFS audit log files is not authenticated. Consequently, the attacker can bypass Eagle and form attack of APT combined with default permissions of Hadoop. In this paper, we analyze the two risks of Eagle, propose two kinds of attack methods that can bypass anomaly detection of Eagle: co-frequency operation attack and log injection attack, and establish threat model of which feasibility is verified experimentally. Finally, we present SeEagle, a semantic-enhanced anomaly detection for securing Eagle, including user authentication and file tagging modules. Our preliminary experimental evaluation shows that SeEagle works well and extra overhead is acceptable.

Keywords: Semantic-enhanced · User authentication · Tagging · APT
User profile · Eagle · Anomaly detection · User activity monitoring
Machine learning

1 Introduction

In recent years, Hadoop [1] has become the most popular distributed system in both industry and academia. For data security, HDFS provides access control to prevent unauthorized access to file data. But in the era of big data, the access control is facing significant challenges [2]: To partition roles for users and to define permissions for roles is difficult.

In response to the challenges of data access control in the era of big data, Molloy et al. [3] proposed to extract roles from the access logs, based on machine-learning algorithms. Zeng et al. [4] proposed an access control model based on the content. Their methods are mostly verified by experimental prototypes, but they are not being in practice. Gupta et al. [5] designed Eagle [6], which can further ensure the security of

© ICST Institute for Computer Sciences, Social Informatics and Telecommunications Engineering 2018
P. Matoušek and M. Schmiedecker (Eds.): ICDF2C 2017, LNICST 216, pp. 221–227, 2018.
https://doi.org/10.1007/978-3-319-73697-6_17

HDFS data through user profile-based anomaly detection. Eagle, which has aroused widespread concern in both industry and academia, has been announced to be a Top Level Project (TLP) of Apache Software Foundation (ASF) [7].

The idea of Eagle is extracting audit logs from applications running on Hadoop systems, such as HDFS which is concerned in this paper, and using machine-learning algorithms to generate user profiles depending on the users' history logs. Based on user profiles, Eagle can detect malicious activities when a user action does not match with the user profile.

Several approaches dealing with anomaly detection for operating system, networks, Web applications and database have been developed, but the behaviors deemed malicious for HDFS are not necessarily malicious for them.

In the database domain, Karma et al. [8] and Spalka and Lehnhardt [9] proposed the method of detecting anomalies respectively. Their work is complementary. [8] focuses on the syntactic aspects by detecting anomalous access patterns in a DBMS, while [9] focuses on the semantic aspects of the SQL queries. So a mature anomaly detection system that designed to better monitor user behaviors should focus on both syntactic and semantic aspects.

However, we notices that the approach in Eagle is closer to that of [8], which both use machine-learning algorithms and focus on syntactic aspects, but there is the lacks of sematic analysis and the authentication of log files owner. If the risks cannot be effectively resolved, they may form the data security issues and attack of APT. Therefore, we propose SeEagle, a semantic-enhanced anomaly detection for securing Eagle, to deal with the risks.

The contribution of this paper can be summarized as follows:

- By analyzing the machine-learning algorithms, we realize that user profiles are models of user operations for operated files, and the KDE algorithm, which only statistically analyzes user operations and does not analyze the objects of operations, focuses on the syntactic analysis.
- Through the analysis of source code, tracking the processes of reading and processing HDFS audit log data in Eagle, we observe that the owner of log files is not authenticated during the process of HDFS log data flow into.
- Based on the two security risks and combined with the default permissions of Hadoop, co-frequency operation attack and log injection attack (see Sect. 2.2) which can bypass the anomaly detection of Eagle are proposed. And the threat model is established to verify their feasibility.
- In order to deal with the two kinds of attack methods, SeEagle,a semantic-enhanced anomaly detection for securing Eagle, is proposed. Based on the general policy framework of Eagle, the user authentication module is added to the entrance of log data flow, and the file tagging module, which based on semantic analysis, is added to the offline training that generate user profiles. Finally, SeEagle which is evaluated experimentally can effectively defend against the attacks and the extra overhead is acceptable.

The paper is organized as follows. Next section analyzes the security risks of Eagle and describes two kinds of attack methods. Section 3 describes SeEagle and shows the results of the experimental evaluation. Finally, we conclude the paper by discussing future work.

2 Challenges of Eagle

2.1 Security Risks

A. The lack of semantic analysis

Through the analysis of machine-learning algorithms in Eagle, we realize that there is a security risk in the offline training of KDE algorithm which lacks semantic analysis. The idea of KDE algorithm is to calculate the probability density of sample data points to evaluate each user by the Gaussian distribution function [10].

By analyzing the KDE algorithm, it is understood that only user operations are analyzed statistically while the objects of operations are not.

For a HDFS user, the HDFS files can be categorized into authorized files and unauthorized ones. Authorized files can be divided into operated files and non-operated files. Figure 1 shows the categorization of HDFS files.

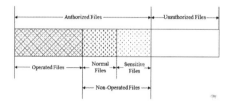

Fig. 1. The categorization of HDFS files

Through the analysis of the machine-learning algorithms in Eagle, it is learned that user profiles are models of operations for operated files. User profiles can effectively detect anomaly for operated files, but they may not defend against the internal threats for non-operated files because the operations for the former may be abnormal for the latter, especially for the sensitive data.

B. The lack of log files owner authentication

By analyzing the source code, there is also a security risk in the process of reading and analyzing HDFS audit logs: the owner of HDFS log files is not authenticated. We illustrate the process of reading HDFS logs as follows:

Configure the path for training dataset of user profiles in the *conf/sandbox-user-profile-scheduler.conf* in the Eagle home directory. From the 34th line in Fig. 2(a), we can know that the training dataset of user profiles is all local HDFS log files whose names start with *hdfs-audit.log* in */var/log/hadoop/hdfs/*directory.

User profiles are generated through reading and analyzing the HDFS logs in *AuditLogTrainingSparkJob.scala*. From the 55th and 65th lines in Fig. 2(b), we can learn that Eagle only judges whether the path is empty, and then reads and analyzes the HDFS logs. However, the owner of HDFS audit log files is not authenticated.

```
# eagle userprofile configuration
userprofile {
    # training audit log input path
    training-audit-path = "
    file:///var/log/hadoop/hdfs/hdfs-audit.log"

    # detection audit log input path
    detection-audit-path = "
    file:///var/log/hadoop/hdfs/hdfs-audit.log"

    # detection output kafka brokers
    # default: localhost:9200
    detection-kafka-brokers = "master.hp:6667"

    # detection output kafka topic
    detection-kafka-topic =
    "sandbox_hdfs_audit_log"
  }
}
```

a. sandbox-userprofile-scheduler.conf

```
54 private def buildDAG(sc:SparkContext): Unit = {
55   if (input == null) throw new
     IllegalArgumentException("input is null")
56
57   val _site = site
58   val _sc = sc
59   val _cmdTypes = cmdTypes
60   val _modelers = modelers
61   val _modelSinks = modelSinks
62   val _aggSinks = aggSinks
63
64   val _period = period
65   val tmp = _sc.textFile(input)
66     .map(AuditLogTransformer(_period).transform)
67     .filter(e => e.isDefined)
68     .map(e =>
     (((e.get.user,e.get.periodWindowSeconds,e.get.cmd),1.toDouble) }} // ((user,period,cmd),count)
```

b. AuditLogTrainingSparkJob.scala

Fig. 2. The source code of Eagle

2.2 Attack Methods

We propose two kinds of attack methods based on the above two security risks:

- *Co-frequency operation attack*: Due to the lack of semantic analysis in Eagle, the malicious behavior that the objects of operation are different can be performed based on the same frequency of operation when an attacker obtains the authority of a legitimate user.
- *Log injection attack*: As Eagle lacks log owner authentication, the attacker can forge the HDFS audit logs according to the operational requirements of getting the HDFS data, and inject them into the Eagle. Once the mendacious user profile is generated, it will cause failure of anomaly detection.
- The relationship between co-frequency operation attack & log injection attack: The former is invalid when the conventional operations in the user profile cannot meet the needs of the attacker. The latter is needed to generate mendacious user profile to meet the operational requirements of the former.

3 SeEagle

3.1 Overview

According to the security risks in Eagle and the two kinds of attacks proposed in this paper, SeEagle, a semantic-enhanced anomaly detection for securing Eagle, has been designed as shown in Fig. 3, including the user authentication and file tagging modules.

The user authentication module is used to defend the log injection attack. We exploit the HDFS audit logs can only be generated by *hdfs* that is the super user of HDFS. Therefore, we increase the user authentication module to authenticate the owner of the HDFS log files whether *hdfs*, which can effectively defend against the log injection attack.

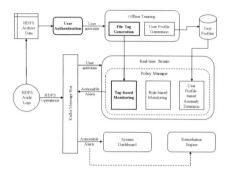

Fig. 3. SeEagle architecture

The file tagging module, which is based on the semantic analysis, is used to protect co-frequency operation attack. In the process of offline training, not only the user operations are statistically analyzed, but also the operated files of the user are tagged with the user name. Then a default policy that an alert is triggered when a user accesses any file without tag of the user name is created for each user through the general policy management framework of Eagle.

The file tagging can effectively protect from the co-frequency operation attacks to access the non-operated files. However, it still cannot avoid the co-frequency operation attack to access the operated files.

In order to protect the operated files from co-frequency operation attack, the default permissions of HDFS log directory and files should be changed and the log files should be defined more granular ACL to prevent the attacker from acquiring the HDFS logs.

3.2   Experimental Evaluation

We mainly from three aspects to test the Eagle and SeEagle overhead: the number of HDFS log files, the number of HDFS users and the number of HDFS logs in Hadoop system. From a large number of experimental data, we draw the following three charts in Fig. 4 to illustrate.

Through the analysis above, we observe that the extra overhead of SeEagle mainly in the generation of file tags and tag-based policies. By combining source code and log output analysis, it is realized that the main overhead is I/O. Considering that on the basis of Eagle, SeEagle has improved its security and has no effect on the performance of online detection anomalies, and the extra overhead is mainly in off-line training. So the extra overhead of SeEagle is acceptable.

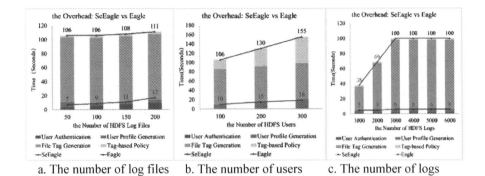

a. The number of log files   b. The number of users   c. The number of logs

Fig. 4. The overhead: SeEagle vs Eagle

4 Conclusions and Future Work

In this paper, we aware the security risks by analyzing the machine-learning algorithms and the source code in Eagle and propose co-frequency operation attack and log injection attack that can bypass anomaly detection of Eagle and form the attack of APT combined with the default permissions of the Hadoop. Finally, we present SeEagle, a semantic-enhanced anomaly detection for securing Eagle, including the user authentication and the file tagging modules. The SeEagle cannot only effectively defend against the above two kinds of attacks, but also the extra overhead is acceptable.

In the future, we plan to further research the response of Eagle when an anomaly is detected. At present, Eagle just generates an alert and informs the related person by e-mail after detecting an abnormal user behavior. It just makes a response after the occurrence of abnormal events rather than making judgment in advance. In addition, during the offline training, the logs of abnormal behavior are regarded as the regular HDFS logs to generate user profiles and Eagle cannot remove them from the HDFS logs. Therefore, we intend to add the appropriate function so that Eagle can generate more accurate user profiles.

Acknowledgements. This work is supported by the National High Technology Research and Development Program ("863" Program) of China under Grant No. 2015AA016009 and the National Natural Science Foundation of China under Grant No. 61232005. The authors would like to acknowledge Xiaoyi Chen, Bin Yang, Dong Huo and Xuxin Fan for their support for our preliminary experiments. We are also grateful to Fenmei Li for her valuable suggestions and thorough proofread for this paper.

References

1. Hadoop. https://hadoop.apache.org/
2. Feng, D.G., Zhang, M., Li, H.: Big data security and privacy protection. Chin. J. Comput. **37** (1), 246–258 (2014)

3. Molloy, I., Park, Y., Chari, S.: Generative models for access control policies: applications to role mining over logs with attribution. In: ACM Symposium on Access Control Models and Technologies, pp. 45–56 (2012)
4. Zeng, W., Yang, Y., Luo, B.: Access control for big data using data content. In: IEEE International Conference on Big Data, pp. 45–47 (2013)
5. Gupta, C., Sinha, R., Zhang, Y.: Eagle: user profile-based anomaly detection for securing Hadoop clusters. In: IEEE International Conference on Big Data, pp. 1336–1343 (2015)
6. Eagle. http://eagle.apache.org/
7. Apache Software Foundation (ASF). http://www.apache.org/
8. Kamra, A., Terzi, E., Bertino, E.: Detecting anomalous access patterns in relational databases. VLDB J. **17**(5), 1063–1077 (2008)
9. Spalka, A., Lehnhardt, J.: A comprehensive approach to anomaly detection in relational databases. In: Jajodia, S., Wijesekera, D. (eds.) DBSec 2005. LNCS, vol. 3654, pp. 207–221. Springer, Heidelberg (2005). https://doi.org/10.1007/11535706_16
10. Gaussian Distribution. https://en.wikipedia.org/wiki/Gaussian_function

Coriander: A Toolset for Generating Realistic Android Digital Evidence Datasets

Irvin Homem[(⊠)]

Department of Computer and Systems Sciences,
Stockholm University, Postbox 7003, Kista, Sweden
irvin@dsv.su.se

Abstract. Triage has been suggested as a means to prioritize and identify sources and artifacts of evidence that might be of most interest when faced with large amounts of digital evidence. Memory Forensics has long relied on simple string matching to triage evidence sources. In this paper, we describe the early developments into our study on Machine Learning-based triage for Memory Forensics. To start off, there are no large datasets of memory captures available. We thus, develop a toolset to enable the automated creation of realistic Android process memory dumps. Using our toolset we generate a dataset of 2375 process memory string dumps from both malicious and benign Android applications, classified by VirusTotal, and sourced from the AndroZoo project. Our dataset and toolset are made available online to help promote research in this field and related areas.

Keywords: Android forensics · Digital forensics · Mobile forensics
Memory forensics · Digital evidence · Datasets · Metadata · Machine learning
Triage

1 Introduction

Digital Investigations struggle with large amounts of potential evidentiary data. Triage [1] has been proposed as a means to help speed up the identification of high priority digital evidence data sources for acquisition, or sections of digital evidence that should be prioritized for analysis [2]. Triaging disk-based evidence to identify files or sections of a disk to be either ignored, or prioritized has been studied widely [3–5]. Triaging of network traffic captures has been less studied, however there are some studies such as [6, 7]. There has been a call for mobile device triage [8] however, to the best of our knowledge little has been done. We thus delve into addressing this knowledge gap, directing our efforts into the triaging of mobile device memory in an automated manner, with a focus on identifying processes in memory that may require further investigation. We propose the use of machine learning techniques as previously used with disk-based [5] and network traffic evidence [7], to aid in identification and prioritization of processes of interest within mobile memory dumps, as part of a triage procedure.

More concretely, in the early stages of this research, we aim to create a significantly large dataset of Android process memory dumps. From these memory dumps, process

© ICST Institute for Computer Sciences, Social Informatics and Telecommunications Engineering 2018
P. Matoušek and M. Schmiedecker (Eds.): ICDF2C 2017, LNICST 216, pp. 228–233, 2018.
https://doi.org/10.1007/978-3-319-73697-6_18

related features (metadata) are to be extracted and used to develop machine learning predictive models to help identify particular processes in memory that warrant further investigation into their activities and interactions with the file system or network.

To aid in achieving our goals, we have developed a toolset (Coriander) in Python to automate the creation of our dataset of Android process memory dumps. Using this toolset we generated a dataset of 2375 Android process memory string dumps using a subset of APK files from the AndroZoo Project [9]. The Coriander toolset and the resulting process memory dataset are the main subject described in this early progress report on our research.

2 Background and Related Work

Some of the methods for triaging digital evidence include removal of known benign artifacts from within the digital evidence dataset. This has been done on *disk* data [2] using: (i) Focused extraction of well known artifacts (E.g. the Windows Registry, File Metadata); (ii) Using string-matching techniques [10]; (iii) Matching files with hash lists of known files or parts of known files [3]; (iv) Using fuzzy hashing to identify closely similar files [4]; and (v) recently also using machine-learning techniques [5]. With regard to triaging *network traffic* evidence, fuzzy hashing has been used to detect files [6] and machine learning methods have been used to identify network protocols within DNS tunneling network traffic [7].

Recently network-scanning tools such as Yara have been deployed to scan memory images as a triage method [11]. This used string-matching techniques, with additional capability of conditional matching of sets of strings through Yara. Visualization techniques have also been developed to help identify areas of priority in the triage process of Windows memory [12].

The triage of mobile devices is largely unexplored and so far only one study [8] has attempted to address this knowledge gap, focusing on the different forms of evidence artifacts available and indicating that there is a lack of tools and techniques for triaging mobile devices, short of "thumbing through" a live device. We thus aim to address this shortcoming by providing a technique for triaging mobile devices with a focus on the processes running in memory.

In the forensic analysis of live memory, an important artifact of interest is the running processes, their interaction with other resources, such as other processes, data in memory, the filesystem, network adapters, the kernel and other peripheral devices drivers. The activities carried out by a process may be malicious or normal benign activity. Within the context of an investigation of live memory, it would be helpful to provide a forensic analyst with a quick method of identifying and differentiating potentially interesting malicious processes from other benign normal process activities. Thus, in this paper, we begin our study towards achieving this triage process on Android mobile device memory.

The identification of malicious Android applications has been studied as malware detection prior to the app running (Static Analysis) with static APK files [13]; while it is running (Dynamic Analysis) [14], or a combination of both (Hybrid Analysis) [15]. These methods are not perfect, and there are ways to beat them [16]. Essentially mobile malware variants can beat detection mechanisms and continue to run undetected. Memory forensics tools such as Volatility and Rekall provide in depth structured analysis, however identification of miscreant processes is left to the discretion of the analyst. With potentially numerous processes in memory it may be a difficult task to identify which processes require further analysis. Whitelisting certain processes based on their name might be one way, however even well known processes may be hijacked to perform malicious tasks. This gives rise to a need for providing more robust, automated techniques for identifying malicious processes on memory images after an incident. To the best of our knowledge the automated identification of malicious processes on memory dumps has not been performed. Thus, we aim to use machine learning techniques to characterize the memory footprint of malicious and benign applications, so as to automate distinguishing between the two classes, and hence provide an automated classifier for triaging malicious processes within memory dumps.

3   The Coriander Toolset

To develop our technique for classifying Android process memory instances we needed a dataset of process memory dumps to identify relevant features. As there is no such dataset available, we set out to generate one. We developed the *Coriander Toolset* to automate this generation of realistic Android process memory dumps from real world APK files. The Coriander Toolset is composed of two major components: The *Coriander* application[1] and the *AndroMemDump* application[2]. The Coriander application coordinates the running of APK files within an Android Emulator and initiates the memory dumping procedure. The AndroMemDump application enables the actual dumping of a given running process' memory space. The functionality of these two applications is described in the following subsections:

3.1   Coriander

The Coriander Python application is made up of 3 main components: *SDK Tools*, *APK Tools* and the *Cookbook*.

1. The SDK Tools package consists of wrappers for the Android Debug Bridge (ADB), the Android Emulator and a class for managing SDK location configurations. It provides a logical abstraction of components of the Android SDK that allow for running, querying and controlling various parameters of an Android device or emulator.
2. The APK Tools package is comprised of two main abstractions: The *APK Store* and the *APK File*. The APK Store serves to maintain the location configurations and metadata extracted from a repository of APK files. The location can be a remote network path, or a local directory on the device running Coriander. The specific parameters are stored in a JSON file within the 'config' directory. The APK File

---

[1] Source code available at: https://github.com/irvinhomem/Coriander.

[2] Source code available at: https://github.com/irvinhomem/AndroMemDumpBeta.

class holds the metadata of a specific APK file, as well as functions for extracting specific metadata out of an APK file. The metadata stored include the *package name*, the *activities* and *permissions*. Other metadata could be captured, but these few are the important ones required to get an Android application to run.

3. The Cookbook package has a single class (*Recipe*) containing the instructions that the Coriander Toolset should run in a given session. There are 2 categories of instructions: Emulator instructions, and ADB/APK instructions. The emulator instructions revolve around the lifecycle of an emulator, that is, setting up an emulator instance, running the instance, resetting the instance, and killing the emulator instance. The ADB/APK instructions involve downloading APK files from an APK Store, installing apps, running app activities, initiating memory dumps, closing apps and uninstalling apps. To achieve these functionalities, the Cookbook calls methods from all other packages (SDK Tools, APK Tools) and the AndroMemdump application.

3.2 AndroMemDump

AndroMemDump is an Android application whose main function is to capture the process memory of a given process. The application is written in Java (using the Android API) and Native C code. The Native C code provides low-level access to the *ptrace* system call, which is used to capture process memory on Linux based systems [17]. When cross-compiled using the Android NDK, we get several flavours of our executable (*memdump*) for multiple process architectures i.e. *x86*, *x64*, *armeabi* and *mips*.

The Java based part harnesses the Android API to provide a simple, portable means of carrying, installing and calling native C executables within an Android ecosystem. The *memdump* binary is carried as an 'asset' within an APK, and is placed in the 'files' directory of the AndroMemDump app on first-run, after which 'execute' permissions are applied on the binary. Using our *memdump* executable AndroMemDump, we can capture process memory and save it onto the device internal memory, the SD Card, or transfer it over the network to a remote location. In conjunction with *Coriander*, process memory dumps can also be stored on the device hosting the emulator. Overall, this enables automating the capture of process memory from numerous APKs allowing us to create a large dataset within a reasonable amount of time.

4 Experiment Results and Discussion

Using the Coriander Toolset, we set out to generate a dataset of process memory dumps. This further required customizing an Android OS image to contain the AndroMemDump app and to avail root permissions. This involved modifying the '/system' partition of a stock Android ROM image to install our app as well as the '*su*' binary and the "Superuser" app by Chainfire (Jorrit Jongma). This was done such that after each run of our customized Android ROM on the emulator, we could wipe the *user* partition, to ensure APKs were completely gone, to avoid different malicious APK's interacting. The assumption made here was that malicious applications would not bypass the Superuser app authorization to gain root privileges to modify the /system partition. This decision was made as a tradeoff to having to install AndroMemDump and the 'su' binary on every round, which would slow the process down. Having these in the system partition and protected by the Superuser app was a good enough tradeoff.

Having all these in place we used the AndroZoo APK repository as our APK Store, extracting only a subset out of the over 5 million APKs available. The reason for using only a subset was due to time limitations and the size of each process memory dump. Each process memory dump took about 3–5 min to capture and store. The first few app dumps ranged between 0.8–1.5 GB in size each, thus we decided to capture only strings from each process memory dump as an initial feature set to reduce the size. The AndroZoo project classified many APKs as malicious or benign using VirusTotal, however not all were classified. Our aim was to achieve around 1000 malicious and 1000 benign process memory dumps. We ran our toolset sequentially through the repository and eventually attained 1187 benign samples and 1188 malicious samples[3]. Numerous apps had problems preventing them from executing, and were this skipped automatically by Coriander. The problems included corrupt manifest files, bugs within the code preventing installation, API level incompatibility and specially compiled native libraries that would not run on our customized ROM. We did not have the time to debug other app developer's code, nor to develop multiple ROMs to cater for the wide variation of compatibility issues in the Android ecosystem. Thus, it took 2321 and 7479 sampling rounds, respectively for benign and malicious classes, in order to achieve the 1187 and 1188 respective samples of process memory dumps from *working* APKs.

We discovered that process memory dumps in Android devices can be significantly large, thus we resorted to extracting only strings. This is acceptable since analyzing strings is one of the initial methods of performing memory forensics. We also saw the large amount of incompatibility issues that plague android apps between different versions of the Android API hindered our dataset collection efforts. Our Android ROM was customized from a stock Android 5.1 (API 22) which was the version commanding about 24% of the market share of Android devices - the 2nd highest at the time. We see the need for our toolset to have other ROMs available to allow for different flavours of the Android OS and thus increase compatibility; however, this comes at a cost of time and effort to maintain the different flavours.

5   Conclusions and Future Work

In this study, we delved into the first stage of our project to perform Machine Learning based triage on Android Memory Dumps. The first stage required a large dataset of realistic Android process memory dumps upon which we could extract features to develop machine learning models. We thus set out to create this dataset in this study. We developed the *Coriander Toolset* in order to help automate the creation of our dataset. From this toolset, we were able to create dataset of 2375 realistic Android process memory dumps, to further our own research and contribute to the larger research area.

---

[3] The dataset is available online at: https://doi.org/10.17045/sthlmuni.4989773.

This study only provides the initial progress into this work and has some limitations. Firstly, more customized ROMs need to be realized to get a better variety of process memory dumps and reduce the APKs skipped. Only strings of process memory dumps were captured; other memory metadata can be captured in future by extending the Coriander Toolset. This will also aid in the eventual feature selection process for the Machine Learning-based Triage goals that we intend to achieve in the future. Algorithms such as k-NN, decision trees, SVM's, neural networks, association rule mining, time series analysis and graph mining techniques are candidates for the classification task for our future work.

References

1. Rogers, M.K., Goldman, J., Mislan, R., Wedge, T., Debrota, S.: Computer forensics field triage process model. J. Digital Forensics, Secur. Law **1**, 19–38 (2006)
2. Roussev, V., Quates, C., Martell, R.: Real-time digital forensics and triage. Digital Invest. **10**, 158–167 (2013)
3. Mead, S.: Unique file identification in the national software reference library. Digital Invest. **3**, 138–150 (2006)
4. Kornblum, J.: Identifying almost identical files using context triggered piecewise hashing. Digital Invest. **3**, 91–97 (2006)
5. Marturana, F., Tacconi, S.: A machine learning-based triage methodology for automated categorization of digital media. Digital Invest. **10**, 193–204 (2013)
6. Breitinger, F., Baggili, I.: File detection in network traffic using approximate matching. J. Digital Forensics, Secur. Law **9**, 23–36 (2014)
7. Homem, I., Papapetrou, P.: Harnessing predictive models for assisting network forensic investigations of DNS tunnels. In: ADFSL Conference on Digital Forensics, Security and Law, Daytona Beach (2017)
8. Mislan, R.P., Casey, E., Kessler, G.C.: The growing need for on-scene triage of mobile devices. Digital Invest. **6**, 112–124 (2010)
9. Allix, K., Bissyandé, T.F., Klein, J., Le Traon, Y.: AndroZoo: collecting millions of android apps for the research community. In: 13th International Workshop on Mining Software Repositories - MSR 2016, Austin, TX, pp. 468–471 (2016)
10. Koopmans, M.B., James, J.I.: Automated network triage. Digital Invest. **10**, 129–137 (2013)
11. Cohen, M.: Scanning memory with Yara. Digital Invest. **20**, 34–43 (2017)
12. Lapso, J.A., Peterson, G.L., Okolica, J.S.: Whitelisting system state in windows forensic memory visualizations. Digital Invest. **20**, 2–15 (2016)
13. Karbab, E.B., Debbabi, M., Mouheb, D.: Fingerprinting android packaging: generating DNAs for malware detection. Digital Invest. **18**, 33–45 (2016)
14. Tam, K., Khan, S.J., Fattori, A., Cavallaro, L.: CopperDroid: automatic reconstruction of android malware behaviors. In: NDSS, pp. 8–11 (2015)
15. Lindorfer, M., Neugschwandtner, M., Weichselbaum, L., Fratantonio, Y., Van Der Veen, V., Platzer, C.: ANDRUBIS-1,000,000 apps later: a view on current android malware behaviors. In: 3rd International Workshop on Building Analysis Datasets and Gathering Experience Returns for Security, pp. 3–17 (2014)
16. Petsas, T., Voyatzis, G., Athanasopoulos, E., Polychronakis, M., Ioannidis, S.: Rage against the virtual machine: hindering dynamic analysis of android malware. In: 7th European Workshop on System Security, pp. 5:1–5:6 (2014)
17. Thing, V.L.L., Ng, K.Y., Chang, E.C.: Live memory forensics of mobile phones. Digital Invest. **7**, S74–S82 (2010)

Author Index

Printed in the United States
By Bookmasters